D1444725

THE FILM 100

THE FILM 100

A Ranking of the Most Influential People in the History of the Movies

SCOTT SMITH

A Citadel Press Book
Published by Carol Publishing Group

A Citadel Press Book
Published by Carol Publishing Group
Citadel Press is a registered trademark of Carol Communications, Inc.

Editorial, sales and distribution, and rights and permissions inquiries should be addressed to Carol Publishing Group, 120 Enterprise Avenue, Secaucus, N.J. 07094.

In Canada: Canadian Manda Group, One Atlantic Avenue, Suite 105, Toronto, Ontario M6K 3E7

Carol Publishing Group books may be purchased in bulk at special discounts for sales promotion, fundraising, or educational purposes. Special editions can be created to specifications. For details, contact Special Sales Department, Carol Publishing Group, 120 Enterprise Avenue, Secaucus, N.J. 07094.

Manufactured in the United States of America
10 9 8 7 6 5 4 3 2 1

Library of Congress Cataloging-in-Publication Data

Smith, Scott, 1964–
    The film 100 : a ranking of the most influential people in the
history of the movies / Scott Smith.
        p.   cm.
    "A Citadel Press book."
    Includes index.
    ISBN 0–8065–1940–1
    1. Motion picture producers and directors—Biography. 2. Motion
picture actors and actresses—Biography. 3. Entertainers—
Biography.   I. Title.
PN1998.2.S592   1998
791.43′0922—dc21
    [B]   97–47101
                                                              CIP

This book is dedicated to my mother, who was never too busy to put down whatever she was doing and rush to the television set to help a ten-year-old boy identify the faces of the B actors who littered the old black-and-white movies we cherished together.

CONTENTS

FOREWORD

Often when I'm asked about my days as an editor on *Citizen Kane,* the questions inevitably turn to whether I had any idea of the impact its innovations would have on the thousands of films that followed it. My recollections of that time are as vivid as ever; while viewing the daily rushes of *Kane,* I could tell that Orson Welles was capturing something extraordinary. The fresh new faces of the Mercury Theater actors, the striking beauty of the sets, and the extreme camera angles all hinted at the marvelous film Orson was creating.

When I began directing my own films, however, I found that anticipating the power and influence of a film is nearly impossible. Only time can tell whether a movie will resonate with audiences, but fortunately, with the aid of books like this one, we can journey into the cinema's past to examine many of the ideas and innovations that have helped make the movies so memorable.

What could easily be lost in the close examination of these tools and techniques is the fact that movies are about stories, but the author has done a commendable job of recognizing the people behind the innovations. He has taken care to relate the stories of these talented men and women, and while each chapter recalls exciting moments in the lives of the most celebrated stars, we are also introduced to some fascinating, hard-working craftsmen and inventors whose contributions took place far from the glittering sets of Hollywood.

Because I've been a director who has worked in many different genres and who has collaborated with many different production crews, I have had the good fortune to work closely with many of these creative individuals. I was happy to see that many of my colleagues are finally receiving the accolades they rightly deserve. The tremendous talents of Saul Bass, Bernard Herrmann, and Gregg Toland, among others listed here, have been highlighted before, but this time, we're given the chance to discover the ways in which their efforts are still having an influence on the films we see today. Better yet, this book may inspire a few filmmakers to find a compelling story, pick up a camera, and make their own mark on the world of film.

Robert Wise

ACKNOWLEDGMENTS

It took nearly one hundred people to assist with the one hundred names found in this book. I regret that I have space enough to mention only a few, but my deepest thanks goes out to everyone involved.

First and foremost, I wish to thank my longtime collaborator Zeke Zielinski. His immeasureable talent—from the award-winning design of the Film 100 website to the inspired concepts of these pages—has made this project very rewarding for me. Also crucial were the roles of Andy Flint and Chris King, who cofounded the website venture that preceded this book. Additional research for the individual biographies was provided by Connie Fernandez, Jason Tsoi, and my mother, Geri Smith. Special thanks are in order for the advice and support of Ed Reilly, Jeff Black, and Valerie Kelly.

Unearthing facts on many of the forgotten heroes of film was accomplished with the generous help of family members, scholars, and filmmakers, many of whom provided great anecdotes and valuable supporting material. One such case was an extended visit to the home of pioneer Linwood Dunn, who graciously led me through his archives and memorabilia on films ranging from *King Kong* (1933) to *Taxi Driver* (1976). At 93 years of age, Dunn is still a master of film gadgetry (he gave me a demonstration of a state-of-the-art 3-D viewing system for broadcast television) and an excellent raconteur. Other sources filled in the blanks for me; in his correspondence from Australia, Arthur Rothafel, a surviving descendent of theater magnate "Roxy" Rothafel, was instrumental in providing facts about the early days of New York's movie palaces. Pulitzer Prize-winning film critic Roger Ebert was particularly forthcoming, and film historian Bob Birchard set me straight on several key points.

A special thanks, as well, to directors Alastair Reid, Caleb Deschanel, and the remarkable Robert Wise, for his thoughtful foreword.

Finally, I owe a large debt to my patient editor at Citadel Press, Jim Ellison, and writer John Simmons, author of the outstanding *Scientific 100*, both of whom lent valuable advice in crafting the final essays.

A WORLD OF FILM LOVERS

A NOTE ABOUT THE INTERNET

The book you are holding represents the first publication of content originally created for the World Wide Web; before *The Film 100* began its life as a book, it was an award-winning website that entertained millions of film fans with biographical sketches, pictures, timelines, film recommendations, and links to other sites on the influential figures listed here.

Working hand-in-hand with the talented graphic designer Zeke Zielinski, I combined a subset of text with his illustrations, the very same that appear on these pages. We posted the list of the Film 100 on the World Wide Web (www.film100.com) in June of 1996. Within weeks, thousands of fanatics visited the site and began writing to me. The overwhelming support of film historians, scholars, students, and critics was both rewarding and reassuring. Even more surprising was the e-mail I received from many of the individuals on the ranking, who helped clarify points and add valuable insights. Critic Roger Ebert was particularly helpful with his informational e-mail messages, and film special effects genius Linwood Dunn's unsolicited electronic greeting was an unexpected thrill; it seems film pioneers never tire of technology.

The Internet also proved invaluable with difficult research questions; the extensive archives of major newspapers and libraries, specifically the Library of Congress Early Motion Picture Collection, were instrumental in completing the essays. Also, many of the descendants and surviving family members of these cinematic legends were easily contacted by e-mail, for instance, Bernard Herrmann's biography was corrected with input from a relative.

Although this volume contains substantially deeper research than is available online, opening up the list to the scrutiny of the world has done the book an immeasurable service. By listening to important criticism from countries other than the United States, I avoided a traditional Eurocentrist perspective on cinematic achievements. Best of all, the Internet gives the list a life beyond the printed page. As filmmakers continue to influence cinema around the world, I'll carry on, changing the rankings to reflect this progress. If ranking film legends intrigues you, try it yourself. Put together a list of a hundred of film's contributors, adopting any criteria you like, and send a copy by e-mail to scott@film100.com. Additionally, I encourage you to visit the Film 100 website (www.film100.com) for links to other online destinations where the accomplishments of these people can be further explored.

THE FINAL CUT

AN INTRODUCTION TO THE SELECTION CRITERIA

Film lovers are sick people.
—FRANÇOIS TRUFFAUT

The idea of ranking people in history by the influence of their accomplishments began with Michael Hart's excellent book *The 100* over twenty years ago. Hart himself had quite an influence, spawning a series of variations including *The Black 100, The Jewish 100, The Scientific 100,* and so on. Upon reading his original text in college, I was struck by the scope of his quest; he took all mankind across all history and whittled them down to an inspirational few. Instantly, I had the idea of ranking film heroes. Certainly, it seemed to me, a more specialized pool of influencers would provide a more relevant comparison to each other. Plus, with movies being documents of record, the influences would be easier to trace and qualify. Best of all, cinema had been my passion since my youth, and the wealth of news clippings, books, magazines, and videotapes I had been collecting for years meant I was up to my neck in valuable research aids.

So I set out to gather a list of film's most influential visionaries. I began by listing only the names of those whose work has been felt by millions. I wanted to unveil the faces behind techniques that are common to all moviegoers today. I wanted to celebrate individuals who, directly or indirectly, created significant changes in the way films are made, seen, distributed, and appreciated. That was my criteria. Using this simple but focused guideline, I jotted down a selection of 350 names I could think of off the top of my head.

Next, I attempted to trace back the ripples of influence to their originators and give credit where credit was due. I was not concerned with the subjective exercise of distinguishing "greatest" or "importance." I consulted other critics, film historians, scholars, filmmakers, and many of the friends, colleagues, and family members of pioneers in the field and modified my initial list against their enlightening feedback. I then started a long and difficult elimination process and was able to limit the group to one hundred names, before assigning the final ranked positions.

It is important to note that, in terms of influence, a single film can easily outweigh a whole career. Consequently, many popular persons are not here; I put Jean Renoir through an exhaustive process before removing him, one of the hardest decisions I had to make. But equally, the accomplishments of some unknown faces will be extremely familiar. Often, the first person to discover an innovation is worthy of inclusion, but many of the inductees were not the first in their craft, simply the ones responsible for the success of an idea. I considered just about every inventor and scientist connected to the industry, but many were edged out by the businessmen who exploited their inventions.

Some other rules trimmed the list further; joint contributions, for example, are treated as a single entry, and large governing bodies like the Screen Actors Guild were not eligible. Advancements that are credited to anonymous persons or are the combined result of generations of slight innovations were not considered. And many of today's finest filmmakers and performers have yet to surpass the achievements that made this prestigious group among the most select in cinematic history.

Simply put, each person ranks above another by the sheer magnitude of his or her influence. For example, the total number of people ultimately affected by the widespread success of the drive-in theater inventor Richard Hollingshead exceeds that of people touched by the inroads of Melvin Van Peebles in the area of blaxploitation films.

Tempting as it may be, I resisted the idea of including an additional list of runners-up at the back of this volume; there is no 101. The arduous process of ranking requires a firm belief in the criteria and a strict adherence to some self-imposed end. What remains is a selection of stellar achievements and the stars behind them.

The mission isn't over; I'll continue to watch films with an eye on influence, both to support my case and to update the list when the contributions of other influential people warrant a change. There are roughly thirty thousand independent filmmakers in the United States alone, any one of whom could instantly become a big hero with just a small film. And a new wave of digital filmmakers are already changing the landscape of cinema; moving pictures will no longer be confined to celluloid.

The careers of the individuals on the Film 100 are far more fascinating than can be explained in the brief space allowed by a book of this format; there was little room for the wealth of Hollywood anecdotes and telling film facts I discovered in my research. If the storied accomplishments of these innovators piques your interest, I strongly encourage you to search out additional material on the lives of these unique and compelling artists and tradespeople.

THE FILM 100

W. K. Laurie Dickson

Born: March 16, 1860, Château St. Buc, Minihic-sur-Ranse, France
Died: September 28, 1935, Twickenham, Middlesex, England

Legend has long established him as the father of motion pictures.
—Thomas Bohn

Had the future of motion pictures been left in the hands of Thomas Alva Edison, there would be no Hollywood, no buttered popcorn, and no *Star Wars*. Edison was reluctant to commit his staff to developing moving images; he thought their only real audience, small children, would tire of them quickly. To turn Edison around, it took the persistent personality of William Kennedy Laurie Dickson, an engineer of Scottish descent with a rare devotion to photography. Working deep within the shadow of America's icon of ingenuity, Dickson advanced each of the critical processes that would show the world the wonder of movies, inadvertently perpetuating the myth of Edison as their lone inventor. Years later, while still alive, Laurie Dickson would be recognized by his contemporaries as the true father of film, and eventually historians would justly record his accomplishments as the most significant work of any single man in the fledgling years of the motion picture industry.

Like many London schoolboys in the 1870s, Laurie Dickson had learned of the legendary achievements of the "Wizard of Menlo Park" through newspapers and comic books. By age nineteen, Dickson was determined to make his way to America and become an inventor. He sent a telegram to Edison in 1881, asking for work in the famous laboratory in West Orange, New Jersey.

Edison's curt reply was an explicit no, but in 1883, Dickson gathered the fare for an ocean liner and came to the States anyway. With experience in amateur photography, Dickson appealed to Edison by offering to take pictures of the Edison family, and by demonstrating an aptitude for the mechanics of the camera, he talked himself into an inconspicuous place among the many assistants in Edison's lab. Then, Dickson waited for an opportunity.

In 1888, the scientific community was giving considerable attention to the experiments of photographer Eadweard Muybridge. Recalling the young assistant's fervor for the hobby, Edison called for Dickson and asked him to examine the progress of Muybridge and other various rival inventors who were recording motion. It was to be an information-gathering assignment only, conducted outside of Dickson's daily responsibilities. Edison made clear that his interest was not in recording movement; he simply wished to apply the optical illusions he had seen in his children's magic lanterns and optical toys to the phonograph, simultaneously putting pictures together with sound.

Dickson took to the task with characteristic zeal and explored every facet of the Muybridge technique. Then, disobeying the directions given him, he spent the next few months searching the world for drawings, pictures, and documents detailing all devices that claimed to make photographs move. Once he felt that the concept of recording images in a single device was viable, he urged his employer to dedicate staff and funding for further research. Edison consented to allow Dickson to tinker, still with a view to adapting some of the principles to the phonograph.

Dickson immediately created several key alliances that would help him proceed. Foremost among these was his relationship with George Eastman's company, which supplied a steady stock of photographic supplies, particularly paper film. Dickson first attempted to attach photographic images to the cylinder of a phonograph by wrapping paper sheets around it. Initially, he used a telescope instead of a lens to look down and view the jittery images rolling under his nose. Building a camera and viewing instrument based on the phonograph proved problematic. First of all, the movement of passing photos was indistinguishable. What was needed was a method to make each still frame stop for a split second, and the phonograph's cylinder could not be made to perform that way. Another concern was the opacity of the paper film. Dickson had read of a product called celluloid, developed by John Carbutt. Carbutt's transparent sheets were being advertised as a replacement for plate glass negatives. Dickson ordered a supply and again tried rolling pieces of the malleable material around a drum, but the celluloid was still too rigid.

Dickson then sought out Hannibal Goodwin, an Episcopalian minister who had perfected a way of applying photographic emulsion to a roll of film. Suddenly, Dickson saw a ray of hope: a more flexible roll of celluloid film, combined with the emulsion process, could become an essential ingredient to commercial success. Befriending Goodwin and Carbutt, Dickson coerced them into relinquishing their patents to the Edison company. Edison's reputation for stealing the ideas of others was firmly rooted by this time, but Dickson assured both men that the prestige and resources of the West Orange lab would help them properly protect and profit from their hard work.

His persuasiveness would have a lasting impact on the future of film in several ways. Immediately, the Edison company received an overwhelming advantage in controlling the technologies required to create images on filmstrips. Furthermore, Dickson's close association with the Eastman company provided it with a substantial lead in manufacturing motion picture film stock; Dickson even traveled to Rochester, New York, to guide Eastman employees through the requirements for coating the celluloid strips with photosensitive emulsion, instructing them to make the rolls 35mm wide and in lengths of roughly 15 meters. And though Carbutt and Goodwin were generously rewarded, their willingness to share their patents would later hurt their chances to receive credit for the discovery of these processes, and ultimately gave Edison legal ownership of film patents for nearly a decade.

By November of 1889, the tenacious Dickson had devised a crude camera to record images on the translucent strips and filmed his first trial, a five-second wonder featuring the movement of fellow assistant Fred Ott. Already, some conventions were being set: the film was 35mm stock from Eastman, it was advanced by sprockets, and the illumination was provided by an electric bulb.

Dickson presented the short film to Edison, calling the peephole machine for viewing them a Kinetoscope. The Kinetoscope was simple; a filmstrip of several images was passed in front of an illuminated lens and behind a spinning wheel. The momentary view gave customers a brief glance at each of forty-six pictures in the course of one second. An optical effect gave the illusion of lifelike motion. Edison immediately relieved Dickson of all other assignments to concentrate fully on the development of motion pictures and put a team of assistants under his supervision. By 1891, Dickson was in complete control of all aspects of Edison's motion picture department.

With the public introduction of the Kinetoscope in October of 1892, the era of the nickelodeon was on. Despite the sensational business the much-hyped Kinetoscope viewers were doing, Dickson knew that they were already being improved upon by inventors abroad. He urged Edison to consider a projection device, but the Wizard was skeptical of the long-term success of the curious films. He saw no need for exhibiting to large groups of people and asked Dickson to cancel further experiments. Edison's shortsighted belief was that the number of images that were interesting enough to warrant capture on film was somehow limited and that, when projected to large audiences in theaters across the country, the novelty—and profits—would quickly fade. He was interested in the mass production of Kinetoscopes, not in the mass production of films.

But while Edison was vacationing in Europe in 1895, Dickson constructed a new camera that tipped the scales at nearly two thousand pounds and had to be housed in a tar-paper shack, christened the "Black Maria," on the grounds of the Menlo Park facility. It was the first motion picture stage. He began recording a variety of films about one minute long, including an early attempt with sound. The experimental tomfoolery created by Dickson over four days, with help from several assistants, was later collected in *Monkeyshines;* the presentation included the famous record of a Fred Ott sneeze that forever made him a fixture in film history. Dickson himself can be spotted in many of these scenes, dancing and playing the violin. Although crude, these films illustrated how a solitary perspective could be used to create many illusions.

Sparked by news that clever French inventors, the Lumière brothers, had previewed a projection device, Dickson once again encouraged an inventor to give up his patents. Thomas Armat had employed intermittent film movement with a rotating arm on a projector, and Dickson successfully convinced him to allow the design to become an Edison property. But the acquisition of Armat's technology would turn out to be the last by Dickson on Edison's behalf. Upon returning from Europe, Edison learned that Dickson had secured the Armat innovations, put them together with existing processes, and was pursuing projection. He and Dickson argued, and despite eight years of collaboration, they decided to part ways.

Several months after Dickson's departure in 1895, Edison displayed a projection system called Vitascope, a bulky but effective camera-and-projector system that sparked a revolution and rendered the Kinetoscope obsolete. Dickson immediately founded his own company and adapted his ideas for a projection system called the Mutoscope, carefully avoiding litigation by working around technologies that might infringe on the existing patents held by Edison. Unveiled in 1895, the system rivaled Edison's with improved image quality and film subjects that audiences found more entertaining. Throughout parlors on the East Coast, Dickson's Mutoscope was the most fierce competitor to Edison's equipment in the first years of the industry, and ultimately a Dickson camera-and-projector system called the Biograph proved superior to the Vitascope, but Dickson lacked the proper sales force to compete with Edison.

Dickson's studio, the American Mutoscope & Biograph Company, known simply as "Biograph," became the model for early studios. Only the second motion picture production company formed in the United States, Biograph became a major producer of features and a springboard for the careers of dozens of film luminaries, including D. W. Griffith, Edwin S. Porter, Mack

Sennett, Mabel Normand, Mary Pickford, Florence Lawrence, Lillian Gish, Wallace Reid, and Harry Carey. The studio's first cameraman was Billy Bitzer, the legendary pioneer who took Dickson's equipment to the streets and quickly mastered early shooting techniques. The first Biograph film released, *Empire State Express* (1896), was not important artistically but became a solid success for the fledgling studio and quickly legitimized the "business" of film production. Laurie Dickson soon sold a portion of his interest in Biograph and retired from the film industry. Ironically, Thomas Edison would purchase the Biograph studio in 1913 and once again overshadow the memory of Dickson's accomplishments; history books often record the company as "Edison's Biograph."

Laurie Dickson proudly returned to his mother in England in 1897. By then, his profound influence on motion pictures was firmly rooted. No single man was more persistent and pragmatic in the pursuit of a working system for the capture and projection of moving images. Dickson brought together all of the necessary technologies from disparate inventors, secured important relationships with Eastman and other materials manufacturers, and managed to carry on with his vision in spite of a lukewarm marketplace and a reluctant boss. Under his passionate guidance, an entire industry was given life, nurtured to strength, and seen through to maturity. His collective achievements add up to nothing less than the bare essentials of moviemaking—the film, the camera, the projector, and the studio.

2

EDWIN S. PORTER

Born: April 21, 1869, Scozia, Italy
Died: April 30, 1941, New York, NY

Editing is the only original and unique art form in film.
—VSEVOLOD PUDOVKIN

Shortly after Laurie Dickson's tenacity helped make the simple mechanics of motion pictures into a viable industry, Edwin S. Porter's cunning would turn the routine process of film production into a truly original art form. Porter's clever method of snipping and splicing celluloid strips into coherent story-pictures became the foundation of film editing.

As a young machinist who emigrated to America in 1895, Edwin Porter put his mechanical aptitude to work for the Vitascope marketing company, setting up equipment for the historic first screening of a projected movie in New York City on April 23, 1896. After a brief side job in the laboratory at Thomas Edison's manufacturing company, he left to become a free-lance projectionist at the Eden Musee theater in 1898. Among his responsibilities was the illegal duplication of George Méliès's films: Porter would clip all identification marks off the French three-minute reels and glue them together to make a single fifteen-minute program.

After failed attempts to build his own camera and projector, Porter returned to Edison's East 21st Street skylight studio in 1900, this time as a "producer" and "director," glorified titles for the men assigned to wander the streets alone to capture new subjects with their hand-cranked contraptions. The experience Porter had accumulated early in his career separated him from the other cameramen, and he was allowed to experiment extensively. While there, he tried desperately to emulate the trick photography of Méliès, beginning with *The Finish of Bridget McKeen* (1901). Porter's other notable efforts of this time were in the first demonstrations of night photography and the first attempts at time-lapsed, 360-degree panoramic recordings, featured in *Pan-American Exposition by Night* (1901). When President McKinley's assassin was scheduled for execution later that same year, Porter staged a dramatized reenactment of the event and juxtaposed documentary footage he had taken at the prison for *The Execution of Czolgosz* (1901).

In the first U.S. documentary film, *The Life of an American Fireman* (1902), Porter once again mixed real footage with performed sequences. In the film, firemen dutifully knock out chores at the firehouse, while across town tragedy awaits. Porter shows the audience footage of a raging fire. He then cuts abruptly to a shot of an alarm sounding, then to more flaming scenery, then back to a fire engine leaving the station, racing toward its destination. Staged scenes of actors heroically saving a trapped child from a smoke-filled set were "intercut" with shots of an actual burning building. The narrative structure was relatively complex, and audiences were asked for the first time to follow two concurrent stories, developing simultaneously. While many people were captivated by the action, others were left bewildered by the frequent repetition of the same activity. The six-minute short is generally considered a landmark of editing technique, although some controversy exists as to its claim of being the first film to intercut between scenes.

However, Porter's next film would definitively illustrate the power of intercutting. Chock-full of film firsts, *The Great Train Robbery* (1903) had a monumental influence on early motion pictures. It was not the first western, but it was the first epic western. It established many of the conventions of the genre: the holdup of a telegraph station, the formation of a posse, a chase, and a shootout. It also featured the introduction of title cards. Plus, it featured a bona fide star in rodeo rider Gilbert "Broncho Billy" Anderson. A qualified "movie," it had a rousing story line complete with sophisticated camera work and a shuddering climax. Shot in just three days and requiring a cast of forty actors, which was considered huge at the time, Porter's most ambitious project used more than 750 feet of film; editing whittled it to twelve minutes. Its running time set the average length of silent western films for nearly twenty years.

More important, *Robbery* was the first use of film to present a cohesive narrative structure, guided by the first use of a script. Hailed as the beginning of modern editing, it revealed film's ability to "jump" to other points of view and scene locations. Low-angle shots, perspective setups, fluid camera movement, and close-up photography all contributed to its majestic power. However, its major achievement was its directional continuity; with the aid of assistant Fred Balshofer, Porter created a series of vantage points and cross-cuts to give the audience a feeling of being led through the story. He also introduced contrast editing: an exterior scene of cowboys chopping down telegraph wires in the desert is followed by an interior scene of a telegraph operator experiencing difficulty in his reception. The result of Porter's editing was cinematic magic that baffled even its creator. When *Robbery* was tested to unsuspecting moviegoers on 23rd Street, in New York's hobo district, the reaction was so overwhelming that the theater had to run it three times to the same audience to avoid a riot.

The film's epilogue, in which a bandit turns a six-shooter straight at the camera, sneers down the barrel, and fires his pistol right into the audience, made the film an international success. Perhaps drawing on the thrill-seeker in all moviegoers, or simply the egocentric excitement of being singled out in a crowded theater, Porter's awareness of the audience in this first-person vantage point has entranced millions. In fact, this scene inspired Hitchcock's famous suicide finale in *Spellbound* (1945) more than forty years later. It also initiated a celluloid obsession with firearms that has never subsided.

The Great Train Robbery's immense success after its premiere in Broadway's Hammerstein Theater signaled to motion picture investors that the movie business was a permanent American fixture. Audiences lined up to see it over and over, and its popularity piqued the curiosity of millions who had never seen a motion picture before. Charlie Chaplin would later cite the film as his first experience with the wonders of the silver screen.

Despite the film's success, Porter nearly abandoned the influential editing techniques in *Uncle Tom's Cabin* (1903), *The Ex-Convict* (1904), and *The Kleptomaniac* (1905). Model animation became a new fascination in *The Teddy Bears*, and Porter experimented with cartoonist Winsor McCay on *Dream of a Rarebit Fiend* (1906), employing Méliès's double exposures and stop-motion camera tricks to simulate surreal dreams, which awaken the hero to an it's-all-a-dream resolution. The dream device is one of the most imitated structures in the history of the movies.

In 1907, Porter purchased some scenarios for one-reel films from an actor named D. W. Griffith. Later that year, he cast the young Griffith in *Rescued From an Eagle's Nest* and launched the film career of one of Hollywood's greatest talents.

Porter left Edison's studio in 1909 to pursue a career away from the assembly-line mentality that was necessary to compete in the fledgling film market. He formed his own production company in 1911, Rex Films, and sold it just one year later. His fame as a pioneer preceded him wherever he went, and he never seemed far from turning out another crowd-pleaser. His *Count of Monte Cristo* (1912), starring Eugene O'Neil's famous father, James, in the title role, was one of Porter's biggest commercial successes.

Riding on his reputation, Porter would join Adolph Zukor to share profits in his newly formed Famous Players, and there he directed several films, including Mary Pickford's *Tess of the Storm Country* (1914), as well as experimenting with various new processes. After directing *The Eternal City* (1915), he retired from moviemaking as one of the most highly regarded innovators of all time. Porter's career represents the important shift from cameraman to director, and he defined the ideal of a master craftsman for such silent-era directors as Griffith, George Seitz, Mack Sennett, and King Vidor. But his most enduring contributions are the seminal editing techniques that form the building blocks of storytelling for the screen.

3

CHARLIE CHAPLIN

Born: April 16, 1889, Walworth, London, England
Died: December 25, 1977, Corsier-sur-Vevey, Switzerland

I don't need interesting camera angles. I am interesting.

—CHARLIE CHAPLIN

For more than eighty years, Charlie Chaplin has been the most universally recognized film celebrity; no other icon so succinctly symbolizes the essence of cinema as the Little Tramp. By age twenty-four, Chaplin had defined the Tramp character through more than sixty films and secured a position as the foremost of all screen stars. His gift for pantomime had a magnetic appeal to people of all languages, and his following was both loyal and demanding. Thus, Chaplin's life traces the path of a creative artist struggling to reach his maturity as a performer in a burgeoning art form, rather than a technologist attempting to discover a new technique. Along the way, he would elevate the standard of sophistication of films, govern the rules of screen comedies, and become the forerunner to such deeply personal filmmakers as Ingmar Bergman and Woody Allen.

The study of Chaplin is the study of one person's growth. Performing on stage at age eight, he grew up among music hall performers, before leaving his mentally ill mother for orphanages and boarding schools. In his teens, he returned to the stage and followed Fred Karno's troupe to America. Mack Sennett discovered the seventeen-year-old Chaplin in a vaudeville act in New York City in 1912 and signed him to appear in Keystone comedies at $150 a week. By 1914, he was Sennett's best-known personality; soon he became

12

loved the world over. As his box office appeal soared, his price tag bulged. Before long, Chaplin would take the helm on his own pictures and exercise total control over nearly every aspect of his work.

Chaplin's career peaked at the perfect time. After the 1890s, the novelty of moving images was gone, and throughout the first decade of the twentieth century, audiences were still viewing movies as sideshow entertainment. Surely, Dickson developed the tools to shine dancing beams of light upon walls, and Porter gave those glistening images a way to follow a continuous story through editing. But Chaplin lent the sheer force of his personality to the medium. His mesmerizing expressions and enigmatic mannerisms gave cinema its most infectious quality. To millions of people abroad, his radiant face was the first they had ever seen in a motion picture. In America, his outlandish performances were responsible for the word of mouth that lured reluctant parents and eager children to a theater for the first time, and his indelible characterizations made moviegoing a habit.

Almost immediately after Chaplin joined Sennett, the character of the Little Tramp took form. The cutaway coat, derby, and cane weren't always present; the little fellow sometimes wore prison stripes, a military uniform, or a clergyman's frock. But the baggy pants and floppy shoes would become as emblematic as the ever-present mustache. The image of the Tramp evoked a complex blend of gaiety, wit, irony, and pathos. The failure of subsequent performers to recapture these nuances points to Chaplin's rare ability to communicate a subtle and poetic range of human emotions. Perhaps the purest example is seen in the cafeteria sequence of *The Immigrant* (1917), where Chaplin juggles three emotional plates—the love interest, the suspicious waiter, and a growling stomach. The elegant resolution of the scene shows thoughtful and painstaking story development that few directors since have demonstrated. The dreams of the Tramp in *The Gold Rush* (1925) show that pathos was not simply a by-product of Chaplin's subtle acting but was deliberately built up through story points. His *City Lights* (1931), considered the highest art of the lowly Tramp, is perfectly structured, as Chaplin puts himself through the wringer to collect enough money to restore the sight of a blind flower girl. The curbside gags are a model of economical editing. And the final scene is pure magic.

The financial milestones of Chaplin's career are simply astounding. By age thirty, he had signed the industry's first million-dollar contract—a sum completely unfathomable in 1918—to direct just eight pictures. One of them, *The Kid* (1921), starring Jackie Coogan, would become the second-highest-grossing film to date behind D. W. Griffith's *The Birth of a Nation,* and each subsequent picture deal would exceed the last with even more shocking signing bonuses and unprecedented creative freedoms. Chaplin's formation of United Artists in 1923 with Mary Pickford, Douglas Fairbanks, and Griffith was a necessity born of the fact that no producer in the world could afford him. He would wind up financing, creating, and distributing his own films for the rest of his career. But Chaplin adapted well to the business side of Hollywood. He had the foresight to preserve and redistribute his own pictures, perpetually keeping his art in front of newer and newer generations of fans. The manufacturing of Chaplin merchandise was a steady growth industry for more than twenty-five years. At the height of his popularity, his portrait graced anything that could be printed on—Charlie books, Charlie toys, Charlie hats, Charlie dishes.

With each new Chaplin film came equal parts of personal and professional notoriety. Off screen, his secret marriages to and public divorces from various leading ladies and child brides got more press than his films. He was rumored to have had affairs with Norma Shearer and Marion Davies, and a scandalous paternity suit in 1944 tarnished the image of the world's favorite clown. As Chaplin's personal politics found a platform in *Shoulder Arms* (1918) and his first talkie, *The Great Dictator* (1940), critics raved over the way his daring antiwar views were presented; *Dictator* skillfully reduced world leaders to buffoons and humorously cut through American sentiment about their leaders. These social satires have been widely imitated, showing up in the films of Stanley Kubrick, Ernst Lubitsch, Woody Allen, and Mel Brooks. The barber scene in *The Great Dictator*, as pantomimed to Brahms's Hungarian Dance No. 5, repeatedly served as the model for some of the best animated cartoon spoofs of the 1940s.

The deeply personal nature of Chaplin's movies revealed motion pictures as a form of expression, and with each new film his admirers witnessed an evolution. As a performer, Chaplin continued to add new meaning to the persona of the Tramp. As a filmmaker, Chaplin seemed to follow his muse rather than trends of the film industry. When studios had abandoned short films for feature length, Chaplin continued to pump out two-reel comedies until he had exhausted the form. When talkies took over after 1929, Chaplin continued with pantomime in *City Lights* and *Modern Times* (1936), well into the sound era. Each picture charted Chaplin's journey into new territory, and this had a significant effect on artists, who would now see film as an avenue of self-exploration.

In 1947, Chaplin rewrote and directed *Monsieur Verdoux* from a draft script by Orson Welles. The movie fizzled, and an attempt to revive the Tramp in *Limelight* (1952) failed as well. Ironically, that same year, after vacationing in Europe, Chaplin—who had never become a U.S. citizen—was denied reentry to the States by federal officials who cited back taxes, Communist sympathy, political activism, and subversive morals. From that point, he lived with his family in Switzerland. His remaining films were produced in Europe, including his final effort, *A Countess From Hong Kong* (1966), with

Marlon Brando. In 1972, after twenty years of exile, Charlie made an emotional pilgrimage back to California to receive a special Academy Award for lifetime service to motion pictures. Queen Elizabeth II knighted him Sir Charles Spencer Chaplin in 1975.

Born of the Jazz Age, a spirited character emerged on the screen to put a kick of humanity in the pants of a world marching toward progress. An inspiration to artists and an ambassador for an art form, Chaplin's Little Tramp embodied the power of cinema: its ability to transcend barriers of language and culture, its strength as a forum for social comment, and its magical way of turning fuzzy shapes of light into a well-defined personality that can make people laugh and cry.

4

MARY PICKFORD

Born: April 9, 1893, Toronto, Canada
Died: May 28, 1979, Santa Monica, CA

*She was the only member of her sex to become the focal point
for an entire industry.*

—BENJAMIN HAMPTON

Mary Pickford's legendary audacity might have been chalked up to youthful impetuousness had it not been for a lasting career that proved her savvy in a ruthless business. At the height of her fame, she was one of the richest women in the world, the first person in history to become a millionaire from the craft of acting, and reigning queen of the box office for more than twenty years. There exists a debate over claims that she was the first movie star, but there is no question that she was the first megastar. The industry term "star system" was coined to describe the efforts to capitalize on her meteoric rise. Pickford was not the result of a star system, she was its genesis.

As a self-styled, self-determined, self-confident girl of fifteen, playing small parts on Broadway, she heard that jobs in moving pictures were paying well. She arranged a trip to the Biograph studio for a spring day in 1909, where she flirted with director D. W. Griffith and begged him for work as an extra. He gave her a role in *The Lonely Villa,* her first film. The studio scale was five dollars a day; but when asked by Griffith to return the following day, Mary insisted on ten. Griffith laughed her off, but when Mary stormed off the set, Griffith stopped laughing. She was back the next morning.

Pickford's naturalistic acting gave Griffith's melodramatic films a much-needed believability. Early Pickford one-reelers like *The Little Darling* (1909) captivated audiences and brought Biograph healthy returns. Sensing her growing importance at each step, she continued to demand incremental raises. By 1911, Pickford had turned away all stage offers to concentrate solely on her screen career. Her mother, a poor widow, came to count on income from Mary's acting and took an active role in her financial affairs. Mary arranged auditions for friends Lillian and Dorothy Gish, who became Griffith's most frequent collaborators. Often the three willful women were above direction, telling their Biograph directors, including the prestigious Edwin S. Porter, how they preferred a take.

Signs of Pickford's international status were manifested in the illegal distribution of her films throughout Europe. Biograph also discovered that distributors in Russia had systematically copied nearly 130 of Mary's films. Despite the loss of income to the studio, the piracy of her Biograph films made Pickford a world-famous celebrity.

By 1913, Mary was the first actress to rise above the stock company of Biograph players and command films and salaries on her own terms. Tired of being overshadowed by the messages in Griffith's work, she accepted an offer to join Adolph Zukor's Famous Players Company. Zukor, an arrogant and tough-minded businessman, was in constant negotiation with Mary and her mother. Using the salaries of the period's leading men as a personal benchmark, she insisted on always outearning them. Jokingly, Zukor once commented that Pickford's films took less time to put together than her contracts. In 1916, an agreement was reached between the two that gave Pickford $10,000 weekly, plus a $30,000 signing bonus and a healthy share of all profits from her films. In addition, Pickford would have choice of directors and cameramen, as well as an unconditional exit clause in case she felt her salary needed to be adjusted to meet market value. She would honor the agreement for less than a year before moving to even greener pastures.

To ensure his payments to Pickford were justified, Zukor forced theater owners to commit to showing the films by signing a contract in advance. In addition, a premium charge to display Pickford films was expected for each new release. Fearful of losing Mary's followers to crosstown rivals, most theater owners agreed to the strong-arm tactic. The "star system" had been officially born.

With an innate sense of her charms, Mary began creating the image of "America's Sweetheart," which would prove an enduring and sometimes restricting screen persona, reinforced in such films as *Tess of the Storm Country* (1914), *Rebecca of Sunnybrook Farm* (1917), and *Poor Little Rich Girl* (1917). The golden curls of Pickford never lost their spring. Millions of people who had never seen a "star" thrilled at a chance to watch a Pickford movie. Practically producing every film herself, she courted the best directors and technicians to her projects, supervised the details of scripts, and tiptoed through precious childlike roles until, at the age of twenty-four, she was not only a millionaire, but Hollywood's first.

Now that Mary was in effect an entire international industry by herself, studios could no longer afford her, and she was not willing to accept anything less than full market value. The only option left was to finance her own films, a prospect that did not intimidate Pickford at all. She knew virtually everything there was to know about the business. Mary discovered that her contemporary Charlie Chaplin, whose financial success she had once used to gauge her own salary demands, was in the same boat. The two came together in 1919, with Griffith, and formed the United Artists Corporation. As a formality, Douglas Fairbanks was included: Pickford had recently married the swashbuckler. The handsome couple, with their massive Pickfair estate in Beverly Hills, achieved a mythic status hitherto reserved only for royalty.

But Pickford, and the rest of Hollywood, would soon learn a valuable lesson about the movie business; she could not shake her girlish image. By *Pollyanna* (1920), Mary was nearly twenty-seven and still playing twelve-year-olds. Longing for more mature, challenging roles outside the stereotype, she defiantly chopped her golden curls into a short bob and began searching for new directors and new parts. She lured German director Ernst Lubitsch to America for *Rosita* (1923), but their fierce battles on the set resulted in an uneven effort: the film was disastrous. Unfortunately, so was *The Taming of the Shrew* (1929), another costly failure. The public would not surrender the notion of her innocence.

But Pickford was now too old to take Cinderella roles. Her natural beauty and restrained expressions still drew audience attention, and even her more sedate performances in later years would reap profit. An adaptation of the Broadway play *Coquette* (1929) afforded the aging screen queen a "serious" role as a mature flapper pressured to give false witness. Her performance was extremely popular and was rewarded with the Oscar. Ironically, the silent screen's greatest star became the first person to receive an Oscar for a talkie.

After her marriage to Fairbanks dissolved in 1935, Pickford bought out her partners and sold United Artists for a substantial profit. Mary remained at Pickfair until her death in 1979. She was honored with a special Academy Award in 1976, long after audiences could comprehend the immense hold she once had on Hollywood and the entire world. A product of her own determination, Mary Pickford was a superstar of rare proportion; her reign in Hollywood has never been matched by any other woman, and, with the sole exception of Chaplin's Little Tramp, no screen persona was ever more beloved.

ORSON WELLES

Born: May 6, 1915, Kenosha, WI
Died: October 10, 1985, Los Angeles, CA

*He was responsible for inspiring more people to be film directors
than anyone else in the history of the cinema.*

—MARTIN SCORSESE

The true potential of Orson Welles is one of cinema's greatest mysteries. A wickedly clever man with unparalleled bravura and innate dramatic flair, he became a pariah in the studio system of the 1940s and sank into a pattern of excessive living and professional bargaining that tainted his genius forever. To this day, his admirers are haunted by what might have been. After all, the only real shot this gifted director ever had to make a movie with the full support of a major studio resulted in the crowning achievement of the film world.

Orson Welles was a classic child prodigy. At eleven, he was directing his prep school plays. At fourteen, he was six feet tall with a commanding voice. At nineteen, he got radio work, dubbing news for the *March of Time* and supplying the deep voice of the Shadow. By the time he was twenty-two, Welles had formed the Mercury Theatre, which presented such high-concept plays as an all-black *Macbeth* and a modern-dress *Julius Caesar.* In 1938, the Mercury Theatre moved to radio, putting on an ultrarealistic version of *The War of the Worlds* that made Halloween listeners believe Martians had actually landed. The notorious broadcast prompted RKO Pictures to offer Welles a film contract giving him unprecedented creative control. Without prior movie experience, Orson traded a microphone for a megaphone and packed for Hollywood. He was twenty-four years old.

RKO made the best collaborators available to Welles; editor Robert Wise, the great cinematographer Gregg Toland, and composer Bernard Herrmann all volunteered to work with the controversial youth. Welles shrugged off RKO's studio actors and instead dragged his Mercury players out west. Most important, Herman J. Mankiewicz, a New Yorker who was a fixture in the legendary literary circles of the Algonquin Round Table, would doctor early script revisions.

The final product was *Citizen Kane* (1941), a film so completely fresh that it would alter the making of every movie that followed it. Critics were at a loss as to how to review the film, but most agreed it was compelling and intellectual. Today, *Kane* is credited with ushering in high artistry in cinema and is the measuring stick of all great films. After fifty years of dissecting its merits, film historians, filmmakers, critics, and buffs routinely return to it for its long list of innovations, including story devices and camera tricks previously unexplored in nearly thirty years of filmmaking. First, there's the absence of titles at the beginning; instead, the film begins with an obituary skillfully presented in a mock newsreel. Next, the script by Mankiewicz, which blatantly mirrors the life of tycoon William Randolph Hearst, adopts the clever "Rosebud" quandary and concentric plot structure to make the examination of a man's life as daunting as piecing together a jigsaw puzzle. The key technical innovation was *Kane*'s optical effects. A special lens, developed by Toland, achieved a complete focus that approximated the ability of the human eye to see characters in the distance and objects close to the camera with equal clarity. Dubbed "deep focus," the effect was revolutionary, allowing audiences to determine what details they wanted to look at in a scene. The technique also allowed Welles to place rich visual metaphors throughout each setting, encouraging viewers to explore the depth as well as the breadth of the picture. In an exemplary image, Susan Alexander, bedridden after a suicide attempt, is seen in the middle of a room, a spoon and medicine bottle on a nightstand in the extreme foreground, and Kane framed by the doorway in the background. The audience is left to make the inferences for themselves.

It is important to note that many of the scenes credited to Toland's deep-focus photography are really the work of special effects pioneer Linwood Dunn. The emblematic overhead view of Kane at the podium in front of a campaign poster was achieved by piecing together clips of a crowd and footage of balcony spectators with the original shot of Welles giving a rousing speech. The three distinct images, combined with the aid of an optical printer, give the effect of deep focus.

Welles shot much of the film with a mise-en-scène aesthetic, in which overflowing action in long, fluid takes was enhanced by the striking use of low-angle shots, claustrophobic architecture, and expressionistic lighting. At other times, however, he used direct cuts, montage sequences, lap dissolves, or special effects as transitional devices. Sound also played an important part in the fascination with *Kane*. Drawing on years of experience in radio, Herrmann developed musical vignettes to suggest the passage of time. Welles's ingenuity with sound techniques came from the stage: off-screen comments, characters talking over one another's words, music that suddenly stops dead on a character's key line, and the use of dialogue to bridge scenes. Suffice it to say that if you blink during a screening of *Kane,* you are bound to miss an innovation.

Clearly, it would be easier to list the moviemakers who have *not* been influenced by this film, and the most difficult part of appreciating its contribution is comprehending just how homogeneous the vast majority of Hollywood films were before *Kane* challenged almost all cinematic conventions. A comparable exercise might be to imagine what all films after *The Jazz Singer* might have been like without sound.

Kane was not without its problems. Upon hearing rumors of *Kane's* satirical look at William Randolph Hearst, gossip reporter Louella Parsons, working for Hearst, wrote scathing columns about the film. Hearst's newspaper chain put pressure on RKO to cease production and destroy the film. RKO resisted and released *Kane* to nervous theater owners. Some favorable notices were published, but RKO took ticket losses of more than $150,000 and shelved the film for seventeen years until a re-release in the mid-1950s.

Still, *Citizen Kane* made stars of everyone associated with it. Joseph Cotten, Ray Collins, and Agnes Moorehead slipped easily into other films. Wise would go on to direct. Herrmann would score dozens of classic films. Toland would forever be revered for deep focus. The authorship of *Kane* later became a controversial issue, but the Academy Award for Best Screenplay (*Kane's* lone Oscar win) went to Mankiewicz and Welles. Often overlooked is Welles's performance, the centerpiece to the film, which has the actor slowly developing the complex personality of Charles Foster Kane from age twenty-one to seventy. He enjoyed plenty of accolades, but only briefly.

His second film, *The Magnificent Ambersons* (1942), was not the finished vision Welles hoped for, but there are still touches of visual beauty, fancy mise-en-scène camerawork, and crisp dialogue in every scene. This film, too, benefited from the *Kane* ensemble, which Welles would never gather again. *Ambersons* was wrested from his control, edited by RKO management, and suffered terribly at the box office. It ranks with Erich von Stroheim's *Greed* as perhaps the greatest unfinished work by a major director. Welles became a Hollywood outcast with a reputation for extravagance and unruliness.

To continue working, Welles took acting assignments in other directors' films; his appearance as Harry Lime in *The Third Man* (1949) has been called the greatest screen entrance ever, and his passionate closing argument as a defense lawyer in *Compulsion* (1959) was widely praised. He tried his hand at bullfighting in South America before becoming an expatriate in Europe for some years. There, he made a spirited version of *Othello* (1956) with a piecemeal cast and crew.

Then came *Touch of Evil* (1958), a B-movie project given to Welles with very few expectations. Upon his return to Hollywood, he was handed a bad script based on a pulp novel, and he was told he had less than eight weeks to prepare. His budget was so small that he was forced to use only natural daylight in all outdoor scenes. Welles had not made a studio picture in more than ten years, but despite these handicaps, he took just forty-two days to shoot and brought in *Touch of Evil* both under deadline and within budget. Dennis Weaver gives a surprisingly strange performance as the weekend desk clerk at an out-of-the-way motel. Charlton Heston and Janet Leigh are overshadowed by Welles's own portrayal of a crooked cop. Marlene Dietrich and Joseph Cotten pitched in as favors to Welles. Featuring handheld cameras, a shocking editing style, sleazy-looking unknowns, and decaying Mexican locations, the film has become a hallmark of low-budget creativity. Embracing the limitations of the production, Welles set the story among dingy rooms, littered streets, and deserted highways. Some of the innovations of *Kane* linger, specifically overlapping dialogue and low-angle shots; however, the film introduces plenty of new tricks. The crackling off-camera blare of radio stations, intercoms, and police dispatchers is used to propel the plot forward without additional actors. Dark, expressionistic lighting is prominent, and the notable flash of buzzing neon lights is cleverly used to enhance the mood.

Touch of Evil has become a cult classic, admired by film buffs and studied by filmmakers. The opening scene, an extended crane-and-dolly shot, has been lifted by a stellar group of directors. The influential technique can clearly be seen in the cat-and-mouse chase through a policeman's second-story apartment in Brian De Palma's *Untouchables,* the long slow glide over the crowded streets of Little Italy and into the back of a refrigerated meat truck in Martin Scorsese's *Goodfellas,* and the entire opening sequence of Robert Altman's *The Player,* to name just a few. Steven Spielberg would use both the crane shot and Dennis Weaver as an homage in *Duel.* And Alfred Hitchcock was so enthralled by the film that he would borrow heavily from it for *Psycho;* the dime-novel plot, the remote motel, the peculiar night clerk, the beaded curtains and braided lampshades as decaying decorations, overlapping dialogue, Janet Leigh, and two key Welles assistants from the *Evil* production are all at work in the terrifying thriller.

Welles lived the rest of his life as a martyr. He continued to pursue filmmaking but struggled to find the proper financial backing to bring his dreams to a satisfying reality. His cameo appearances and commercial endorsements helped fuel his hope, but his projects never got past the planning stages. By the mid-1970s, renewed appreciation by college students and critics led to both a special Oscar and a Lifetime Achievement Award from the American Film Institute. At the end of his life, confined to radio and television voice work, a bitter Welles confounded interviewers with inconsistent and outlandish fabrications about his contributions, though his sharp sense of humor made even the lies eminently printable.

Perhaps the untapped genius of Welles, the films that will never be seen, is what inspires so many people to be filmmakers. Small pieces of his films have proved more influential than the entire careers of many directors. A single line of his dialogue may have inspired others more than the lifetime output of a successful screenwriter. His innovations are the most pervasive in modern filmmaking; his body of work is arguably the most studied; and his bittersweet legend is both a warning and a challenge to all aspiring directors.

6

ALFRED HITCHCOCK

Born: August 13, 1899, Leytonstone, England
Died: April 28, 1980, Bel-Air, CA

Hitchcock was the rare director who was familiar to audiences.

—FARLEY GRANGER

Even before Alfred Hitchcock pulled his greatest surprise, the chilling movie *Psycho* (1960), he was already the most recognizable director of all time. By defining an entire genre, and tailoring it to his own unique gifts, he had become the de facto master of suspense films. He was famous even to those who had never seen one of his films. His trademark humor and experimental techniques were easily identifiable. His directorial style became the most imitated ever. More precisely, his name became synonymous with a spirit of moviemaking; to be "Hitchcockian" was to keep people clutching firmly to the edge of their seats.

Hitchcock began his career as an illustrator of title cards for the silent films of Jesse Lasky's London studio in 1919. After advancing to art direction, he began picking up tips on screenwriting and editing, until his appointment as assistant director in 1922. His debut with a Jack the Ripper story, *The Lodger* (1926), provided an early hint at a personal style, featuring a mistaken-identity motif that he would use repeatedly. Thrillers quickly became his forte, and *Blackmail* (1929) was the first British talking picture to reap a profit.

A prototypical Hitchcock web of intrigue was weaved in *The 39 Steps* (1935). By this time, Hitchcock had formed the habit of meticulously outlining his productions with extensive notes, hundreds of drawings, and an airtight script. The result was a tense chase film highlighted by unique characterizations from almost every player. An editing style was also apparent: Hitchcock closes in on a woman's scream before cutting to a train whistle, an old radio effect that translated well to the screen. By *The Lady Vanishes* (1938), Hitchcock was streamlining his suspenseful techniques and adding large amounts of humor. An endless learner, he experimented with camera movement and restricted views to maintain prolonged tension. Hand-wringing audiences were soon becoming accustomed to his trickery, and Hitchcock's reputation was met with Hollywood offers.

In 1939, producer David O. Selznick signed Hitchcock to a Hollywood contract that would begin with *Rebecca* (1940). Like other Hitchcock films, *Rebecca* stemmed from the fiction of mystery writer Daphne du Maurier. But Hitch was unhappy with the casting forced on him for his first American production, and for his secoond, *Foreign Correspondent* (1940). His panache seemed to have gone missing; then he adjusted to the studio system. *Suspicion* (1941) took the Master of Suspense into the sanctity of the family home for the first time, and audiences responded by coming to the theater. Suddenly, Hitchcock was a bankable director.

His success led to more creative freedom. On his next film, *Shadow of a Doubt* (1943), Hitchcock initiated a device that would become one of the most-used character clichés in all of cinema: the gentleman-killer. Attending a screening of *Citizen Kane,* Hitchcock was impressed with the ability of the meek actor Joseph Cotten. Cotten so epitomized the everyman, Hitchcock felt, that he effectively disappeared from his films, allowing ordinary folks to connect with extraordinary circumstances. Hitchcock soon cast Cotten as the villain in *Shadow of a Doubt,* a quiet suburban mystery that takes a unique approach to suspense by presenting Cotten as the quintessential "good" uncle who turns out to be a deeply disturbed predator of elderly spinsters. Cotten's expert handling of the polite, unlikely murderer created a stereotype that has since become a staple of suspense films, repeated most memorably in *Night of the Hunter* (1953), *Taxi Driver* (1976), and even Hitchcock's own *Psycho.* *Shadow of a Doubt* forced the audience to look twice at their neighbors and relatives, and perhaps for this very reason Hitchcock often cited the film as a personal favorite among his work.

Hitchcock's uncommon talent, it seems, was his ability to compel onlookers to project themselves into the shoes of the bumbling innocents he engulfed in sinister situations. His films are the most effective demonstrations of how moviegoers empathize with screen characters.

Rope (1948) and *Strangers on a Train* (1951) both were inspired by the Leopold-Loeb murder case, as were a dozen other Hollywood films of the fifties. They received high praise as well as dependable box office, and Hitchcock was safely out of the meddling hands of producers; now a household name, he was coming into his own as a filmmaker. He was hailed by French New Wave theorists André Bazin and François Truffaut as the consummate film visionary. Hitchcock's films looked remarkably distinct; the obvious special effects of the time didn't demean the overall film—in fact, they combined to create a recognizable style. This consistency was largely due to Hitchcock's training as an artist. On most films, he never bothered to employ an art director, and he was very fond of using storyboarding techniques in planning. Film executive David Brown claimed "he would no more improvise during shooting than the conductor of the New York Philharmonic would improvise while conducting." His penchant for storyboarding became legendary, and later filmmakers, among them David Lean and Steven Spielberg, adopted this habit of visualizing every scene with detailed drawings.

Suddenly, bigger budgets and marquee stars were at Hitchcock's beck and call, and his best films followed. *Rear Window* (1954), *Dial M for Murder* (1954), *To Catch a Thief* (1955), *Vertigo* (1958), and *North by Northwest* (1959) all received the lush Hitchcock look. He also began lengthy collaborations with costumer Edith Head, composer Bernard Herrmann, and designer Saul Bass, all of whom helped polish his projects to perfection.

True to form, Hitchcock shocked his fans once more with *Psycho* (1960), a startling leap forward in suspense movies. The film became an instant classic and a primer for the use of point-of-view camera angles and quick cutting. Hitchcock's studio, Paramount, didn't want him to make it; they didn't like the plot, the title, the ending, anything. They felt an unexpected amount of suggested nudity and graphic violence was as foreign to Hitchcock fans as the absence of black humor. Hitchcock, however, took on a new direction and delivered a movie that blurred the line between horror film and psychological thriller.

Two key scenes have had a lasting impact on the way horror films instill terror in audiences. The famous shower scene, in which a knife attack on a vunerable hotel guest is presented as a rapid flash of disjointed images, gives viewers a dizzying perspective on the explosiveness of murder. The scene creates additional tension by frustrating viewers with cutaway shots of a static showerhead and running water in the midst of the violent act. The second influential scene involves the ambush of a private detective at the top of a staircase. In a moment of absolute silence, Hitchcock abandons the first-person perspective and shoots the set from overhead. This technique allows the audience to discover the location of the attacker just seconds before the victim does. Both of these mesmerizing scenes have been duplicated endlessly in the so-called splatter films of the horror genre.

Hitchcock followed with the eerie *The Birds* (1963), but struggled with difficult stars and shrinking budgets throughout the sixties. His final film,

Family Plot (1976), was a well-received and fitting end to his career, applying his trademark wit to an exposé of the fashionable resurgence of clairvoyance. In 1979, the American Film Institute gave him a Life Achievement Award, and shortly afterward he was knighted by Queen Elizabeth II.

Alfred Hitchcock had earned his place in film history so early in his career that he lived with the "Master of Suspense" moniker for most of his professional life. He was a rare thing: a living legend, greatly appreciated in his own time. Since his death, the suspense genre has produced no worthy successor, although the techniques of Hitchcock are still present in the films of Brian De Palma, John Badham, and Peter Yates, among many others.

7

WALT DISNEY

Born: December 5, 1901, Chicago, IL
Died: December 15, 1966, Los Angeles, CA

*The whole success of the Disney operation was Walt's
demand for high quality.*

—WARD KIMBALL

The entire first decade of Walt Disney's career was extremely rocky. He had locked himself and his company into poor business arrangements. His studio wasn't producing anything unique. The rubbery look of its characters was unimpressive, and the rival studio across town, headed by producer Max Fleischer, was making cartoons that were often more innovative. Still, Disney remained optimistic. His commitment and energy helped him become an industrialist whose product was entertainment and whose brand name stood for imagination. And today, "Disney" is a household word symbolizing the best of American values in family entertainment.

Throughout the 1920s, Disney's sole effort was to keep his *Alice in Cartoonland* (1923–26) series alive. But after a brief year of Oswald the Rabbit shorts, Disney felt he needed an edge on other cartoon studios to make a name for himself. He told his lead animator, Ub Iwerks, to create an animated character that would capitalize on the coming sound era. Iwerks's creation was Mickey Mouse. Originally scheduled to appear on the same bill as *The Jazz Singer* (1927), Mickey's debut in *Steamboat Willie* (1928) put the Disney studio in the spotlight.

The sudden fame of Mickey Mouse forced Disney to shuffle responsibilities.

A cattle call went out across the country for anyone interested in becoming an animator, and a flood of talented illustrators poured into Hollywood. Many of these people would be trained under Disney's roof and blossom into some of the biggest names in animation. To meet his demands for improved quality, artists were asked to specialize in certain job functions. Disney wanted a team concentrated on technical improvements. He wanted a special effects department. He put animators through life-drawing lessons and brought live animals into the classrooms, all in a search for realistic motion. He asked the creators of Donald Duck, Goofy, and Pluto to give their characters more emotions and vitality. Most of all, he asked everyone to contribute to story development.

An important by-product of Disney's reorganization was the use of storyboards to plan a movie's production. A storyboard is a series of individual pieces of paper, each displaying an illustration of a scene, outlining every action in a film. Pinned to a wall or mounted on an easel, storyboards became "picture scripts," allowing groups of animators to analyze each scene long before committing ideas to ink. Simply put, the storyboard made Disney films great. It eliminated unnecessary work. It made writers a part of character creation. It kept stories focused on their themes. Breaking artists into different teams, Disney would have ideas developed independently before bringing a number of storyboards together in one room, where he could excise redundancies and smooth out transitions. The films created with this process were far superior to any other cartoons, and storyboards went well beyond animation circles. They are being used today in advertising agencies and television studios; among film directors, such meticulous planners as Alfred Hitchcock, George Lucas, and Steven Spielberg have relied on storyboards to communicate their ideas to others and keep projects on track.

In spite of many critical successes, Disney continually struggled for profits. During World War II, his studio survived only on propaganda films made under government contracts. Disney's deals to merchandise Mickey watches, dolls, and shirts helped to stave off the effects of the Depression, until he could complete his company's transformation. In 1931, he signed an exclusive agreement with Natalie Kalmus to use Technicolor on every film for a period of seven years. No other cartoon studio could use the three-color process, and Disney capitalized on the novelty of color with the majestic debut of *Flowers and Trees* (1932). As the end of this agreement approached, Disney feared other color cartoons would catch up to his quality. He hurried to release *Snow White and the Seven Dwarfs* (1938) to further distance Disney quality from the pack and establish the studio as a feature film shop.

Although he would continue to produce theatrical shorts for many more years, full-length spectacles became Disney's hallmark. The most important of these was *Fantasia* (1940), the marriage of a Leopold Stokowski–conducted score with abstract and experimental animation. A controversial film, it initially performed dismally at the box office. Classical music fans shuddered at the idea of hippos dancing all over Tchaikovsky, and common folks avoided its pretentious aim by simply staying away from the theaters. However, years after *Fantasia*'s brief theatrical release, admirers begged Disney for another screening of the film. Haunted by the huge losses from his *Pinocchio* (1940), Disney was eager to squeeze every last dime from his features, so he agreed to a repeat showing. The re-release became the first of many, and the lesson learned from *Fantasia* would help the studio reap millions over the years. Soon, Disney would also discover the value of merchandising his entire stock of films and characters.

Beginning in 1937, Disney's films were under the exclusive control of a fourteen-year distribution deal with RKO Studios. But in 1953, Disney freed himself of major studios by releasing his cartoons through his own distribution company, Buena Vista. Immediately, the cartoon king set out to see if he could expand his empire. Grossing $1 million with *The Living Desert* (1953), Disney proved that his name was marketable beyond animated shorts. This led to live-action TV programs in 1954, like the popular *Zorro* and *Davy Crockett* series. *The Wonderful World of Color* also became part of the weekly habit of television viewers. And the much anticipated Disneyland theme park, opened in 1955, quickly climbed the list of favorite vacation destinations.

Innovations in both animation and live-action technique were present in *Mary Poppins* (1964), a huge success that garnered five Academy Awards and became the last big film that Walt Disney would have a hand in making. But his studio would stand firm well after his death, continuing with feature-length films, television specials, and eventually cable programming. The leadership of the Disney studio in the animation industry remained steady throughout the 1970s, but the future of animated films looked bleak until the breakthrough films *Beauty and the Beast* (1991) and *The Little Mermaid* (1992) sparked renewed interest among moviegoers in Disney animated features. These films succeeded by returning to the strong story lines and songs that Walt himself had insisted on.

Like many giants of industry, Walt Disney overcame early failures, restructured his ailing organization, perfected key processes in manufacturing, and excelled. The detailed storyboarding techniques he used in planning his films are a lasting contribution, used in almost every movie made today. His unforgettable characters are often an extension of his personal values; the image of Mickey Mouse has become a universal symbol of spirited optimism and goodwill. The logo signature of Walt Disney graces literally millions of products; however, the name now stands for more than merely excellence in animation. His competitive drive and unflagging standards set a benchmark for quality in family entertainment, and for more than half a century audiences have been eager to watch anything carrying his seal of approval.

8

D. W. GRIFFITH

Born: January 22, 1875, Floydsfork, KY
Died: July 23, 1948, Hollywood, CA

*We regarded him as a leader; and I think the leader of our whole
business. We've never had a leader since.*

—ALLAN DWAN

As a child, David Wark Griffith was mesmerized by his father's tales of the
Mexican wars and readings of Dickens and Shakespeare. Nineteenth century
literary works further fascinated Griffith while working as a clerk in a
Louisville bookstore around 1890. Exposed to the local poets and community
theater actors, Griffith became fixated on adapting Elizabethan poetry to the
stage. He began acting in amateur groups and received a professional position in the stock company of Temple Theatre, where he wrote some plays
without attribution. But the sale of some of his scenarios to pioneer Edwin S.
Porter in 1907 changed the course of his life. In a letter to Porter, Griffith
expressed admiration for the influential editing techniques that he had seen
in *The Great Train Robbery* (1903). Flattered, Porter offered Griffith a job as
an actor at Biograph in New York.

Narrative structure had been left largely unexplored by the Biograph staff;
most directors were merely cameramen with seniority, so their films were
generally straightforward recordings of poorly acted vignettes. Porter, who
knew this, saw in Griffith a man with stage experience, a sense of the dramatic, and, best of all, no mechanical aptitude. Griffith proved to be a rather
gawky and inanimate actor for silent films, but his suggestions for improving

productions caught the attention of Porter, who promoted the thespian to
director and assigned an experienced cameraman, Billy Bitzer, to keep
Griffith's ambitions on solid ground.

Griffith's skills were honed under a hectic pace. In his first five years, he
made more than four hundred one-reelers, each about twelve minutes long.
He averaged twenty-one productions a week, using a stock company of actors
that included Lillian and Dorothy Gish, Mary Pickford, Blanche Sweet, Mack
Sennett, Mae Marsh, Lionel Barrymore, and Harry Carey. However, his
greatest collaborator was Bitzer, who would remain with Griffith for almost
every film of his career and held a unique role as confidant and mentor.
Together, they discovered film language through experimentation.

Technically, Griffith's films were ambitious. His refinement of motion picture techniques, including the close-up, the long shot, panning, and cross-cutting, provided new ways of telling stories. He continually used parallel
plotlines and cut between the different stories; audiences who watched *A
Corner in Wheat* (1909) or *The Lonely Villa* (1909) were often confused by
such back-and-forth storytelling. But Griffith's films contained such raw emotional impact that unsophisticated moviegoers overlooked these faulty trials.

His successes piled up, and Griffith became the first director to establish
a following among theater patrons, largely due to his thematic choices.
Although his stories were largely based on the melodramas he admired as a
young man, Griffith's movies were a vital bridge between antiquated Victorian
values and the blinding modern age as he focused on issues of inhumanity
and social injustice in modern society. Foreign filmmakers soon duplicated
his scenarios, and the entire world was taking in the subjects that Griffith
alone conceived. By 1913, he was an international celebrity, commanding
absolute rule over his productions.

At this time, two crucial developments in the motion picture industry
would crystallize Griffith's reputation: studios instituted a division of labor
among its staff and placed its craftsmen in units, and unions responded by
organizing around these new trades. Gone were the days when the camera
could be cranked by anyone willing and able. Suddenly, a cameraman was a
cameraman. A stuntman was only a stuntman. And a director was exclusively
a director. Each specialized field had its heroes, and Griffith became the quintessential director. Many of the stereotypical conventions of the Hollywood
director were modeled after his eccentricities: shouting instructions to actors
through a megaphone; giving direction from a folding chair; wearing flamboyant hats and riding pants to the set; throwing temper tantrums; handing
down orders to set crews through assistants; using experts to lend authenticity to scenery and costumes. The position has never escaped these influences.

In 1913, Griffith fervently debated with Biograph executives over the running time of *The Massacre*. The fighting drove Griffith from the company.
Interested only in feature-length films, he joined Reliance-Majestic studio

and prepared in secrecy for *The Birth of a Nation* (1915) with only Bitzer as a conspirator.

The release of *The Birth of a Nation* brought Griffith more infamy than acclaim. President Woodrow Wilson originally praised it, then succumbed to pressure and denounced its racial violence. Banned in eight states, it was cut and censored by other theater owners. Even audiences sensitive to Griffith's casual depiction of the Ku Klux Klan were startled by the force of the epic. Most films had only a hundred different shots in their entirety, but *Birth* consisted of 1,544. In all, more than three million people came to see the battle sequences and historical re-creations, making it the most popular film up to that time. Filmed for under $125,000, it netted profits in the millions. Sergei Eisenstein, Cecil B. DeMille, and Fritz Lang cited it as a major influence. However, Griffith was angered by the critics' outcry of racism. He campaigned against the dangers of censorship and extolled the role of the director as visionary.

He hurried to finish *Intolerance* (1916) as an answer to his doubting public. Wrapping four historical stories around the theme of man's inhumanity, *Intolerance* was both an artistic achievement and a huge flop. Of its four interwoven stories, only one had a happy ending. Audiences were perplexed by the quartet of battle sequences, and the torrent of overlapping images was mind-boggling. To salvage his spiraling losses, Griffith yanked the film from theaters after a short twenty-two weeks and cut the Babylonian scenes into separate features, *The Mother and the Law* and *The Fall of Babylon* (1919). *The Intolerance* editing style was not completely wasted, however; Eisenstein and others recalled it as brilliant and inspirational.

In 1919, Griffith joined Mary Pickford and Charlie Chaplin in forming United Artists, a corporation that would allow him even greater control over his work. He settled into his craft and made some of his more palatable features, including *Way Down East* (1920), *Orphans of the Storm* (1922), and *Isn't Life Wonderful* (1924), a forerunner to the location shooting style of Vittorio De Sica's neorealist "street" films. Griffith's final film was *The Struggle* (1931), a haunting story of alcoholism that tackled taboos Hollywood would repress for another thirty years. After only two talkie efforts, Griffith retreated from the film industry disheartened and unfulfilled. In his later years, he became a symbol of the passing silent era and was shunned by the new blood in Hollywood. After spending more than a decade in isolation at the Hollywood Knickerbocker Hotel, he died in 1948.

Celebrated as one of the century's great renaissance men, D. W. Griffith was the first ideal of the film director. His presence can still be seen in the working methods of contemporary directors. The camera techniques and basic narrative structure of every film made today contain fundamental elements that he first explored nearly a century ago. In a career that spans almost 550 films, Griffith took the existing techniques of moviemaking and turned them into a "grammar" of film.

9

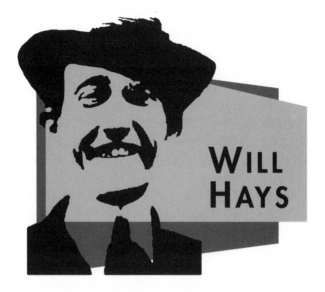

WILL
HAYS

Born: November 5, 1879, Sullivan, IN
Died: March 7, 1954, Sullivan, IN

It wasn't just a job that had been offered to him. It was a challenge, a duty.
—RAYMOND MOLEY

At the height of the Jazz Age, the film industry faced its first major offensive from moral arbiters. By the early 1920s, forty million Americans were making weekly trips to the movies, and half were minors. Films with racy plots, dark themes, and cynical endings became an increasing concern. Making matters worse was the involvement of major Hollywood names in a wave of off-screen scandals: Fatty Arbuckle was acquitted in the rape and murder of a Hollywood starlet; William Desmond Taylor was found shot to death; popular comedian Wallace Reid died of a drug overdose; and swashbucking idol John Gilbert had turned to alcohol and drank himself to a premature death.

Community leaders across the country responded by organizing local censorship boards. Frightened by the prospect of making movies that would have to meet standards in states as vastly different as Iowa and New York, Hollywood put out the word that it would police itself. Leaders of the studios, headed by Louis B. Mayer, successfully thwarted the possibility of government regulation by banding together in 1921 to form an organization to curb questionable content in films, the Motion Picture Producers and Distributors of America, Inc. (MPPDA), but to quell the increasing pressure from the media, they needed a president who would appear fair and objective. The job was offered to Will Hays.

Hays, a politically active lawyer from Indiana who had headed the Republican National Committee in 1918, was rewarded the position of U.S. Postmaster General in Warren Harding's administration in 1921. A respected and dignified elder in the Presbyterian Church, Hays readily accepted the position as the new head of the MPPDA a year later. He was immediately embraced by studio bosses eager to show their compliance with the public's demands and desperate to improve the image of their troubled industry. Hayes went to work immediately, blacklisting Hollywood regulars, writing moral clauses into studio contracts, and campaigning in highly visible forums about the changes he was instituting.

Certain celebrities, however, were too powerful or too clever to be scared by Hays. Cecil B. DeMille found the whole business offensive and turned out such flesh-and-blood spectacles as *The Ten Commandments* (1923) simply to prove the ineffectiveness of Hays. Ernst Lubitsch used slyer means, littering his comedies with double entendres and sexual innuedo so skillfully that Hays and his staff of censors seldom caught the references.

In 1930, after it became obvious that a public relations campaign was not enough, Hays outlined a set of strict guidelines for moviemaking: the Production Code, commonly called the Hays Code. Through it, Hays wielded his power until he had single-handedly reshaped the image of Hollywood. The Code, revised to an even greater scope in 1934, detailed unacceptable screen portrayals and required all scripts to pass through censors. No films made from 1930 to 1966 could show the inside of a woman's thigh under any circumstances, nor could a dead body appear on the screen. Drinking, gambling, and narcotics use were banned. The gangster's tommy gun was out, as was lace lingerie. Because the Code was extremely specific, censors were able to follow it to the letter. With little room for interpretation, Hollywood screenwriters were forced to avoid its no-nos, and costume designers, cameramen, and directors learned it inside out. Some attempts bordered on the ludicrous: when censors suggested that Clark Gable's famous line in *Gone With the Wind* be altered to "Frankly, my dear, I don't care," producer David O. Selznick became livid and stonewalled the production until Mayer spoke to Hays.

Although the Hays Code was officially in place until 1966, several landmark films tested its rigidity over the years. Sex goddess Mae West used her voluptuous lips to utter risqué innuendos, in films like the notorious *Klondike Annie* (1936) and became quite skillful at passing scripts through censors, then applying sexual meanings through clever delivery of her lines while filming. Many of these lines found their way into the vernacular, sparking the Hays Office to battle her over virtually every other word of dialogue. At the peak of the actress's popularity, the Production Code was nicknamed "the Code of the West." Ultimately, censorship damaged West's career, but the controversy inspired others to join the battle.

Two landmark challenges were made by director Billy Wilder, first in *Double Indemnity* (1944), which featured a steamy plot to bump off a husband for insurance money. The femme fatale gets away with murder, a strict violation of the Code, but after much wrangling Wilder was allowed to keep the ending. Such small acts of leniency encouraged other filmmakers to push the limits of the censors. A principal character in another Wilder picture, *The Lost Weekend* (1945), was an unabashed drunk, a portrayal routinely tolerated by the Hays Office. *Lost Weekend,* however, exposed a double standard: by detailing the devastating effects of alcohol abuse, the powerful film was instrumental in exposing the hypocrisy of the Code.

Nevertheless, the influence of the Hays Code was significant—it altered the creative product of Hollywood for more than thirty-five years. Hays maintained his advisory role with the MPPDA as president until 1945. By then, the self-regulatory rules were firmly in the hands of studio executives, and Hays returned to his native state. In 1966, the Code had become outdated and was feared to be ineffective against the changing social mores of the liberal 1960s. It was altered to curb sexual content in broader terms, and definitive language requirements were made. In 1968, an adjusted system was developed by the Motion Picture Association of America (MPAA, the MPPDA's successor) rating films according to their suitable audience: it set up G (general, for all audiences), M (mature), R (restricted; children under eighteen must be accompanied by an adult), and X (over eighteen only). Soon PG (briefly GP) was added as a parental guidance signal, replacing M, and since 1984 PG-13 has cautioned parents of stronger content. After much debate, NC-17 replaced X in 1990 to ensure that no children under seventeen are admitted to films of an adult nature. Besides the rating system, the MPAA works to develop international distribution of films, advises studios on special tax issues, and continues public relations efforts for the entire industry. But the Hollywood blacklists of the 1950s and the recent attacks by politicians on the values of Hollywood filmmakers echo the beliefs of the original MPPDA founder. The Hays legacy lives on.

10

THOMAS EDISON

Born: February 11, 1847, Milan, OH
Died: October 18, 1931, West Orange, NJ

Patents have ceased to give any protection to inventions.
It's cheaper to steal them.

—THOMAS EDISON

Thomas Edison's profound effect on the film industry goes well beyond any of the world-record 1,093 patents he held for gadgetry. His international reputation as a great innovator was instrumental in consolidating the bright minds and the vital inventions that comprised the first camera and projector. He became the ambassador of a new art form that he himself hardly appreciated. As the world's fascination with movies became undeniable, he sought to control the entire industry. Eventually, his efforts to profit from the movie craze led to the darkest period in film history.

Stories of the brash inventor are the stuff of myth. Hearing problems motivated the tinkering young Thomas to develop the telephone transmitter, mimeograph machine, and phonograph. His most lucrative invention, the stock ticker, provided the funding for the New Jersey labs that would lend him the nickname "the Wizard of Menlo Park." There, a large staff of creative minds worked together in think tanks on key technologies.

Although the mechanics of the phonograph became the basis for his experiments with recording moving pictures, the incandescent lamp was perhaps the more significant Edison contribution. Using it in combination with low-voltage batteries, Edison's team of assistants, headed by the zealous

W. K. Laurie Dickson, was able to illuminate photographs that flickered past
an eyehole in the first Kinetoscope, introduced in 1892 in New York.

Although the Kinetoscope launched the motion picture industry, the
images were displayed in nickelodeon theaters to one customer at a time.
Dickson urged Edison to build a projection system to display films to large
groups of people at one sitting. But Edison regarded the Kinetoscope as a
toy, best suited for curious children who were willing to pay five cents to
watch a six-second performance of a dancing woman or a jumping dog.
Adults were not interested, he argued, and therefore there was no money in
projection. He ignored the protests of Dickson, occupied himself with other
inventions, and failed to file his patents in a timely manner. Imitations of the
Kinetoscope sprouted up almost overnight, and its rapid dissemination across
America and Europe cut deeply into Edison's profits.

So, heeding Dickson's advice, Edison pursued a projector system, called
the Vitascope upon its introduction in 1895. This time, Edison patented the
intermittent movement of his projector, made possible by a synchronized
shutter. However, there was still a problem feeding film through the device;
a revolving Maltese cross ripped through the sprocket holes of the celluloid
when the reels pulled the film through the aperture, destroying the strips
completely. Edison himself brilliantly solved this problem by creating a
simple loop in the feed that allowed enough slack to prevent the ripping.
These few small innovations made the Edison equipment reliable enough to
become the choice of theater owners by 1895.

But cries of patent infringement followed the Vitascope's success. While
developing the new system, Dickson had persuaded other inventors that
Edison's stature was respected and marketable and he urged them to file
their patents under the Edison name. Although most of the men were paid
handsomely, and the process conducted legally, it is clear this method was
unscrupulous, and the advances of some pioneers were likely stolen when
they could not be coerced. "Everyone steals in industry and commerce,"
Edison said in his own defense. "I've stolen a lot myself. The thing is to know
how to steal." Inflamed over these claims on his patents, Edison began a
vicious legal war, seeking full credit for the invention of motion pictures and
a ban on the use of any film equipment not manufactured by his company.
But a Supreme Court ruling of 1902 concluded that Edison's contributions
did not constitute the actual invention of motion pictures. The combined discoveries of others were deemed critical.

Furious over the decision, Edison vowed to win in the marketplace.
Though he had a substantial share of commercial moviemaking devices, he
wanted more control. In 1908, he solicited several companies representing all
major producers and distributors in the industry: Vitagraph, Biograph,
Essanay, Selig, Lubin, Kalem, Pathé, Méliès, and Gaumont. Together, these

giants formed the Motion Picture Patents Company (MPPC) in 1909, commonly known as the Edison Trust. The Trust was a puppet organization in which Edison pulled all the strings, and his demands were tyrannical. He insisted that films be limited to no more than two reels, believing movie audiences wouldn't sit for twenty minutes at a time. He also wanted there to be no screen credit for actors, fearing their popularity might significantly raise the salary structure.

Most stunning, Edison forced independent filmmakers, including Adolph Zukor and Sam Goldwyn, to sign restrictive contracts that guaranteed the camera and projection equipment used in their motion picture production would be manufactured by the Trust companies exclusively. No producer was allowed to buy or rent any materials from other companies without suffering retaliation. Key to the power of the group was the inclusion of George Eastman, who refused to sell negative stock to filmmakers who did not cooperate with the guidelines set by the Trust. Producers who, like Thomas Ince and Jesse Lasky, refused to go along with the Trust decrees and found clever ways to continue filming were physically threatened by Edison's hired henchmen. In a series of events that seem straight from a gangster movie, the MPPC sent muscular thugs around town to all movie sets to ensure that producers were complying. When they came across equipment that was not manufactured by a Trust company, they destroyed it and roughed up the crew. Rather than buckle, several studios decided to make pictures overseas until the situation came to a resolution. Others packed up their operations and moved to Texas or California to escape the violence. This exodus west is responsible for the formation of Hollywood.

But some independents stayed and fought. William Fox, who led the charge against Edison and his cronies, broke their monopolistic practices in a highly charged court case in 1917. Shattered and embarrassed, Edison retired to his laboratory and dropped his interest in film entirely. Ironically, Edison's life would later be honored in films made by some of the same studios he once attempted to stifle; *Young Tom Edison* and *Edison, the Man* were both made by MGM in 1940.

The influence of Thomas Edison on motion pictures is dichotomous. His prestige was crucial in corraling the patented discoveries necessary to make a workable camera and projector. His earliest inventions became essential in illuminating moving pictures. He also contributed important solutions to the problems of intermittent film movement. But his eight-year campaign of terror against independent filmmakers was perhaps more widely felt, and in the end it strengthened their resolve to maintain creative freedom. Had he succeeded in stamping out his detractors and gaining a permanent grip on the movie business, his single-minded focus on making money might have prevented film from ever becoming a canvas for the expression of ideas.

11

JOHN WAYNE

Born: May 26, 1907, Winterset, IA
Died: June 11, 1979, Los Angeles, CA

There is no one who more exemplifies the devotion to our country,
its goodness, its industry, and its strengths than John Wayne.

—RONALD REAGAN

For nearly seventy years, the personality of John Wayne has shaped the moral code of the western genre and dominated the spirit of American moviemaking. His legendary persona exemplified both the law of the Old West and the politics of the Cold War. In movie theaters, he became the ideal patriot to millions of children and adults. Beyond the screen, he stood as a symbol of the righteousness and fortitude of America for the rest of the world. More than poets or presidents, this actor became the most effective ambassador the United States ever had, appearing before millions of people in hundreds of countries, disseminating a vision of the American ideal through his immensely popular films. No other man ever embodied the values of an entire country as succinctly as John Wayne.

Wayne began his film career as Marion Morrison, a young college football star who found work doing odd jobs at the William Fox studio in the late 1920s. Soon, he changed his name to the more masculine John Wayne and captured several bit roles in serial westerns. Though his first big break came when director Raoul Walsh gave him the lead in *The Big Trail* (1930), Wayne spent most of the decade in low-budget horse operas until a reluctant John Ford was persuaded to cast him as Ringo Kid in *Stagecoach* (1939).

The film raised the sophistication level of westerns by incorporating strong ensemble characterizations and daringly realistic action sequences into the standard cowboys-and-Indians formula. *Stagecoach* was a widespread success and brought much attention to the easygoing grace of the young Wayne, making him an instant action hero.

Although famous for his saddle work, Wayne would also lay a foundation for his legend during the 1940s playing a string of tough sergeants, brave aviators, and marine commanders in wartime classics such as *Flying Tigers* (1942), *The Fighting Seabees* (1944), and *Back to Bataan* (1945). These roles were critical to the development of John Wayne's public image during World War II, for they brought his patriotism into the present day and allowed homefront moviegoers to attach a heroic face to the American soldiers fighting in foreign lands.

As a Hollywood commodity, Wayne was a unique box office phenomenon. At least one of his films finished in the top ten every year between 1949 and 1972. And though his rolling gait and likable manner were mainstays, he wasn't afraid to explore off-type roles and keep his work fresh. Movies like *Red River* (1948) and *The Searchers* (1956) gave him opportunities to explore darker themes and present himself as an antagonist. He made noble attempts in romantic comedies and costume dramas, sometimes playing the unlikely barbarian or Roman; even drawling through the role of Mongolian emperor Genghis Khan in the critical flop *The Conqueror* (1956) could not tarnish his box office crown.

Still, the Wayne persona would remain most powerful and consistent in westerns. Under the care of director John Ford, who nicknamed the actor "Duke" and hoisted him back in the saddle, he made a long string of stellar films set in the picturesque landscape of Arizona's Monument Valley. Through three decades, Ford cast Wayne in such outstanding films as *Fort Apache* (1948), *She Wore a Yellow Ribbon* (1949), and *The Man Who Shot Liberty Valance* (1962), ultimately redefining the western genre and molding Wayne into an American icon. John Wayne made only thirty-one westerns, but in these roles he established the code of the screen hero—free, fair, decisive, and determined. His man-of-action was a rugged individualist who said what he meant and was ready to defend his words. Previous western heroes lacked these governing rules, and the western actors that followed were obliged to stay within the moralistic boundaries that audiences found so appealing in Wayne's performances.

Off-screen, his personality was neither rigid nor brash. An affable man with a self-effacing sense of humor, John Wayne spent his private time in quiet leisure, preferring the serenity of sailing to the raucous parties of Hollywood. When he wasn't relaxing, he honed his craft by tirelessly rehearsing. The monologues that seemed to roll effortlessly off his lips on film were in fact the result of laborious practice. Wayne's neighbors recalled seeing him spend long sessions in the backyard of his home, wandering the length of the property with a script in hand, memorizing his lines and repeating even the smallest phrase hundreds of times to determine the appropriate delivery.

Eventually the line between his personal views and his screen image blurred beyond recognition. His active membership in organizations like the Motion Picture Alliance for the Preservation of American Ideals allowed him to use his celebrity to further causes he deemed worthy. In the 1950s, Wayne joined Walt Disney, Clark Gable, and other entertainers to assist U.S. Senator Joseph McCarthy and the House Un-American Activities Committee in exposing Communists working in the film industry. He began hand-picking roles and financing the production of certain films, like the heavy-handed *Big Jim McLain* (1952), which made overt anti-Communist statements. These "message films" would often cost him, both personally and professionally; Wayne lost a small fortune on the Vietnam War film *The Green Berets* (1968), allowing an errant sense of patriotism to oversimplify the story of soldiers conducting covert military actions in Southeast Asia. As television images exposed the horrors of battle to Americans, the film's romantic portrait of "gung-ho" optimism was often cited as an example of how completely out of touch Wayne and many of his conservative contemporaries were with the complexities of the conflict.

Many of his critics felt John Wayne became encircled by his own legend and behaved as if he were truly the renegade he often portrayed in the movies. In a telltale example of Wayne's forcefulness, he virtually willed into being the Academy Award nominations for *The Alamo* (1960), a film he directed himself. *Alamo* was not an especially deserving piece of work; many people felt Wayne produced the project as a way of giving himself the heroic role of Davy Crockett. When rumors circulated that the Academy would pass the picture over, Wayne became enraged. He felt that *Alamo* was an important film, because it espoused American ideals in the midst of rampant Communism, and should be included as a Best Picture candidate. He enlisted the help of Russell Birdwell, the public relations showman who had successfully staged the search for the perfect Scarlett O'Hara in anticipation of *Gone With the Wind*. Wayne and Birdwell figured out that votes from just a few hundred of the Academy's two thousand members would swing a nomination. Targeting the 180 publicists in the voting body, Wayne drafted a 183-page press release that appealed to their patriotic side, and he spent $150,000 of his own money on an unprecedented campaign that placed hundreds of ads in trade dailies over several months. His persistence paid off; *The Alamo* received six nominations, including one for Best Picture. Many in Hollywood felt Wayne's personal crusade undercut the chances of such worthy films as *Inherit the Wind, Psycho, Spartacus,* and *Exodus,* none of which was nominated. However, the campaign became the blueprint for Oscar-stumping, and today's studios follow Wayne's plan to the letter, spending heavily on slick marketing campaigns to bolster the chances of winning a statuette, which can instantly double an actor's salary and add an estimated $25 million to the grosses of a film.

One of the hardest-working actors of his day, John Wayne made ninety-three films and was still in demand as a leading man well into middle age. Just as audiences felt he was becoming a pathetic has-been, he playfully poked fun at his own image in *True Grit* (1969). The role of the craggy curmudgeon Rooster Cogburn would bring Wayne his first Oscar at age sixty-two. A few years later, he gave his final performance, as a dying gunman in the elegiac *The Shootist* (1976), a painful reminder that Hollywood's greatest cowboy and film's most splendid genre were both passing.

Among cinematic icons, Wayne looms above all but Charlie Chaplin as an instantly recognizable international symbol of movies and a consistent box office champion. He was to the western what Chaplin was to silent comedy, what Alfred Hitchcock was to suspense, and what Lon Chaney was to horror. In fact, so pervasive is the influence of John Wayne on the cowboy picture that it's close to impossible to separate one from the other. It is equally difficult to recall the history of the American West without summoning many of the dramatic overtones that are present in the Duke's memorable performances.

12

J. R.
BRAY

Born: August 25, 1879, Addison, MI
Died: October 10, 1978, Bridgeport, CT

The first successful cartoonist to become a successful cartoon producer.
—LEONARD MALTIN

The first animated cartoon to contain a structured story, *The Dachshund and the Sausage* (1910), is credited to a young newspaper artist named John Randolph Bray. By day he worked as a senior artist on the *Brooklyn Daily Eagle,* and at night he fiddled with the idea of giving life to his drawings. But it was not artistry that would endear J. R. Bray to legions of animators, it was inventiveness. While moonlighting one evening, Bray toyed with sketches he had draped over a lampshade and was struck with the idea of a drawing process that would prove fundamental in making animated films commercially feasible.

At the beginning of the century, animated films were a tremendous drain of time and energy. Each character had to be drawn on individual pieces of paper in a series of slightly progressed poses, while retaining a consistent look throughout. Then, a tedious task would ensue: a background of scenery would have to be hand-drawn over and over again on each sheet of paper. The more elaborate the scenery, the more time-consuming the work. The number of hours required to complete just a few seconds of screen time made any prospect of profiting from cartoon distribution an utter impossibility.

By 1914, Bray had devised a system whereby a single image of scenery would be printed on hundreds of sheets of tracing paper, eliminating the need to duplicate backgrounds by hand. Then, after animating his characters on plain pieces of paper, he would overlay the translucent scenery onto the cartoons, giving the appearance of a cohesive scene. However, after these drawings were filmed, the trees and mountains of the background seemed to jitter when projected onto a screen. To fix this, Bray established one of the first important conventions of quality animation—registration pegholes. Most animators of the day were filming stacks of drawings by lining up their edges against the inside of a box. This was not a reliable way to ensure perfect alignment. Bray pushed two stubby hatpins through a piece of pressboard, turned it over, and affixed it to his drawing table. By placing the paper over the pins and puncturing each sheet in two separate places, he secured them for drawing. Each successive piece of tracing paper would be punctured directly over the previous sheet, and the artist would draw on top of his last illustration. When the drawings were all completed, Bray mounted a camera directly over the table, pointing it down in the direction of the pins, and threaded each drawing back through its original holes. The system worked magnificently. Bray's cartoons contained the steadiest images to be found anywhere.

He then joined with Earl Hurd, another newspaper cartoonist, who had independently experimented with a similar process using clear celluloid sheets instead of translucent paper. Hurd's approach differed from Bray's in that the background was a static painting and the characters were inked onto the celluloid material, called cels. Bray shared his peghole registration technique, and together the two men had the makings of a cel-based animation process that could reduce production cycles enormously and cut costs dramatically. Their first cartoon short, *The Artist's Dream* (1913), proved that the method was a sound success. Suddenly, animated cartoons were no longer a labor of love for starry-eyed cartoonists to create in their spare time. They were an industrialized product.

To capitalize on the idea, Bray first showed the process to Pathé Films and promised to roll out a steady supply of cartoon shorts. Studio head Charles Pathé was thrilled and contracted Bray to create the first animated cartoon series. *Colonel Heeza Liar* (1914) was based on a fashionable comic strip about an adventurous braggart, a thinly disguised caricature of Teddy Roosevelt. Bray did the first sketches himself but later hired young Walter Lantz, the soon-to-be creator of Woody Woodpecker, to complete much of the animation until 1916. As commissions for more cartoons poured in, Bray began to hire almost any artist who could hold a pencil. Animation experience was not required, and Bray preferred to teach the cel process to fresh thinkers. Many of the world's finest animators, including Max and Dave Fleischer, got their start in the Bray studios. He invited his competitors to learn the process, even offering to train many of their animators at night. There were naysayers who doubted the efficiency of the Bray-Hurd system, but it quickly became the standard for cartoon production, spreading to every animation studio in the world. In fact, Bray's 1914 patent on the process forced every studio to pay a licensing fee and required every cartoon made until 1930 to include in its opening titles the phrase "Licensed by Bray-Hurd Process Company."

Bray enhanced the cel method further with the introduction of multiple layers of celluloid, each carrying a separate element of the scene. For example, if two cartoon characters entered a scene from different edges of a frame, each character was inked onto his own celluloid sheet. The two sheets would be placed in register over the background painting and appear as a single integrated picture. The beauty of the multilayer method was that Bray could assign a dedicated illustrator to each character in a scene, once again reducing the time it took to finish a cartoon. By 1922, Bray's studio became a forerunner of the modern assembly-line process, separating tasks—like inking and painting, for example—into distinct departments. Other animation studios were stymied by his pace.

Artistically, Bray's studio never matched the level of his competitors; the skills of his illustrators were generally poor, and the stories were second-rate. Even his lone attempt at developing a franchise personality, *The Debut of Thomas Cat* (1920), was not memorable. But the financial success of the Bray studio allowed the artists time to experiment, and they introduced a number of sophisticated firsts for cartoons: the use of gray tones, camera dissolves between scenes, iris close-ups, surreal gags, and even live-action integration long before Max Fleischer's studio made it famous.

But the greatest gift was the cel process itself. Its basic concepts—independent movement of objects, and overlapping levels of action—have been utilized in every facet of filmmaking. For the next sixty years, almost all title cards and screen credits were achieved through some variation of the cel process. The principles of cel animation easily applied to other assembly techniques used in special effects departments; the optical printer uses a variation of the method to sandwich images together before filming. Ultimately, the multilayer concept would even be applied to many of the computer software programs that produce today's special effects.

The cel process alone accounts for Bray's lofty position in this ranking. Without it, the entire animation industry would not have been commercially viable, and the areas of special effects and title sequences would have been dramatically limited in their ability to produce many of the cinematic experiences we see daily. Additionally, the division of labor that Bray instituted in his studio became the worldwide model for the mass production of animated shorts; the separate tasks performed by animators has remained relatively unchanged. Bray's other technical innovations also support his reputation as one of film's most significant pioneers.

An ironic footnote to Bray's contribution to cartoons is the explosion in the late 1980s of vintage hand-painted animation cels as collectible items. As you read about one of these original cels being auctioned off for thousands of dollars, consider the many sheets that were discarded or unwittingly wiped clean after their initial use over seventy years ago.

13

BILLY BITZER

Born: April 21, 1872, Roxbury, MA
Died: April 29, 1944, Hollywood, CA

The greatest inventor among cameramen was perhaps Billy Bitzer.
—KENNETH MCGOWAN

In the dawn of motion pictures, there were no directors, only camera operators. And the quintessential pioneer among fledgling cameramen was Johann Gottlob Wilhelm Bitzer, better known as "Billy." Though he joined the Biograph company as an electrician in 1901, Bitzer swiftly advanced to cameraman and served his apprenticeship by photographing train arrivals, piano recitals, and boat christenings for the sputtering nickelodeons at the turn of the century. It was Billy Bitzer who explored the possibilities of the camera, and his timeless discoveries are the fundamental building blocks of filmmaking, evident in every movie made today.

The turn-of-the-century cameraman was a lone operator, an entire production crew on foot. Each day, Bitzer would fold up his tripod and hoist the camera over his shoulder, then set out onto the streets of New York to capture a short film. He had total control of filming: loading the reels, choosing the setups, hand-cranking the footage, and controlling the exposure. When the demands of his assignments increased, Bitzer packed up a horse-drawn wagon with additional cameras and drove around with assistants to faraway locations. He captured many of the day's most important news and sporting events in a journalistic fashion. A highlight of Bitzer's days as a newsreel cameraman was his filming of William McKinley's presidential nomination, a reel that became the first Biograph film presentation. As the first cameraman to record moving pictures in battle, Bitzer covered the Spanish-American War for the Hearst newspaper chain.

Bitzer was behind the camera on nearly all of Biograph's landmark films, honing his craft and toying with film exposures. In his years of filming news reports, Bitzer had learned to introduce a "fade to blackout" into shots by placing an opaque piece of black paper over the camera lens and letting the reel wind for a few feet, allowing less light into an exposure. This gave the final film a graceful break between subjects. By doing this several times a day, Bitzer became quite skillful at fading in and out of shots, sometimes winding the film canister back a few feet to overlap exposures.

When Biograph yanked him off his street duties and assigned him to watch over a talented new director, it was the beginning of a historic collaboration that would spark Bitzer's inventive mind and set him free to experiment. He would become D. W. Griffith's personal cinematographer, spending the next sixteen years working side by side with the director on close to four hundred film projects. He personally cranked the camera on nearly all of the Griffith classics—prominent among them, *The Birth of a Nation* (1915), *Intolerance* (1916), and *Way Down East* (1920).

One lucky consequence of this partnership was the application of Bitzer's streetwise camera effects on Griffith's straightforward narrative films. The fades and superimposed images began to shape the narrative structure, acting as smooth transitions and suggesting time lapses between scenes. Suddenly, the Griffith films took on a sophistication unseen in any other director's. Bitzer would continue to create these in-the-camera effects, which never required the help of editing. He introduced the famous "iris" fade effect, where the movie frame closes in from all sides to encircle a telling detail, prop, or facial expression. He developed a diffusion screen for lenses to produce a soft-focus look, used in later years to hide the wrinkles of aging stars. He would eventually master other optical tricks, including the freeze frame, which is found decades later in François Truffaut's *The 400 Blows* (1959), Martin Scorsese's *Goodfellas* (1990), and scores of other films.

Two other areas of expertise made Bitzer the perfect cameraman to capture Griffith's classics: he was as adept at filming close-ups as at taking long shots. The famous spectacle *Intolerance* (1916) gets most of its attention because of its huge sets, but Bitzer was responsible for capturing them on film. Master of the long shot, he often strapped the camera to the front of a car and rode, straddling the hood, through the gargantuan Babylon.

It can fairly be claimed that Billy Bitzer put a roof over Hollywood's head. In the earliest days of silent pictures, all films were shot outside; if an interior shot was required, three walls were haphazardly erected in a clearing. Pioneering studios were built with removable ceilings that rolled away to expose the set to daylight. But Bitzer was the first to use artificial light, photographing completely indoors without the benefit of sunlight, as early as 1909. This took films off the streets and into enclosed studios where cast and crew were sheltered from the elements.

After years of developing a sense of the proper film exposures required in natural light, Bitzer had to learn to adjust indoor lighting to meet the needs of the film stock. In this way, he became the first true cinematographer. He also instituted the classic three-point lighting setup that most films since have used without variation: a key light on the actor, a fill light on the set, and a backlight to help separate the actor from background elements. Backlighting instantly became an important cinematic concept, and Bitzer developed the first foil-covered reflectors for directing backlight into strategic positions. These findings were both critical to controlling the look of a film and to creating an appropriate mood. He was also the first to play with special lighting effects; he would cast flickers of light onto the set to give the illusion of candlelight, firelight, or morning sun. Among the hundreds of cameramen who contributed to the earliest discoveries of motion pictures, none came close to matching the numerous advancements that Bitzer stumbled on through his endless tinkering.

His trove of tricks and techniques usually brought more fame and credit to his directors and colleagues than to himself. Bitzer would go on to turn several of his assistants into fine cameramen and directors, notably Karl Brown, Erich von Stroheim, and Todd Browning. As the ace cameraman of the industry, he helped form the photographers' unions both on the East Coast and in Hollywood. Until his death in 1944, he spent his retirement restoring some of the world's earliest film recordings under the care of New York's Museum of Modern Art, many of which he had originally filmed himself. Shortly after his autobiography was published posthumously in 1973, the Billy Bitzer Awards were established by the International Photographers Guild in New York to honor those who have made a lasting contribution to the film industry.

For more than one hundred years, cinema has benefited from the seminal camera work of Billy Bitzer. Although the moviegoing public revered the talented Griffith for many of Bitzer's innovations, the close-knit circles of the industry had only the highest respect for the contributions of this legendary cameraman.

14

JESSE
LASKY

Born: September 13, 1880, San Francisco, CA
Died: January 13, 1958, Beverly Hills, CA

*At that time, Hollywood had just one policeman, and he
generally stood at the corner of Hollywood and Vine.*

—JESSE LASKY

By 1913, the film industry had a solid group of quality studios turning out movies at a regular clip. In fact, most of the motion picture business was controlled by large companies, principally Biograph, Vitagraph, Essanay, and Lubin. To break into moviemaking, a young producer like Jesse Lasky had two choices: he could join a studio and do it their way, or he could head out on his own. Lasky was among a new batch of filmmakers who became "independent" producers—those who made movies with whatever equipment they could afford and distributed them directly to theater owners. It was these "indies" that Thomas Edison's aggressive organization, the Motion Pictures Patents Company, was determined to drive out of business. At first, Lasky refused to buckle under the pressure, but when Edison sent goons to physically threaten him, Lasky packed his entire company and headed for California to an inconspicuous, undeveloped town called Hollywood.

Setting up shop in a small office on Sunset Boulevard in Los Angeles, Lasky became the founder of a new industrial mecca, the center of world film production for the next eighty years, and a good distance from the Trust thugs who threatened his small studio. Lasky simply couldn't afford to let Edison present huge problems for his biggest production, the historical

51

Squaw Man (1914). The first film to be made in Los Angeles, it featured the talents of director Cecil B. DeMille.

DeMille and Lasky discovered that Hollywood was an ideal place to make movies. First of all, it was equidistant from ocean vistas, mountainous terrain, and stark deserts—and not very distant, at that; almost any location or climate could be simulated within a few hours of the Sunset Strip. Initially, the citizens of the town didn't appreciate the influx of "movies," a derogatory term for the hoards of rodeo riders, circus performers, and thespians who found work there. But soon other studios followed Lasky to Southern California, staked out their lots, and began building their movie empires.

Lasky, helming his newly formed Feature Play Company, was now safely making movies in Hollywood, and with backing from his brother-in-law, Samuel Goldwyn, business was taking off. To ensure that his films would be exhibited, he teamed up with W. W. Hodkinson in 1916 and discussed a merger with distribution czar Adolph Zukor. They agreed to combine Zukor's Famous Players Film Company with Lasky's Feature Play Company and, after several name changes, eventually called the joint venture Paramount Corporation after another small company they had folded into the acquisition.

Instantly, Paramount became a major studio and Hollywood became a boom town. Lasky and Zukor paid lucrative fees to lure established stars such as Mary Pickford, Fatty Arbuckle, Gloria Swanson, and Rudolph Valentino to California and paid their handsome salaries by charging theater owners a premium to display their films. Then, they actively discovered or stole nearly all of the emerging stars of the twenties and thirties, including Carole Lombard, Marlene Dietrich, Mae West, and Gary Cooper. Directors of the stature of Ernst Lubitsch and Rouben Mamoulian were plucked out of Europe, and promising writers, including Preston Sturges and Billy Wilder, were later groomed for directorship in the family atmosphere of Paramount. Lasky also had a keen sense for innovators in peripheral areas; he gave career breaks to documentarian Robert Flaherty, wide-screen pioneer Fred Waller, and cinematographer Karl Struss.

Most important, Lasky continued to play an active part in the development of Cecil B. DeMille. He personally handled DeMille's film choices, moving him from the famous epics *The Covered Wagon* (1923) and *The Ten Commandments* (1923) to heralded romantic comedies. The energetic David O. Selznick was another favorite of Lasky's, gaining a position at Paramount after MGM had let him go.

In 1932, at the height of Paramount's output, the company suffered a financial disaster when several of its investments failed in the Depression. Lasky and Zukor were both ousted for mismanagement, and Paramount declared bankruptcy in 1933. Reorganized as Paramount Pictures in 1935, it continued on with Zukor as a powerless figurehead and Lasky out on the street. Lasky found work in a familiar role as an independent producer on *Sergeant York* (1941) and *Rhapsody in Blue* (1945), but he retired with a huge tax debt in 1950, the same year his former employee Billy Wilder honored the Hollywood pioneer with a mention in *Sunset Boulevard*.

It's most appropriate that Lasky ranks as the highest producer on this list; he defined the spirit of independent filmmaking. He was an unabashed opportunist who would proudly beg, borrow, or steal to ensure he was making movies that promised enormous financial return. His search for the unique film was driven by the desire to stay ahead of the competition. Finally, Lasky was the father of Hollywood; he gave birth to a place and an industry, he instilled the values it would retain for life, and he was respected as its leader until the fledging community could stand on its own.

15

GEORGE EASTMAN

Born: July 12, 1854, Waterville, NY
Died: March 14, 1932, Rochester, NY

*Eastman improved on Edison's idea by making celluloid flexible
so it could be wound on a spool.*

—DONALD HERALDSON

A bank clerk with a passion for amateur photography, George Eastman purchased a camera at age twenty-three and began learning how to master the difficult wet-plate process that had become the standard for capturing images. After much frustration with these messy wet plates, Eastman invented his own solution: he made a prototype machine that coated glass plates with a dry chemical emulsion that was light-sensitive. This new process was welcomed enthusiastically by photographers, and the dry plates sold well. However, the heavy glass plates proved too cumbersome to carry in quantity, and their higher price made them even less desirable. Eastman needed a better product.

A key development was the 1884 Eastman patent on a paper film, provided on a roll and made to wind through a camera so that it collected pictures as it moved past the lens. Originally, these pictures were captured one at a time; photographers had to expose an image, wind the film forward, then expose another image. The invention would launch the successful company known today as Eastman Kodak and make possible the Brownie snapshot camera, introduced in 1888.

The Brownie was the first portable camera simple enough to be used by amateurs, and it released thousands of new photographers into the world.

These snapshot experts simply sent the cameras back to Eastman for developing, and they were promised complete service through the advertising catchphrase "You push the button, we do the rest." Sure enough, the Eastman company churned out thousands of photos the first year.

The entrepreneurial Eastman, looking for more ways to sell his roll film, was happy to provide some in response to inquiries from the pioneering spirit of Thomas Edison's workshop, Laurie Dickson, who was experimenting with recording moving images. The paper film broke easily when Dickson attempted to send it through his viewing machine, and he told Eastman that he would require a stronger film that could mold to a cylinder for rotating through the viewer. Eastman, to his regret, could not oblige.

Luckily, Dickson had heard about a process discovered by the Reverend Hannibal Goodwin of Newark, New Jersey, for making a strip of film on a nitrocellulose or "celluloid" base, coated with a photosensitive emulsion. Dickson told Eastman of the Goodwin invention and suggested that this might be better suited to his needs. Dickson explained that the rolls should ideally be 35mm wide and perforated. Tempted by the prospect of supplying the regular needs of Edison's blossoming film business, Eastman did some testing and soon found a way to manufacture the first flexible transparent film on a celluloid roll. By 1889, the film was commercially available, and the specifications have changed little since.

The greatest achievement of the Eastman company, however, was its ability to keep pace with the changes in the film industry, despite its explosive growth in other markets, such as amateur photography. It is the only vendor to have supplied the film industry continually since its inception (except for a four-year period, when Eastman's participation in the Motion Picture Patents Company prevented him from servicing certain customers). Eastman gave the film business his unflagging support, investing heavily in any technology that was deemed important to the advancement of film. He was skillful at hiring talented inventors to keep his products of the highest quality. His organization was swift in edging the competition and quick to raise capital when needed. His support in the infancy of motion pictures was vital, particularly in seeing that busy producers from Edwin Porter to Mack Sennett received steady shipments of film stock.

In 1902, a significant patent case threatened Eastman's company. Hannibal Goodwin sued Eastman over the infringement of his 1887 patent on flexible celluloid film. The case, which dragged on until 1914, possibly altered the course of film history. It is clear that Goodwin knew of the limited shelf life of his nitrate film, and he had made significant steps toward developing an alternative. But the eleven-year legal battle with Eastman tapped the resources he needed to manufacture a better film stock, and an accident ended Goodwin's life prematurely. Nitrate developers continued to be the standard for film processing—and today present the greatest threat to the preservation of classic films.

Again in the 1920s, a patent dispute plagued Eastman; when Hollywood embraced the Technicolor process invented by Herbert T. Kalmus, Eastman hurriedly prepared his company for competition in color film stock. However, Technicolor enjoyed a lengthy patent protection period that effectively locked out Eastman for decades. So while Eastman waited for Kalmus's reign to end, the engineers at Kodak labs devised a system that substantially lowered the cost of developing three-color film. On the heels of the patent deadline, Eastman representatives made backlot deals with most of Hollywood's studios, and by 1953, producers were abandoning the Technicolor process for Eastman Color. George Eastman, however, never lived to see its success. After a long bout with illness, he committed suicide in 1932.

The legacy of Eastman carried on. Shortly after his death, the George Eastman House was founded to become a permanent archive of international motion pictures; today, one of the oldest film archives in the United States, it houses over seventeen thousand cinematic treasures, including silent films, Technicolor negatives, documentaries, shorts, newsreels, amateur films, still photographs, lobby cards, advertising posters, music sheets, and scripts. In the late 1950s, Kodak did for wishful young home-movie makers what it had done for photographers with the Brownie snapshot camera: the company released a low-cost 16mm Instamatic movie camera and projector for amateurs, giving hope to a generation of dreamers that included Steven Spielberg, George Lucas, and Francis Ford Coppola.

Innovations such as celluloid roll film and amateur movie cameras illustrate the profound influence of Eastman. He spent a good portion of his time and resources on perfecting the technical aspects of film and promoting its worldwide use. His organization was a cornerstone of the industry that would provide cameras and film made at his Rochester, New York, headquarters for more than a hundred years. George Eastman's commitment to motion pictures, coupled with a competitive drive to dominate its equipment and materials, earns him a top position among film influencers simply because his dedication to the industry was instrumental in the rapid progress of the art form.

16

SERGEI EISENSTEIN

Born: January 23, 1898, Riga, Latvia
Died: February 11, 1948, Moscow, Russia

*Any two pieces of film stuck together inevitably combine to create
a new concept.*

—SERGEI EISENSTEIN

Arguably, the most powerful ten minutes in movie history belong to Russian director Sergei Eisenstein. His flashing images of a massacre in the landmark film *Battleship Potemkin* (1925) shocked the film world and ushered in a remarkable and controversial style of editing. It was no happy accident that *Potemkin* contains such raw emotional energy; Eisenstein was a thoughtful director who had been preparing to make the film his greatest illustration of the art of "montage" editing. Montage showed filmmakers a new way to glean meaning from their footage, to weave messages into their stories. Though Eisenstein would manage to complete just seven films, all of which demonstrate the potential of montage, the concept would catch on quickly and take hold in films around the world.

Sergei Eisenstein was first and foremost a student of movies. An intense fascination with the editing style of D. W. Griffith led him to the production of his own short films, including a parody of newsreels in *Glumov's Diary* (1923). The young director spent long hours at the editing table, cutting miles of footage into different combinations to achieve new effects. Many of his creations were shown to friends who seemed to humor his particular bent, but when he edited the avant-garde film *Strike* (1924), he sparked the public's imagination with the first display of a new cinematic grammar. The film had scenes in which a series of conflicting shots abbreviated time spans and overlapped the meaning of images. *Strike*'s best example of the new "montage" editing style was a scene in which rioting factory workers are gunned down; intercutting between the massacre and shots of cattle being butchered, Eisenstein was able to draw a parallel with images that borrowed an emotional response from one shot and applied it to another. This power of suggestion is the essence of montage.

The enormously influential *Battleship Potemkin* (1925) was only Eisenstein's second film, but it became the perfect demonstration of the editing style—a montage masterpiece. *Potemkin* remains to this day the highest achievement of its kind. The story is about Russian sailors who refuse to accept maggot-infested provisions while docked in the city of Odessa. Enlisting the support of the townspeople, they rise up against czarist troops and face a violent end in the film's climactic scene. Eisenstein's script was based on an actual account of the 1905 mutiny that incited the Russian Revolution. Splicing close-ups of suffering faces with the boots of marching soldiers in the legendary "Odessa steps" sequence, Eisenstein used a rapid-fire technique of fast cutting between babies, mothers, and guns in scenes so shocking that audiences believed they were watching newsreel footage of a brutal wartime uprising. The film featured no memorable characters, and the quick succession of human faces served to symbolize the power of the masses rather than the thoughts of an individual. For example, the devasting effects of the revolution are insinuated by shots of anonymous people: a grieving mother embracing a dead child, an elderly man running for shelter, and, most famous, the seemingly purposeful stumbling of an untethered baby buggy through a barrage by vicious infantrymen. The ten-minute montage sequence manages to say more about the senselessness of aggression than any two hours of dialogue from a script ever could.

Battleship Potemkin pushed cinema to a new standard. It is surpassed in its editing influence only by *The Birth of a Nation,* and the exceptional cross-cutting is one of the true original additions to the art of film. Eisenstein basked in the worldwide reaction, calling himself a premiere illusionist. The film displayed its political ideology so convincingly that it was banned in several countries. However, Eisenstein became the legendary filmmaker of his country, overshadowing the accomplishments of such other Russian talents as Dziga Vertov, Vsevolod Pudovkin, and Alexander Dovzhenko.

The montage style became the predominant technique in many films, and it is used in thousands of contemporary films to execute most of the transitional devices that audiences now take for granted. The most commonly seen example of montage is a collage of images that conveys the passing of time or events: for example, the stereotypical shot of printing presses running with superimposed newspapers falling on top of one another, each showing a new headline. Another example, by now a visual cliché, is the use of overlapping shots of the same car in front of different landmark tourist locations to mean a character is traveling around the country; the editing style compresses the entire trip into just seconds of film time. These concepts are so ingrained in the visual language of film that most viewers never stop to question their long-established purpose.

However, there is a more sophisticated execution of the montage editing style, often referred to as intellectual montage, and this is the style most closely associated with Eisenstein's work. Intellectual montage juxtaposes several images through the use of shock cuts or dissolves, to pull from the scene a deeper meaning. Symbolism and visual metaphors are often the result, but the technique is also a way to create penetrating thematic points that would be awkward or difficult to portray otherwise. Sometimes these sequences can take on a slow, majestic feeling; the opening montage sequence of *Citizen Kane* superimposes iron gates and NO TRESPASSING signs over the castle of Xanadu as a metaphor for the reclusive millionaire living inside. Other times the suggestive power of montage is best served by shock cuts: the famous shower scene in Alfred Hitchcock's *Psycho* brings together startling clips from several vantage points to simulate the surprise and confusion of a brutal attack. Eisenstein's influence can also be seen in the sacrificial ritual at the conclusion of Francis Ford Coppola's *Apocalypse Now,* in the space dogfights in George Lucas's *Star Wars*, and in the peyote-induced visionquest of Jim Morrison in Oliver Stone's *The Doors.*

Eisenstein's direction became internationally renowned. The overwhelming curiosity over montage forced him to articulate his filmmaking aesthetic to the world, and he became known as the greatest thinker among film theorists. The Stalin regime, growing weary of the attention Eisenstein received, took out their disfavor on his subsequent films. *October* (1928), originally commissioned for the anniversary of the 1917 revolution, was plagued by party politics, and Eisenstein was ordered to change his style of editing.

When the sound era approached, Russian filmmakers feared they would be left behind and urged their government to let them explore sound technologies. Eisenstein was sent to Europe in 1929 to investigate recording techniques for sound films and was welcomed as a hero by the film community. He met his own hero, Abel Gance, scientist Albert Einstein, and author Gertrude Stein. From Europe he continued on to Hollywood, where he formed an immediate friendship with Charlie Chaplin, Walt Disney, and his mentor, D. W. Griffith.

Inspired by the documentaries of Robert Flaherty, Eisenstein detoured to South America in 1930 before returning to Russia. He filmed *Que Viva Mexico* and sent the footage ahead to Moscow for editing, where it mysteriously disappeared; it was never seen again. After years of frustration over Russia's interference with his work, Eisenstein suffered a nervous breakdown in 1932. The Communist government continually refused to allow the production of his ideas until 1941, when Eisenstein was commissioned to make *Ivan the Terrible,* based on the sixteenth-century historical figure. He proposed a three-part epic that eventually became mired in problems and hastened the end of his career as a director. In later years, he worked as a professor in the Moscow film school. His selected essays dissecting the different applications of montage in film direction, as well as his books *The Film Sense* and *Film Form,* were published in the sixties and widely read. He died just days after his fiftieth birthday.

The four cornerstones of basic film techniques were laid by Eisenstein, Porter, Welles, and Griffith. Together, these four men discovered the essential elements of composing, shooting, and editing, and discovered important ways of combining images to inject powerful new meanings into their stories.

17

ANDRÉ BAZIN

Born: April 8, 1918, Angers, France
Died: November 11, 1958, Paris, France

Just to be scolded by him was a pure delight.
—FRANÇOIS TRUFFAUT

The word "auteur" has been applied to filmmakers ever since legal battles were waged in the French film industry of the 1930s to determine who deserved credit for a film. Many critics of the time felt the screenwriter should be considered the original author of a finished movie. Others argued for the contributions of editors and producers. The question was extended beyond the courts in 1951, when film theorist André Bazin founded *Cahiers du cinéma*, a quarterly journal devoted to studying the art of motion pictures and hailing its greatest contributors. In the magazine, Bazin trumpeted the motion picture director as the sole claimant to ownership of films. As the principal instigator of the "auteur theory," Bazin contended that, since film is an art form, the director of a film must be perceived as the principal artistic creator of its unique and distinctive style. This highly influential opinion formed the persistent notion among movie buffs that the director is the driving force behind every image.

As university clubs and film societies sprouted up in the 1950s, a new generation of film lovers closely followed Bazin's criticisms, and an underground critical movement was born. His viewpoints redefined a set of critical tools for the people who watched movies, and his reviews of contemporary films, as well as his lengthy examinations of techniques used in classic films, formed the foundation for a new way to evaluate and appreciate filmmakers.

Others influenced by Bazin's critical essays were critics and filmmakers themselves. Many of the French New Wave directors, who often congregated in the Paris theaters of Henri Langlois while viewing selected classics from his extensive film archives, were listening to Bazin at the same time they were shaping their ideas about a new cinema. Among the film critics who came under his tutelage were four men who would go on to become the most famous directors of postwar French cinema: François Truffaut, Jean-Luc Godard, Jacques Rivette, and Claude Chabrol. These young enthusiasts took to the streets with 16mm cameras and applied to filmmaking their own vision, largely based on the aesthetics articulated by André Bazin.

A prolific writer, Bazin was also a consummate voyeur who dissected each film with a discerning eye. An important principle championed by Bazin's writings was "mise-en-scène," a style of filming that emphasizes long takes, the placement of the camera, and the precise choreography of action. In mise-en-scène sequences, several elements come together to give a scene the director's personal touch: lighting, color, scenery, the proximity of actors to each other, the camera's movement and angles, and transistions within the same frame. More than any other factor, the placement and use of these elements speak to the control of a director over his vision, Bazin emphasized, and through them the style of an artist emerges. When successfully executed, the residual effect of this technique is the all-encompassing feeling that a whole world is in motion far beyond the reaches of the frame. Bazin said, "The camera should be able to spin suddenly, without picking up any holes or dead spots in the action."

An effective example of mise-en-scène appears in Orson Welles's film *The Magnificent Ambersons* (1942). A conversation between two gentlemen begins at a fireplace, moves across a crowded dance floor, picks up two other interested parties, and moves into another room. In one continuous shot, the focus of the discussion turns away from the two men and zeroes in on a young couple who speak a few lines before joining the dancing throng. The scene, completely choreographed to happen in a single take, ebbs and flows with the intimate close-ups of people talking and the establishing distance shots of the ballroom. Another memorable mise-en-scène shot is witnessed in Martin Scorsese's *Goodfellas* (1990), when a man escorts his girlfriend through the back door of a busy nightclub and winds through a maze of kitchen helpers, coatcheck girls, bouncers, and bartenders to find their seats in front of the performers' stage. Careful planning and skillful direction are required to maneuver through dozens of actors who genuinely appear to be unaffected by the couple. The scene lends a believability through its utter complexity.

Bazin argued that mise-en-scène compositions are preferable to the radical montage scenes of Sergei Eisenstein, for they show that the director was planning all cuts before the editing stage. Bazin pointed to the works of Jean Renoir, Erich von Stroheim, Orson Welles, and Ernst Lubitsch as the finest examples of mise-en-scène direction, and a renewed interest in their careers soon followed.

He particularly revered directors who succeeded in experimenting and improving their methods despite the strict budget constraints, stock players, union crews, script revisions, and impossible deadlines imposed by their producers. Taking his lead from film critic James Agee, Bazin argued that the highest purveyors of the form were the fiercely independent American directors who continued to stamp their personalities on films in the midst of the assembly-line mentality of Hollywood's studio system. His respect ran deepest for film pioneers like D. W. Griffith, Ernst Lubitsch, and Charlie Chaplin, and Bazin's analysis of their accomplishments gave film lovers a greater understanding of their influences. A sudden interest in the films of Alfred Hitchcock, John Ford, William Wyler, and particularly Howard Hawks stemmed from Bazin's unique perspectives on their careers; throughout the 1960s, film appreciation classes and revival theaters showcased the work of these directors, and many of these "auteurs" were finally honored for their achievements.

Appropriately placed on this list as the highest-ranking nonfilmmaker, André Bazin had a significant impact on cinema as both a theorist and a critic. He completely turned around all thinking concerning the art of film, setting criteria by which film buffs could evaluate the efforts of an entire generation of filmmakers. His adamant support of the auteur theory remains the most pervasive position in film criticism; almost all films seen today are viewed with a sense of a sole originator, the director, as an omnipresent force driving the entire production. This predisposition has cast much notoriety on the directors who have developed their craft in the wake of Bazin's influence. Today, the director takes the credit and the director takes the blame. Contemporary directors are often more popular and more controversial than the cast or crew of their films, and many, such as Stanley Kubrick, Oliver Stone, Spike Lee, Francis Ford Coppola, and Martin Scorsese, are now known to audiences by their distinctive styles.

18

IRVING THALBERG

Born: May 30, 1899, Brooklyn, NY
Died: September 14, 1936, Santa Monica, CA

His record is too excellent for me not to regard him as the master.
—DAVID O. SELZNICK

The emerging studio system of the 1920s shifted power from stars and directors to omnipotent producers, whose job it was to make formulaic pictures that were assured of success. To do this, studios sought experts in efficiency and profitability, the best of whom was Irving G. Thalberg. At the pinnacle of his power, Thalberg's dominion over the entire Metro-Goldwyn-Mayer operation was complete. He controlled the finances, hired and fired directors, discovered new screen personalities, coordinated with artists and technicians, and, nearly all by himself, transformed MGM into the most profitable and respected studio in the industry. He carved out a position as the prototypical modern producer of motion pictures and instituted many of the tests that gauge audience reactions to films as a way of improving their financial prospects.

Irving Thalberg's rise through the ranks of Hollywood was meteoric. He began as a humble secretary at Universal, and before reaching the age of twenty-one he had been promoted to general manager. (One anecdote relates that Universal executives assigned a special bookkeeper to assist Thalberg because he wasn't yet old enough to have check-signing authority.)

He left Universal to join Louis B. Mayer's production company, building a reputation as a boy wonder. When Metro Pictures merged with several other small production studios to become Metro-Goldwyn-Mayer in 1924, investors insisted that an independent party keep an eye on the manner in which Metro boss Louis B. Mayer would run the new venture. Thalberg got the assignment, largely due to his reputation for high-quality films, and his inclusion was packaged with the deal. The rocky relationship between the jealous president and the wunderkind didn't affect productions at first, but soon Thalberg's emerging power threatened Mayer.

To ensure that MGM completed the merger smoothly, the studio elevated Thalberg's stature to supervisor of production, giving him total control over all projects. His autocratic style perfectly suited the needs of the assignment. He had an innate sense of entertainment, he was an organized and meticulous taskmaster, and he did his homework. To keep in touch with trends, Thalberg frequently sat through movies with the general public.

His first real challenge on the job was corralling the costs of flamboyant director Erich von Stroheim, the studio's biggest talent and biggest spender, and with whom Thalberg previously had conflicts at Universal over excessive costs and unmanageably long film lengths, replacing him midway through the production of *Merry-Go-Round* (1922). On the mammoth silent film *Greed* (1924), Thalberg and Stroheim clashed in a scene that has become Hollywood legend. Discovering the excessive indulgences of Stroheim's production, including bills for imported caviar and champagne, Thalberg stripped the film of the director's control and edited a ten-hour film to just 140 minutes. In one swift move, Thalberg essentially ended Stroheim's career, ruined his reputation, and established the lengths to which MGM would go to deter excessive costs.

If Thalberg was a fabled cost-cutter, he was even more the legendary census-taker. His greatest contribution to motion picture production was the audience litmus test. Seeking to ascertain public interest, Thalberg first used *The Big Parade* (1925) to collect opinions and reactions to the film's story, stars, costumes, and settings. He followed up intensive preproduction questionnaires with a series of preview screenings designed to predict box office success. Exit polls were conducted on everyone who saw the film, then he unwaveringly filmed retakes to bend to the tastes of moviegoers. He would not hesitate to change an ending or eliminate a character completely on the basis of feelings he perceived from audiences. Gauging the line between commerce and art, Thalberg made all decisions on gut instinct but tempered his whims with the reports he collected. The result was such hits as *Mutiny on the Bounty* (1935), *A Night at the Opera* (1935), and *San Francisco* (1936). This screening process was faithfully applied to all MGM productions and is still in widespread use today.

Second only to Thalberg's acute sense of public opinion was his reliance on talent. He personally handled the careers of MGM's greatest stars, including

Lon Chaney, Greta Garbo, Jean Harlow, Clark Gable, Spencer Tracy, and the Marx Brothers. Having great respect for the immeasurable value of the production crew to his assignments, he favored a hand-picked group of specialists, including director Victor Fleming, writer Anita Loos, and art director Cedric Gibbons.

The Good Earth (1937) was his last hurrah, featuring a stunning film cast, and cut with Thalberg's input at nearly every turn. It was the only film in which Thalberg gave himself an on-screen credit. A persistent heart condition slowed him in 1933, and in the middle of production for the Marx Brothers' *A Day at the Races* (1937) he caught pneumonia and died at the age of thirty-seven. Today, the Thalberg Memorial Award, instituted in 1937, is given by the Academy of Motion Picture Arts and Sciences to distinguished efforts in production. A celluloid biography came by way of Elia Kazan's adaptation of the F. Scott Fitzgerald novel *The Last Tycoon,* starring Robert De Niro in the role of the young impresario.

Ironically, Thalberg ranks just slightly ahead of production pioneer Thomas Ince: while Ince became famous for bending films to his strict production system, Thalberg was willing to bend his productions to the whims of the audience. Years later, studios continue to favor the Thalberg method, and his influence resonates throughout studio films that are screened for audience approval. In fact, the legacy of Thalberg is still present in the modern-day film producer—adhering to the practices of responsible budgeting, and shaping films by keeping a finger on the pulse of the public.

19

THOMAS INCE

Born: November 6, 1882, Newport, RI
Died: November 19, 1924, Hollywood, CA

Being able to give orders without giving offense made Ince's method work.
—THOMAS BOHN

As well as being one of the towering figures in Hollywood's early days, Thomas Harper Ince originated the film industry's most basic movie production techniques; he fathered the concepts of budgets, shooting scripts, multiple camera units, and set crews made up of specialists. Through his iron grasp on hundreds of films, he became the early model of a Hollywood producer, and his groundbreaking production innovations have remained relatively unchanged for eighty years.

Ince's entrance into and exit from moviemaking are two of Hollywood's most bizarre stories. In 1910, he was a struggling performer whose last performance was in one of D. W. Griffith's first Biograph films. Frustrated with screen acting, he decided to produce movies independently, and he quickly displayed an aptitude for pulling a team of filmmakers together. His new enterprise got the attention of the Edison Trust, which was systematically putting independents out of business; just two months after his precarious start as a producer, he was off to Cuba to escape their brutal tactics. Along with him went fellow Biograph star Mary Pickford; after directing her in a comedy short, he was more than ever determined to make a living in the volatile film industry.

When it was necessary to return to moviemaking in the States, Ince traveled to Texas and eventually settled in California, where, like Mack Sennett, he set up a small studio to meet demand for shorts. By 1912, Ince had himself a movie factory, turning out hundreds of reels a year. The popular western one-reelers Ince specialized in forced him to construct bigger surroundings, and his new location became the first major studio built in Hollywood.

The Ince compound was an eighteen-thousand-acre facility outside Culver City. Built to resemble Mount Vernon, George Washington's plantation-style home, it was the predecessor of the modern studio, with individual offices for writers and directors, sound stages, dressing rooms, a cafeteria, and warehouses, all enclosed by a giant fence that spurred the playful Mary Pickford to refer to it jokingly as a "lot." Others mocked its enormous stretch by dubbing it "Inceville." The antebellum feel of the buildings later prompted David O. Selznick to film much of *Gone With the Wind* there.

Along with a new location, Ince's mammoth operation needed a new discipline. Traditionally, the budgets on early silent films were so low that many studios didn't bother to clearly define all of their costs. But Ince insisted that every penny be meticulously documented. Accountants were hired to keep a close eye on efficiency and ensure strict compliance with budgets. To avoid duplication of effort, Ince divided film production crews into several shooting units that each worked on a variety of projects. Every day, he assigned one team to travel to the nearby mountains and handle the location shots for several westerns while other teams were on the lot shooting barroom or bunkhouse interiors; actors and directors moved in and out according to the dictates of his detailed schedules. Instituting these streamlined processes, Ince was following the trend that was taking hold in industries all over America: he was applying Henry Ford's principles of assembly-line automaking to films. In his quest for strict accountability, the artistry of his films became secondary to sheer business sense.

The most useful contribution of Thomas Ince, however, was the detailed continuity script. A rigid guideline for filming, it broke down every detail of a movie by numbering scenes, suggesting camera setups, outlining costume and prop needs, recommending camera angles and lighting, and hinting at postproduction details such as special effects and titles in scribbled notes throughout the margins. The Ince script became gospel, and he exerted his creative and financial control through it. He often used a detailed script as a way of changing a scene without having to confront a volatile director: in a note delivered by messenger, he would order the director to hold all shooting on a certain sequence in the script until costs could be evaluated and approved, then secretly order a second-unit team to shoot the scene exactly as written in the detailed script, and finally tell the director that the scene had already been shot.

As a "director-general," Ince could review many projects simultaneously, writing scenes and making comments. He watched daily rushes and groomed actors for stardom. A capable storyteller and technician, Ince was more responsible for his studio's final output than the film's director, and he often took credit with "Thomas H. Ince Presents" above the title. His centralized management techniques were so successful that other studios adopted his methods immediately, particularly his incessant note-writing. David O. Selznick would become an infamous memo-writer, and the young Irving Thalberg developed Ince's penchant for shooting schedules and budget worksheets.

One consequence of Ince's methodology was the introduction of labor unions. Most producers in those days allowed a person to contribute to a film as an actor, writer, director, or crew member, often doing several jobs on the same production. Ince would no longer provide those opportunities. His highly structured system clustered craftspeople by specialty, creating a division of labor. Soon, trade organizations were formed to represent the interests of each group. By the early 1920s, the film industry was heading smack into the era of the studio system.

Thomas Ince was regarded among his contemporaries as a true visionary. At times, he partnered with such luminaries as Mack Sennett, Allan Dwan, and D. W. Griffith. One such collaboration took place in 1915, when Ince formed the Triangle Film Corporation in concert with Sennett and Griffith. They produced a string of famous and commercially successful westerns starring William S. Hart. However, Ince could not get the diffcult Griffith to adhere to his rigid schedules, and the troubled studio faltered after *Intolerance* (1916) failed to recover costs.

In his later years, Ince dissolved his interests in motion picture studios and looked for work as a hired gun on big productions. He was sought by Paramount and MGM for his efficiency and became a forerunner to such modern independent producers as David O. Selznick, Darryl Zanuck, and Alexander Korda. Throughout his life, he remained one of the most prominent and influential producers in Hollywood.

The death of Thomas Ince was shrouded in mystery and confusion. Although only forty-four years of age, Ince was already a puffy-looking man of frail health. Ulcers and liver problems had plagued him for years. One night, he boarded publishing magnate William Randolph Hearst's yacht for a seafaring celebration of his appointment to head Hearst's new production company. When the boat returned to shore, a seriously ill Ince was hurried to a train in Del Mar en route to a family doctor. His condition was critical enough that his body had to be placed on a stretcher and passed through the window of the train. When he arrived at home, a family physician cared for him for two days before a heart attack supposedly caused his death. A coroner's certificate that listed the reason for his death as "natural causes" started rumors about the true nature of the events on the yacht. Gossip columnist Louella Parsons seized a chance to fuel speculation by alluding to "Hollywood's darkest scandal" in a fabricated story that had Ince fatally shot aboard the yacht by the jealous newspaper tycoon. In a persistent and unfounded piece of movie lore, Ince was allegedly mistaken for Charlie Chaplin, whom Hearst believed to be involved with his mistress. Hearst is said to have put a bullet into Ince's abdomen in the heat of passion, causing him to slowly bleed to death. In the absence of any supporting facts, the scandal is rumored to have been completely covered up by Hearst. The story is vehemently denied by Ince's family, who insist that his stomach problems were preexisting and that his death was not at all dramatic or mysterious. Still, that depiction continues to taint the memory of Ince as one of the true pioneers of motion picture production.

20

MARLON BRANDO

Born: April 3, 1924, Omaha, NE

With Brando, you feel something smoldering, explosive, like a
furnace door opening, with the heat coming off the screen.

—JOHN HUSTON

By the time famed acting coach Lee Strasberg dissolved his Group Theatre in 1940, he was the monarch of the modern "method," having learned it straight from a Moscow disciple of its originator, Konstantin Stanislavsky. The Stanislavsky method was a series of techniques used to invoke the emotional experiences and life memories of an actor to add authenticity to a role. When Broadway director Elia Kazan and his cohorts decided to stage experimental plays under the name Actors Studio, Inc., they lured Strasberg as their artistic director. From 1948 until his death, Strasberg's New York workshop was home to an exclusive membership of dedicated recruits. The most famous of these was Marlon Brando.

But Brando's roots in method acting actually started in 1943, when he enrolled in the Dramatic Workshop at the New School for Social Research. His teacher was Stella Adler, another Stanislavsky teacher, who trained many of Hollywood's finest actors, including Robert De Niro. Brando became Adler's greatest pupil, developing the distinctive performances that characterized the method as highly improvisational and raw. After a few brief appearances in Broadway plays, Brando left the Dramatic Workshop for the Actors Studio, where he first rubbed elbows with filmmakers. Though actor John Garfield had brought the method to Hollywood years earlier, it was

Brando's role as Stanley Kowalski in the film version of *A Streetcar Named Desire* (1951) that drew attention and praise to the performance style. Alongside the theatrics of Vivien Leigh, his brooding intensity and teeming sexuality painted him as a rough-hewn primitive and struck chords in both male and female audiences. The plaintive screams of "Stella!!!" and the deflated muscular figure draped by a ripped T-shirt created an indelible moment in cinematic acting.

Brando became an overnight celebrity, accosted at every turn by curious and crazed fans. Immediately, Hollywood tabloids began reporting on his unusual preparation for roles and his rebellious sex life. But the paparazzi didn't distract Brando from his work. Including *Streetcar,* he received four consecutive Oscar nominations for earthy, visceral performances, in *Viva Zapata* (1952), *Julius Caesar* (1953), and *On the Waterfront* (1954). His magnificent role as a punchdrunk boxer in *Waterfront* guaranteed his place in film history with the oft-quoted "I coulda been a contender" and won him the Oscar. For a new wave of actors—Anne Bancroft, Rod Steiger, Patricia Neal, Sidney Poitier, Marilyn Monroe, and legions more—the method's value had been confirmed.

So natural and charismatic was Brando that a riveting turn in *The Wild One* (1954) made his strong portrayal of a vulnerable rebel the symbol of post–World War II angst before James Dean came along. As a sexually charged antihero, the moody Brando perched atop a motorcycle wearing a leather jacket and riding cap and spoke for all youths. "What are you rebelling against?" a character in the film asks him. "Whaddya got?" replied Brando. This rebellious spirit had a significant influence on the way teens were portrayed in films for nearly two decades.

A decade of mercurial performances and studio wrangling began with *One-Eyed Jacks* (1961) and *Mutiny on the Bounty* (1962). By the time these films had reached the theaters, both the method and Brando's temper were labeled by film executives as bad for business. Brando was apparently more concerned with exploring the depths in his film characters than with the films themselves, and his peculiarities soon added up to costly delays on a number of projects. As his reputation became a source of ridicule, he became sullen and retreated to an island home in Tahiti to live the life of a recluse.

Good roles eluded him until he heard that the young director Francis Ford Coppola was making a movie about an organized crime family from a bestselling novel by Mario Puzo. He pestered Coppola for a shot at *The Godfather* (1972). Originally, Coppola was interested in Laurence Olivier, but after Brando sent a videotaped audition, which featured large cotton balls shoved deep into his cheeks, Coppola was convinced. The film brought Brando another classic line in "I made him an offer he couldn't refuse" and another Oscar. At the Academy Awards ceremony that year, he did not accept the award for Best Actor, sending instead a young squaw to announce Brando's refusal as a way of protesting the treatment of American Indians.

Last Tango in Paris (1973) gave Brando the opportunity to use his experiences as a disenchanted American expatriate to add nuances to his character. Playing a lonely, self-loathing man who plays juvenile sexual games to mask his own insecurities, Brando claimed the emotional strain of the method nearly killed him. The film was an internationally recognized success, reaping several awards and the highest critical praise. Brando's roles in the 1970s had a tremendous impact on the acting styles of Al Pacino, Robert De Niro, Harvey Keitel, Jon Voight, Dustin Hoffman, and countless others. Establishing himself once again as a sensation, Brando held out for enormous salaries for bit parts in *Superman* (1978) and *Apocalypse Now* (1979).

His last Oscar nomination, for *A Dry White Season* (1989), renewed interest in Brando for a whole new generation and sparked a recent flurry of undistinguished work, including a superficial role in *Don Juan DeMarco* (1995) and a bizarre title part as an androgynous mad scientist in a remake of the H. G. Wells story *The Island of Doctor Moreau* (1996). But Brando's unique and surprising characterizations continue to influence the best work offered by today's American film actors; Jason Patric's animalistic pugilist in *After Dark, My Sweet* (1990), Sean Penn's confessional killer in *Dead Man Walking* (1996), and Nicolas Cage's self-destructive drunk in *Leaving Las Vegas* (1996) all borrow the brooding intensity and self-examination that made Brando's acting such a mesmerizing experience for filmgoers.

Marlon Brando represents the highest-ranking performer on this list who didn't make his mark by establishing a character cliché in a cinematic genre. His impact on fellow actors took shape in his portrayal of diverse characters in a wide variety of films. Better yet, Brando seems to transcend his most memorable parts to symbolize a style of performance, a feat that few actors ever achieve; he is the embodiment of method acting, a form that initiated sweeping changes in the way screen actors communicate.

21

LOUIS B. MAYER

Born: July 4, 1885, Minsk, Russia
Died: October 29, 1957, Los Angeles, CA

*Talent is like a precious stone, like a ruby or a diamond. You take care
of it. You put it in a safe, you clean it, polish it, look after it.*

—L. B. MAYER

Louis B. Mayer joined his father's junk business in Boston right out of high
school, but an offer in a 1907 advertisement put him into the nickelodeon business at a bargain price. By 1918, he was Massachusetts's largest movie theater
owner, specializing in the presentation of top-quality films for wealthy patrons.
Mayer started expanding his empire by distributing D. W. Griffith's *The Birth of
a Nation* (1914) in the New England area and made a small fortune from its
popularity. To further speed the supply of pictures to his theaters, he moved his
operations to Hollywood and opened the Metro Pictures Corporation in 1917.
He began production with his only star, Anita Stewart, in *Virtuous Wives* (1918).

A three-way merger in 1924 gave Sam Goldwyn, Marcus Loew, and Mayer
a new company, Metro-Goldwyn-Mayer (MGM). Largely because of the production savvy of Irving Thalberg and the consistent style of Cedric Gibbons,
MGM dominated the film industry during the twenties and thirties, and
Mayer's salary signaled the financial strength of the movie industry; in 1938
he was the highest paid person in a U.S. corporation, taking home more than
a million and a quarter dollars.

Another sign of Mayer's power was his ability to quash the careers of his
employees, no matter how successful or beloved they had become. Director

Erich von Stroheim, actor John Gilbert, and seductress Mae West all suffered the wrath of Mayer's short fuse and saw their careers ruined prematurely and forever. Even producer Irving Thalberg, whose inherent likeability and business acumen were legendary, was suffocated by the jealousy of his boss. However, these displays quickly established the power of studios in the days of the "star system," and Mayer and his contemporaries exerted much of their control through restrictive contracts that put actors at the mercy of their bosses.

Mayer's leadership within the film industry was critical to the formation of the Motion Picture Producers and Distributors of America, Inc., a puppet organization conceived by Mayer to duck government regulation by convincing lawmakers that the picture business itself could police the objectionable subject matter in Jazz Age films. The MPPDA, which created the Hays Office and the Production Code, became the perfect venue for Mayer's conservative politics, often the subject of discussion at the massive parties he held for the organization at his palatial residence.

One such discussion at his home was the impetus for the founding of the Academy of Motion Picture Arts and Sciences. Seeking to recognize the contributions of the industry's growing number of trade unions, Mayer felt a group of representatives from each union could form an "academy" and select a member who exemplified the best of the year's output through a lavish event. The first Oscar award ceremony was held in 1927. For several years, the Oscars were hand-picked by a small group of union members and studio executives—and, of course, Mayer himself. In fact, he held an uncontested veto power over who received Oscars until 1941, when an outstanding performance by Bette Davis was passed over at Mayer's insistence, inflaming the Screen Actors Guild. Since then, the Academy has adopted a formal-based nomination process and a secret ballot for the final vote. The winners' names are sealed in envelopes that are not opened until one fateful night of each year. The Academy Awards was a stroke of genius, giving the industry a much-needed unity and giving great achievers a chance at worldwide recognition.

Looking for every opportunity to sway industry affairs, Mayer even became California's chairman of the Republican Party in the 1930s. After a brief and failed attempt in 1937 by Thalberg and William Fox to stage a coup and dethrone Mayer, he continued on at MGM until he stepped down from the helm of his own volition in 1948. He remained as vice president and general manager until 1951, also acting as adviser to Mike Todd's Cinerama corporation briefly before retiring completely by 1953.

Few individuals have ever controlled so many aspects of the film industry as L. B. Mayer. As the absolute ruler of the fabled Hollywood star system, he ran Metro-Goldwyn-Mayer like a grand patriarch, ruthlessly punishing disloyalty among his children and indefatigably defending the members of his family against scandal and rumor. His personal values shaped the films of MGM in their heyday; Mayer was famous for removing all controversial material from popular novels to turn them into pure escapist fare. In keeping with the virtues of patriotism and family, MGM pictures generally reflected Mayer's penchant for wholesomeness. Mayer was committed to the best talent money could buy, and he scouted pretty girls and dashing men the world over, discovering Greta Garbo, Joan Crawford, Rudolph Valentino, and Clark Gable. Grooming these stars became his everyday mission. Molding public opinion became a sideline passion. Reigning over Hollywood became an obsession. L. B. Mayer was the most powerful executive of the largest and most prestigious film studio for more than forty years.

In 1932, when the famous platinum blond starlet Jean Harlow went home to find her husband dead from suicide, the first call she made was to Mayer, who quickly rushed over to comfort Harlow and defuse any potentially adverse publicity. A scandal was thwarted, and Harlow's career continued on unaffected. The paternal Louis B. Mayer had taken care of everything.

22

GRETA GARBO

Born: September 18, 1905, Stockholm, Sweden
Died: April 15, 1990, New York, NY

Her indifference to public opinion made her career unique.
—ALEXANDER WALKER

During the silent era, Hollywood was eager to distribute its films to wider audiences and considered international markets a prime source for additional box office profits. To tap them, studio heads set out to find foreign actors and directors who had established a following, bring them to America, and place them in movies that had universal appeal. Talent scouts first began scouring the European film community for emerging stars. In 1925, MGM founder Louis B. Mayer went shopping for directors in Stockholm and found Mauritz Stiller, fresh off the success of *The Saga of Gösta Berling* (1924). Stiller returned to the United States with Mayer, under the condition they bring a promising young actress with them. Within a year, Mayer would send Stiller back to Sweden and begin to mold his protégé, Greta Garbo, into one of his top stars. Before long, Garbo would become one of the world's most recognizable faces and leave a lasting impression on the world of cinema.

Greta Garbo's film career was quite unlike that of any other Hollywood actress of the time; she did not work her way up through hundreds of auditions and dozens of bit parts. Her stardom was manufactured by L. B. Mayer and the staff at Metro. Mayer decided to make Garbo an instant star, and her first day in Los Angeles was spent at the salon of makeup artist Max Factor, who created a special look for the actress that accentuated her trademark features—pale complexion, thin lips, arched eyebrows, and long lashes. Despite Mayer's best efforts, Garbo's first film, *The Torrent* (1926), went relatively unnoticed. However, her second, *The Temptress* (1926), marked two important beginnings: it began an exclusive contract with MGM that would lock her into a lucrative but tempestuous relationship with Mayer for years to come, and it started a lengthy collaboration with photographer William Daniels, who would capture the famous Garbo gaze in nearly every film she made.

Much has been made of Greta Garbo's statuesque beauty; her looks are purported to be appreciated even more by women than by men. She was graced with a face that photographed well from any angle and deep, penetrating eyes that gave her a great range of expression, an invaluable asset for silent films. Her instincts as a performer were unerring; she knew the right amount of emotion to display in front of the camera. She has been said to convey both intense passion and complete indifference at once, and much of the fascination with her acting stemmed from her ability to reveal intimate thoughts while remaining aloof. Her screen persona was a sophisticated mixture of icy remoteness and aristocratic fortitude. This complexity made Garbo one of the most compelling actresses in film history and allowed her to portray some of the strongest female roles ever filmed.

When she was teamed with MGM's top leading man, John Gilbert, in *Flesh and the Devil* (1927), a reported affair between the two fueled the success of the picture, and Garbo's popularity soared. As their off-screen relationship generated greater public attention, the demand for more of their films intensified. Their second film together was perhaps the most anticipated event in the silent era. However, before pairing with Gilbert in *Love* (1927), Garbo demanded more money and top billing from Mayer—and got them.

Mayer guarded his prized commodity very carefully, and the romance of Garbo and Gilbert, his two finest stars, would become a sore point with him. When Garbo eventually tired of Gilbert's affections, Mayer was asked to act as a liaison between them, and the relationship between Mayer and Gilbert quickly became strained. Gilbert felt Mayer was encouraging Garbo to leave him, and Mayer grew tired of Gilbert's constant accusations. As their discussions became increasingly heated, the two men elevated their enmity into a well-publicized feud. The breakup of Garbo and Gilbert ultimately led to the release of Gilbert from his MGM contract, but they remained close until Gilbert's early death in 1936.

After thirteen silent films, Garbo was uncomfortable with the transition to sound. She felt uncertain about the reaction to her voice, deep and thickly accented. But her first talkie, *Anna Christie* (1930), ended her worries. She crossed over to sound films with tremendous box office success and was nominated for the Best Actress Academy Award that year. Despite her beauty, she could easily handle the masculine determination required for *Queen Christina* (1938). It was not her finest film, but *Christina* did capture Garbo's incredibly magnetic allure. Although she spent much of the film walking around in pants, her femininity didn't wane. The final shot of her courageous, pensive countenance staring into the sea is one of film's most enduring images.

As critical successes mounted, Garbo bargained with MGM until she eventually became the highest-paid woman in the United States. Her largest paycheck came in 1930, a whopping $275,000. She was given her choice of director, preferring MGM's sure-handed craftsmen like Clarence Brown, who directed most of Garbo's twenty-seven films. Whether at home in the poignant melancholy of *Grand Hotel* (1932), or trying her hand at cynical desperation in Ernst Lubitsch's *Ninotchka* (1939), Garbo also welcomed any chance to showcase her more-lighthearted skills. In *Ninotchka*, Lubitsch stripped away the old, brooding Garbo to create a sophisticated yet fussy performance that revealed her gifts for comic timing and delivery.

Timing would, in fact, turn out to be her most legendary quality, for in 1941 she made a career move unique in the history of cinema. After sixteen years in film, at the age of thirty-six, Greta Garbo withdrew completely from the public eye, becoming a staunch recluse until her death in 1990, and leaving only her flickering images to sustain her memory.

Greta Garbo, Hollywood's greatest European import ever, was arguably the world's most popular actress and the most celebrated woman of the silent era. Although Mary Pickford ranks higher on this list for her all-around contributions to the earliest days of Hollywood and for her seminal role in the star system, Garbo perhaps achieved greater international recognition during her heyday because of the maturation of the industry and the greater number of filmgoers worldwide. Throughout her career, she enjoyed the rare stature of a goddess; Garbo set a standard for sex appeal in the movies that has rarely been matched. Also, an important part of Garbo's legend is her reclusiveness. She shunned public events and rarely was seen outside of her films. This enigmatic quality, coupled with her regal features and glamorous air, added to her celebrity, and she has become a cinematic mystery, baffling millions of admiring fans with her complex and magnetic persona.

23

ROBERT FLAHERTY

Born: February 16, 1884, Iron Mountain, MI
Died: July 23, 1951, Dummerston, VT

Flaherty edited his raw films into a new and creative experience.

—FRANK MANCHEL

Working as a surveyor and mapmaker for a fur company, Robert Flaherty often brought his trunk of amateur photography equipment with him during explorations of the Belcher Islands in 1917. When the company purchased a motion picture camera, Flaherty showed enthusiasm for its possibilities and carried it with him throughout the Arctic. He would use it to become the first man to popularize a form and style of shooting known as documentary filmmaking.

He shot his first film of Eskimo life for a personal project in 1919, using a makeshift film-developing lab in his Hudson Bay cabin. He would start a small log fire to heat his processing chemicals to an exact temperature for successful processing of the negatives. Flaherty learned the mechanics of his equipment through necessity; the moist weather conditions forced him to disassemble the camera and wipe away any condensation before using it again. He had collected nearly seventy thousand feet of film when a cigarette butt accidentally ignited the nitrates in the film canisters, destroying everything. Flaherty, intent on re-creating his movie, returned in 1921 and befriended a village of natives while he filmed their daily activities for one year.

The edited result was the sixty-nine-minute *Nanook of the North* (1922), a painstaking chronicle of an Eskimo family's struggle for survival. Filming the daily life of hunter Nanook the Bear, Flaherty captured poignant moments of the children at play with their father, the hunters chasing down a walrus, the fighting dogs who keep their master company, and the gruelling procedure of building an igloo from scratch. Using only such simple camera techniques as close-ups, tilting, and panning, Flaherty captured scenes of Nanook at a traders' outpost, investigating a gramophone record by biting its edge, and he juxtaposed those shots with images of Nanook biting the fishes he catches and kills with his teeth. The most compelling sequence comes at the film's finale; a hunt for the Great Seal takes viewers across rushing waves with the Eskimos in their kayaks.

Flaherty staged many of the scenes to give *Nanook* a narrative structure. His clever selection of special orthochromatic stock was perfect for capturing the blue-green tones of Arctic life. And though he established many long-standing conventions of documentary filmmaking, he manipulated many of the situations he was filming and paid almost all of his subjects to perform their normal routines. Flaherty even instructed the Eskimos to create an oversized igloo without a ceiling so that he could capture their "natural" habitat with enough sunlight for proper exposures.

Nanook became the first travelogue feature film to claim international success. British critic John Grierson would later coin the term "documentary film" in a 1926 essay examining *Nanook,* and Flaherty would forever carry the moniker "the father of the documentary." Flaherty became a celebrity in Hollywood, and studios were eager to finance explorations of other cultures. Audiences craved more information about the unassuming hunter and his family, but as Flaherty documented in his book *My Eskimo Friends* (1924) Nanook had starved to death on a gruelling deer hunt long before the film made its debut.

Paramount agreed to send Flaherty to Polynesia for another documentary, *Moana* (1925). An important development in *Moana* was the application of panchromatic film, which was first used here in feature length and later became the industry standard; Flaherty chose it not for technical reasons but simply because he liked the way the Samoans' skin looked in the experimental emulsion used in developing it. *Moana* was at first lauded by critics until it became evident that Flaherty was not a pure documentarist. He was making his features more attractive by manipulating his subjects and their settings. Like filmmaker Leni Riefenstahl, Flaherty learned a bitter lesson about the social responsibility that audiences assign to them. When he was justly attacked by anthropologists for making a poetic fantasy rather than an accurate representation of island life, Flaherty changed his approach completely.

He collaborated with W. S. Van Dyke and F. W. Murnau on more narrative features, including *White Shadows in the South Seas* (1928) and *Tabu* (1931), using scenarios to guide the filming. He rejected large crews and big budgets and longed for a personal, simple process, all the time making significant and influential advancements in documentary filmmaking. His most successful film, *Man of Aran* (1934), watched an Irish fisherman's daily work and was recognized by historians as his most accurate account.

As his films were seen internationally, he became a popular figure in Europe and was introduced to filmmakers wherever he went. Flaherty was instrumental in helping Sergei Eisenstein bring his masterpiece *Battleship Potemkin* (1925) to the United States. He also introduced the Russian director to admirers Charlie Chaplin, D. W. Griffith, and others. The challenge for Flaherty came when movies went to sound and he was forced to write traditional scripts and record narrations for his films. Silent movies were no longer acceptable to paying audiences, and his films ceased to be popular. Hollywood studios thought it was a reflection of the subject matter Flaherty was choosing.

Returning to America in the forties, Flaherty was reduced to taking grants from the U.S. Information Service to make public information films for the Mental Health Film Board and private commissions from Standard Oil to make, respectively, *The Land* (1942) and *Louisiana Story* (1948). These films opened new markets for documentary films, providing a generation of amateur directors an opportunity to seek corporate funds for their projects.

Flaherty's position in film history is firmly rooted; as the father of the documentary film, his ignorance of editing and techniques was overlooked, and his natural instincts are still the ideal among documentary films. His inventiveness and persistent searches for foreign subject matter have sparked the imagination of filmmakers since he first took to the Arctic ice. *Nanook* still stands as the most vivid and powerful example of how films can connect cultures and introduce moviegoers to distant, mysterious lands. It has been consistently listed as the single most inspirational work in documentary filmmaking.

24

LON CHANEY

Born: April 1, 1883, Colorado Springs, CO
Died: Aug. 26, 1930, Los Angeles, CA

No matter how grotesque the makeup was, you kept watching him.
—MICHAEL BLAKE

Like many other actors in the silent era, Lon Chaney came to personify an image that audiences would never relinquish. He made the most indelible impression on horror films of any actor, and his name became synonymous with a genre that has remained one of film's most mesmerizing. The child of deaf-mute parents, he learned to master the art of pantomime, joined his brother as a propman in a traveling show, and rose through Hollywood's ranks to become a legendary chameleon known best as "the man of a thousand faces."

Beginning as an extra in 1913, Chaney took any bit part he could land, and before long he had made over seventy films. A memorable role in *The Miracle Man* (1919) made him a star. His extraordinary talents attracted director Tod Browning, who used Chaney extensively in such films as *Wicked Darling* (1919), *The Unholy Three* (1925), *The Blackbird* (1926), and *The Road to Mandalay* (1926). In *The Unknown* (1927), he played an armless knife-thrower who dazzles circus crowds with his feet; a startled Joan Crawford was his favorite target. Conversely, he played a man whose legs had been amputated in *West of Zanzibar* (1928); Browning liked the effect so much that he used a legless character in *Freaks* years later.

By the early twenties, Chaney's pictures were made on his terms; he was powerful enough to choose his own director and command complete script approval. That probably accounts for the adaptation of Victor Hugo's piercing novel *Hunchback of Notre Dame* (1923). Stripped of its politics and left with the relationships, it reflects the nature of Chaney himself: nonconfrontational. This fundamental story of maiden and monster is the origin for all imitations, including Chaney's own later films.

In another Beast and Beauty story, *The Phantom of the Opera* (1925), Chaney demonstrated his profound influence with the stiff, slow movements of the title character. These jerking, eccentric motions, usually accompanied by the display of outstretched, clawing hands, would later influence the character shadings of Dracula and Frankenstein. His compelling performances in these grotesque roles put him forever in the nightmares of horror fans.

A trademark of Chaney's films was incredible physical transformations, beginning in *The Penalty* (1920) when he strapped his legs behind his body and put himself through excruciating pain when leaping off tables to land on his knees. However, a common misconception is that Chaney was a reckless contortionist who put celluloid in his cheekbones and pins in his nose for roles like the Phantom. A proclaimed seventy-pound rubber hump for *Notre Dame,* for example, was actually revealed to be just twenty pounds of plaster. Although his disfigurements were complicated and strenuous, they certainly were not masochistic; such stories were exaggerated and perpetuated by studio executives to heighten interest in his pictures.

In the 1929 edition of the Encyclopedia Britannica, Chaney generously contributed a general description of contemporary motion picture makeup techniques. However, he left out many details; by leaving fans to speculate on the methods behind his particular transformations, he prolonged the life of his illusions. In fact, Chaney was careful not to let his characterizations rely heavily on makeup. He developed a great screen presence, using his ability to examine the darkest aspects of the human condition. In one of his biggest hits, *Tell It to the Marines* (1927), he used no disguise at all, and the critical response was tremendous.

Dual roles also became another trademark, as in the lost film *London After Midnight* (1927), where vampire and policeman roles are both played by Chaney. Carefully picking a project for his debut into the sound era, he filmed a remake of *The Unholy Three* (1930), in which Chaney played all of the leading characters. The film opened to rave reviews and instant box office success. He had made a brilliant transition to talkies and was ready for a new challenge. Unfortunately, *The Unholy Three* was his last picture and his only sound effort. Shortly before his death, Chaney was set to work with Tod Browning on a sound version of *Dracula* (1931). Universal Pictures had acquired the rights to the Broadway play, a box office smash starring an unknown named Bela Lugosi. When throat cancer claimed Chaney's life in

1930, at the age of forty-seven, the role of the famous count reverted to Lugosi.

Unfortunately, the gallant efforts of film preservationists have failed to keep many of Chaney's films in front of film fans. Of his 150 spectacular films, a paltry forty-three still exist, many of them fragmented or in jeopardy of permanent damage from the effects of nitrate chemicals. James Cagney performed scenes that Chaney had originated in a tribute to the master of horror entitled *The Man of a Thousand Faces* (1957). And though Creighton Chaney, son of his first marriage to Cleva Creighton, would keep the horror alive through his performances as "Lon Chaney Jr.," he could not match his father's macabre characters. Lon Chaney's unique performances are still the standard among screen entertainers. The humanistic view of monsters and freaks set a precedent for screen portrayals from Boris Karloff's Frankenstein to Steven Spielberg's ET.

At Chaney's funeral, Irving Thalberg gave the eulogy, saying, "There are few who possess his peculiar magic, that extraordinary ability to make us feel, to lift us out of our own existence and make us believe in the world of make-believe. But let's examine him closely, look behind the makeup, the many masks, and see what happened to this strange and interesting man to give him those sharp edges, those facets that made him glitter, that made him great. Great not only because of his God-given talent but because he used that talent to illuminate certain dark corners of the human spirit."

25

ANITA
LOOS

Born: April 26, 1893, Sissons, CA
Died: August 18, 1981, New York, NY

She was the first practitioner of the wisecrack for the screen.

—GARY CAREY

Perhaps the most unsung creative artist in motion pictures was Anita Loos. No other writer in film history can lay claim to her sheer artistry. Her terse, clever title cards came to define screen personalities in the silent era. Loos was in tune with moviegoing audiences and knew exactly which linguistic approach would send them into howling laughter. Mastering the ability to make audiences anticipate her next comment, she would surprise and delight them with unexpected wordplay or double meanings. Her words had the power to create stars and level governments. She was the unspoken "voice" of Lillian Gish, Mary Pickford, and Douglas Fairbanks, and she crafted a tone and delivery that established the essence of Hollywood dialogue.

Surrounded by performers all of her life, Anita Loos grew up on the streets of New York playing with childhood friends Helen Hayes, Adele Astaire, and Paulette Goddard. At the age of sixteen, she went to work for D. W. Griffith writing a script for the Mary Pickford film *The New York Hat* (1912). One of the first film scenarists (most then were women), she received fifteen dollars a week for her story ideas, many of them humorous. She wrote a staggering 105 scripts in the next three years, including several of Biograph's early commercial successes.

After seeing simple title cards used in early films for exposition, Loos urged Griffith to let her explore them as dialogue cards. Griffith, although partial to her humorous writing, was unimpressed with the prospect. His position was that "people don't go to the movies to read," but Loos persisted. After she presented some examples, he reluctantly conceded, and Loos was soon writing witty phrases that are credited with helping make Douglas Fairbanks a star in *His Picture in the Papers* (1916). It was the introduction of satire to silent film. Griffith was converted, Fairbanks was transformed into a star, and title cards were a permanent fixture.

Loos's silent wisecracks seemed to mock the Victorian values of most silent productions and drew humor from the moviegoing experience itself; in a Fairbanks adventure that featured a villain with an unpronounceable name, she tickled audiences with a title card that said, "Those of you who read titles aloud, don't attempt to pronounce his name. Just think it." Theater patrons sat up and eagerly awaited her next screen gem. Loos was the first writer to make sexual innuendo an integral part of highbrow film comedies. She was also one of the first known to the public by name, and she playfully winked at her followers by giving herself equal billing with the authors of classic literary works: a title card for *Macbeth* read "Written by William Shakespeare and Anita Loos." Today's flippant one-liners spoken by action stars after climactic moments are pure Loos. Her spirit is present in the smug "Hasta la vista, baby" of Arnold Schwarzenegger in *Terminator 2* (1994) or the cynical "Go ahead, make my day" of Clint Eastwood's Dirty Harry in *Sudden Impact* (1983). Loos turned wisecracking into movie language distinct from stage wit.

Until 1920, the writers of title cards attempted to mimic the sharp-witted humor that Loos initiated, and many failed dismally to reproduce her talent for deft understatement. More important, other silent films were becoming tiresome and repetitive; it seemed Loos had added a personality and bite to them that moved the art form into a new era of maturity. Her subtitles strongly supported characterization and suggested a speaker's "tempo." Good subtitles, she demonstrated, could clarify the action in a scene and help propel the plot forward.

Loos developed a prestigious reputation for her writing on more than two hundred films, including Griffith's *Intolerance*, several Shakespeare adaptations, and a popular treatment of Clare Booth Luce's play *The Women* (1939). Sought after by other studios, including Reliance, Lubin, and Metro, she would remain one of the most prolific and well-paid writers in Hollywood, finally accumulating more than 250 screen credits in her career. Her success drew attention to the screenwriter as a creative artist equal to the director and allowed audiences to see that movies were written and not merely ad-libbed, and her biting wit paved the way for Dorothy Parker and other women writers who came to assume similar prominence in Hollywood.

Screenwriting led her to other forms of writing—a 1925 comic novel, *Gentlemen Prefer Blondes*, became a bestseller, which Loos subsequently adapted for the screen in 1928.

In 1929, Loos joined MGM at the request of Irving Thalberg. Female screenwriters then outnumbered males by nearly ten to one, and she was instrumental in guiding some of the talented young screenwriters of the era, especially Preston Sturges, while pounding out scripts for sound films. Actress Jean Harlow became a recipient of Loos's cynical banter in *Red-Headed Woman* (1932) and opposite Clark Gable in *Riff-Raff* (1935) and *Saratoga* (1937). The breezy lines of Loos's script slipped off the sexy lips of Harlow with ease and became her trademark delivery.

Despite penning the exploits of characters in all kinds of exotic settings, Loos rarely traveled outside the country, dividing her entire life between New York and Hollywood. A diminutive woman of four feet, eleven inches, she died at the age of eighty-eight. In her old age, she assisted historians in restoring many of her films in the 1970s and was careful to remind them of the contributions made by women screenwriters.

Few have ever matched the style of the teenage scenarist who literally set the tone of movie dialogue. Among other gifted screenwriters of the day, including such pioneering females as June Mathis, Frances Marion, and Jeanie Macpherson, she was the most successful at creating a voice and personality for the stars of the silent screen. The clever banter that Hollywood scripts favor is the direct result of her prolific lines. A telltale anecdote of her influence comes from a *Photoplay* interview in 1917. Reporter Julian Johnson was interviewing D. W. Griffith, and when the name of Anita Loos came up, the stately director placed a finger over his mouth, paused to collect his thoughts for a moment, smiled, and said simply, "The most brilliant young woman in the world."

26

GEORGE MÉLIÈS

Born: December 8, 1861, Paris, France
Died: January 21, 1938, Paris, France

I owe him everything.

—D. W. GRIFFITH

The life of George Méliès is the stuff of great fiction. As a child, Méliès found an escape from his family's machinery business by skipping off to a Paris theater in the afternoons, where he was captivated by the optical illusions of magician Robert Houdin. By the age of thirty-four, Méliès would own the Houdin Theatre, and he himself would perform startling illusions there. As an amateur magician, he explored new ideas to keep his youthful patrons coming back for more.

In 1895, Méliès went to see a demonstration of the Lumière brothers' Cinématographe in Paris, the first public display of motion pictures. In the audience that day was another future film pioneer, Alice Guy Blaché. The two were both amazed and inspired by the possibilities of moving images. Each would conceive of a new direction: Blaché would become the first to capture a narrative on film, while Méliès went on to become the most influential celluloid storyteller of his day.

After unsuccessful attempts to purchase a system from the Lumières, Méliès rushed home to build his own camera-projector. He presented a selection of film shorts made at the Edison studio in conjunction with a live program of magic at his Houdin Theatre just four months later. However, the Edison features, like the Lumière previews, were sixty-second recordings of typical daily scenes—such scenes as factory workers leaving for home. This was not the bill of fare a magician could combine with live theater to entertain children, so Méliès set out to make his own films.

He built a studio and designed elaborate sets and costumes for his fantastic stories. He crafted scripts and recruited pretty French girls. By trial and error, he learned to make performers disappear by stopping his camera in midshot, removing the actors, and continuing on. He learned of the wonders that appeared on the screen after he wound the negatives back and exposed the film twice. He played with different shutter speeds and discovered more magical effects while experimenting with such camera tricks as slow motion, dissolves, fade-outs, and superimposition. Better yet, Méliès let his imagination dictate the best applications of these newfound techniques; his story films showed the touch of both a curious inventor and a science fiction writer.

Most of the early Méliès stories began as staged magic shows. As the master of ceremonies, Méliès often dressed as a conjurer who could sever the limbs of victims through special effects. His output at this time was astounding; he worked at a rapid pace, following his own muse when creating original stories or adapting classic literary works as in his mini-epics *Cleopatra* (1899) and *Hamlet* (1908). His hurried pace, however, often resulted in shoddy craftsmenship. He hand-painted colors onto many of his films and placed awkward sliding cards between frames to signal transitions. But what Méliès's entries lacked in theme and execution, they made up for in energy and imagination. His films were highly successful and show his knack for sheer entertainment.

At one time Méliès was the world's most prolific producer, and his films were widely successful in the United States and imitated all over the world. Other directors surpassed him quickly with new narrative devices, but Méliès commanded the lion's share of the market with a steady supply of entertaining shorts. He made over five hundred films in all, financing, directing, photographing, and acting in nearly every one. Most of these films were less than ten minutes long, and a great majority of them have since been lost. Both Porter and Griffith expressed their admiration of Méliès and cited his films as a major influence on much of their early work.

By 1900, illegal duplication of Méliès's films was so common that the filmmaker was forced to put a small trademark in the corner of every frame. Many U.S. distributors would simply hire employees to paint out or cut off the trademark before copying the prints. Piracy became such a problem that Méliès felt compelled to hand-carry the prints of *Trip to the Moon* (1902) to the United States, where he began a ridiculous ruse to expose the perpetrators of this crime. Posing as a European theater owner, he visited several U.S. distributors, including the Lubin Company, where he was taken to a screening room and shown a duplicated print of his own film, with his trademarked signature covered by opaque paint.

The enormous popularity of *A Trip to the Moon* changed the course of motion picture production. The Jules Verne story would be universally acknowledged as the great-granddaddy of all science fiction films. Never again would a Méliès film reach such heights. His *Baron Munchhausen* (1911) failed to make money, and although he created an intriguing and frightening Abominable Snowman in *The Conquest of the Pole* (1912), audiences generally were tiring of Méliès's lower-quality productions and looking for more sophistication in both effects and storytelling.

Continued piracy and rising costs of independent distribution caught up with Méliès in 1905, and before World War I his film career was over. Although he had become the first man to strike it rich in the film industry, he died penniless at seventy-seven. A last contribution would be his meticulous record-keeping; he was the first filmmaker to document his work through still photography. Méliès's trove of drawings and notes outlines his frantic method and leaves us with the pieces of one of the first great stories of feature filmmaking.

Inspirational leaders like Méliès are rare in any industry; his imagination was the wellspring from which almost all early films were born. Other filmmakers split their time equally between making their own movies and watching the ones made by George Méliès. To the language of film, he contributed the photographic tricks; to the spirit of film, the fantastic and the supernatural. His need to explore his dreams through the art of filmmaking is the fundamental force that today drives such visionary directors as Stanley Kubrick, David Lynch, George Lucas, Ridley Scott, Tim Burton, and Steven Spielberg.

27

ADOLPH ZUKOR

Born: January 7, 1873, Risce, Hungary
Died: June 10, 1976, Los Angeles, CA

*Zukor bought up as many film adaption rights as he could
and enticed big names away from the theater.*

—ANDRÉ BAZIN

Fifteen-year-old immigrant Adolph Zukor didn't take long to discover opportunity in America; he started a nickelodeon in 1903 and eight decades later, he was still a vital part of show business. He teamed up with Marcus Loew in 1904, and they began purchasing theaters in New Jersey, Philadelphia, and Boston, systematically gobbling up their competitors before forming the largest chain of semipalatial theaters on the East Coast, Loew's Consolidated. As treasurer of the company, Zukor guided the expansion of the company into a national chain of theaters that founded a film empire.

However, Zukor was more interested in the distribution of films than their exhibition. In 1912, he left Loew to finance film productions of famous Broadway plays. Zukor's idea was to recruit stage actors to repeat their performances, a concept he would master over the years. His first success came after he bought the distribution rights to *Queen Elizabeth* (1912), a British four-reeler starring the respected Sarah Bernhardt. The film was a hit in America, and the profits afforded the creation of Zukor's Famous Players Company with a new partner, Edwin S. Porter, who directed many of their first productions. Together, they signed superstar Mary Pickford and forced theater owners to pay premium prices for her films.

Now immersed in the film production business, Zukor became a shrewd talent scout and promoter. He turned Pickford's "America's Sweetheart" image into an international campaign. Later, his handling of the "It Girl," Clara Bow, would extend her career to more than fifty features during the Roaring Twenties. He merged again in 1916, this time with Jesse Lasky and his Feature Play Company. Lasky produced the first feature film made in Hollywood, *The Squaw Man* (1914), and had a stable of talent including idol Gloria Swanson and director Cecil B. DeMille.

After a series of financial reorganizations, Zukor and Lasky merged with a few smaller companies in 1935 under the name Paramount. Zukor arranged for a $10 million loan to buy up more theaters, more book rights, and more actors. Nobody in Hollywood had a keener sense of talent or a more astute notion of distribution. He offered Roscoe "Fatty" Arbuckle a million-dollar contract to join Paramount and direct comedies. He also secured long-term contracts from actors like Claudette Colbert, Wallace Beery, Bob Hope, Gary Cooper, Bing Crosby, Dorothy Lamour, Marion Davies, Alan Ladd, Veronica Lake, Fred MacMurray, Ray Milland, and the Marx Brothers. Almost every other studio had to deal with him in one capacity or another; they borrowed his stars, they purchased from his huge collection of story rights, and they attached their films to his "blocks" of theater bookings, i.e., renting their films to theaters in packages of features, shorts, and cartoons.

Zukor was also responsible for the exodus of foreign filmmakers to Paramount in the 1930s. The studio became known for its exotic stars such as Marlene Dietrich, Maurice Chevalier, Pola Negri, and Emil Jannings. Setting up production facilities in Europe, Paramount created a testing ground for emerging directors, including Alfred Hitchcock and Hans Dreier. Others were simply imported to the U.S. by Zukor, who dragged Ernst Lubitsch, Rouben Mamoulian, and Billy Wilder to Hollywood.

A special Oscar in 1948 honored his vast contribution to the industry. From film exhibition to film distribution to film production, Zukor steered his companies through the glory days of the silent era and made his impression felt in the coffers of Paramount. He restructured the company in 1932 after attempts by Lasky to unseat him were foiled. He remained president during the Depression, becoming a figurehead chairman of the board in 1936, and continued to show up for work daily until 1973, the hundredth anniversary of his birth. Zukor died at age 103. As the head of Hollywood's most consistently powerful studio, Adolph Zukor was a key figure in the film community for more than eighty years.

28

JOHN GILBERT

Born: July 10, 1895, Logan, UT
Died: January 9, 1936, Los Angeles, CA

His absolute disregard for the powers of the studio has all but wrecked his career.

—LOUELLA PARSONS

In the late 1920s, John Gilbert was the screen's greatest idol, appearing in one hit after another. Following the death of the legendary Rudolph Valentino, Gilbert was being groomed by Metro-Goldwyn-Mayer to replace him in macho adventures and bedroom dramas. An article of the day in *Cinema Art* magazine proclaimed that "John Gilbert stands alone at the topmost pinnacle of film fame. There is no one who can approach him." He was receiving gushing praise, collecting $10,000 a week, and romancing a modern-day goddess. Then, after a row with MGM boss Louis B. Mayer during a cocktail party, Gilbert was cast out of the picture business forever. The event signaled a major shift from an industry dominated by powerful stars to an industry controlled by studio heads. Mayer used John Gilbert to effectively demonstrate the ease with which he could destroy an actor's career.

Gilbert's sudden and complete excommunication from the film industry shocked his fellow actors, who immediately speculated as to the real reasons behind his troubles. Stories started to circulate about the fateful night Gilbert attacked Mayer. Rumors began about his voice tests for sound movies. Gossip columnists shared their thoughts on his absence from the screen. Actors paid close attention to the news of Gilbert's subsequent heavy drinking and destitution. Then, the March 20, 1934, issue of *Hollywood Reporter* was published, featuring an ad placed by Gilbert himself that shamelessly declared: METRO-GOLDWYN-MAYER WILL NEITHER OFFER ME WORK NOR RELEASE ME FROM MY CONTRACT! The power shift in Hollywood was complete.

The downhill slide of Gilbert was the steepest of any actor in film history. Having acted on the stage under the name John Pringle, he broke into films in 1915 through his family's connections and was billed as "Jack" Gilbert for his first bit part, in the Thomas Ince production *Matrimony* (1915). He starred opposite Mary Pickford in *Heart o' the Hills* (1919), then in a string of action adventures that got him a contract with William Fox. He was prominently marketed as a dashing swashbuckler in such films as *Monte Cristo* (1922). His status as a budding screen idol grew with each picture.

His blockbusters came at the close of the silent era and included *He Who Gets Slapped* (1924), *The Big Parade* (1925), and *The Merry Widow* (1925), a smash hit and a boon to his clout as a Hollywood star. By the time he teamed with Greta Garbo in *Flesh and the Devil* (1927), he was MGM's hottest property, demanding bigger pay and better roles. His heated romance with Garbo made their pairings in *Love* (1927) and *Woman of Affairs* (1928) eagerly anticipated events and international hits. Gilbert's real-life infatuation with Garbo is often credited with bringing forth her on-screen sex appeal.

Contrary to rumors that the fabled romance had fueled Mayer's dislike of Gilbert, the two men had clashed several times before Greta Garbo entered the picture. Mayer's puritan upbringing made him uneasy with Gilbert's unflagging infidelities and his coarse manner. An unfortunate incident at an MGM production office one day found Mayer questioning whether Gilbert's mother had been married before his birth; Irving Thalberg and a bodyguard were required to restrain the two men. Following that, Thalberg kept the peace between his vindictive boss and his most popular star.

As the affair with Garbo turned sour, Gilbert and Mayer found more opportunities to argue. An exchange between them at the wedding of King Vidor to Eleanor Boardman on September 8, 1926, set off one of the most bizarre incidents in Hollywood's history. To spite Gilbert, Garbo had become engaged to another man and had asked Metro chief Louis B. Mayer to break the news to the doting Gilbert at the reception dinner. There, in a heated discussion, Gilbert viciously attacked Mayer, hitting him in the face. In front of a roomful of movie stars and producers, Mayer, enraged, threatened to ruin Gilbert's career.

For the next several weeks, Thalberg attempted to act as a buffer again, telling Gilbert that he should cling to the terms of his contract and that Mayer would eventually relent. When Mayer tried to renegotiate Gilbert's weighty $250,000-per-picture contract, Gilbert refused to budge, insisting that MGM live up to its agreement. Then, Mayer simply declined every proposed project with Gilbert's name on it, claiming his salary was a budget-killer. After Thalberg convinced Mayer to allow a sound debut for Gilbert to utilize his talents, *Redemption* (1930) became the star's first talkie. However, Mayer delayed its release for a year, sending rumors around town that the recordings of Gilbert's voice made the film laughable. In its place, Mayer agreed to send out *His Glorious Night* (1929), a film that was badly edited and poorly recorded. He then assigned Gilbert to roles requiring foreign accents. Reviews were not bad, but grosses sank and the trade papers began to eulogize Gilbert prematurely. Alleging that Gilbert's vocal qualities were unsuitable for sound films (an exaggeration of enormous proportions), Mayer fired him.

The advent of sound films ushered in a new generation of actors who didn't have to combat silent stereotypes, and there was little hope for a reversal of Gilbert's declining fortunes. Garbo attempted to help him with a role in *Queen Christina* (1933), and Marlene Dietrich campaigned for his inclusion in *The Garden of Allah* (1936). He drank himself into depression and became something of a village idiot, lumbering around sets, looking up old costars, all the time reminiscing and bellyaching about his dire financial future. Literally drinking himself into poor health, John Gilbert died of a massive heart attack in 1936. He was only forty-one years old.

The demise of John Gilbert's career is now so clouded in legend that separating the cause from the effect is critical to an understanding of his place in Hollywood history. It is clear that before the wedding scuffle, Gilbert was at the height of popularity. His pictures were breaking attendance records, and many of his five-year-old films had been re-released internationally by William Fox to full houses and enormous grosses. But despite Gilbert's unforgettable charm, no producer dared to recruit him. Gossip columns clung to the story of his high, squeaky pitch, and some guessed his misfortune was a result of the downfall of romantic silent dramas, but the point was bell-ringing clear to other actors—the studio heads had demonstrated that they had the power to make stars and to ruin careers at will. Gilbert was the most compelling example yet of how studio heads had turned the tables on powerful stars. The film industry would no longer be ruled by the force of its creative talent, but instead by a system of managers and executives who would determine all aspects of filmmaking—a system that has remained a permanent part of Hollywood since the tragic end of John Gilbert's career.

29

MAX FLEISCHER

Born: July 19, 1883, Vienna, Austria
Died: September 11, 1972, Woodland Hills, CA

*Without Max's pioneering spirit and additions to the technology
of animation, few, if any, of us would be where we are today.*

—WALT DISNEY

Like many animators in the cartoon industry, Max Fleischer began his career as an errand boy. Working alongside animation pioneer J. R. Bray on the *Daily Eagle* newspaper in Brooklyn, New York, in 1901, Fleischer spent his days punching holes in paper until moving up to become a cartoonist. In a prophetic step, the inventive artist with a passion for mechanical objects, then took a job at *Popular Science Monthly* magazine, eventually quitting to join the ranks of artists who flooded the animation scene in 1915. During a brief World War I commission, Max was joined by his brother Dave to make instructional films for Bray. Together, the Fleischers and Bray would produce a bizarre and inventive collection of animated classics, and the technical advancements they discovered in making these films, primarily fueled by Max's curious and competitive nature, would keep their films interesting and enduring.

The Fleischers made immediate waves with a popular series of animated shorts featuring Koko the clown. The first of them, *Out of the Inkwell* (1916), earned them a contract with Paramount-Bray Pictographs for a regular supply of shorts; more than fifty were eventually produced. Brother Dave would soon take over the stories, supervising the development of such unique personalities as Betty Boop, Bimbo, and Popeye the Sailor, a profitable cast that would afford Max a chance to branch out into other areas. These characters were among the first in animation circles to strike a chord with both moviegoers and fellow animators. Bray, Disney, and other studio heads realized that strong cartoon personalities ensured steady work.

By 1920, the Fleischers were ready to start their own studio. The freewheeling animators of the Fleischer crew, such talented men as Ted Sears, Grim Natwick, Doc Crandall, and John Culhane, demonstrated a highly experimental, surrealistic quality in their work that was more sinister, more racy, and much less rigid than Walt Disney's output in this period; these early Fleischer classics include *The Herring Murder Case* (1931), *Chessnuts* (1932), and *Swing, You Sinners* (1930). Their interpretations of the slinky Boop as the quintessential flapper were never more seductive than in *Mysterious Mose* (1930) and *Bamboo Isle* (1932). These films were watched more closely by the Production Code censors of the Hays Office than any Mae West movie; in *Bimbo's Initiation* (1931), a sexy Betty Boop sequence has her slapping her own buttocks coyly to lure a stray dog closer.

Although the Disney and Fleischer studios both pioneered the use of cartoons set to music, Fleischer's popular *Minnie the Moocher* (1932), featuring the wailing Cab Calloway and Rudy Vallee, started a trend of setting animation to hit recordings. Later that year, animators drew Betty Boop and Bimbo singing and dancing to "I Ain't Got Nobody," "Just a Gigolo," and Irving Berlin's Broadway tune "Oh! How I Hate to Get Up in the Morning." These wildly popular musical shorts, the earliest examples of synchronized dance numbers, are the direct forerunners of today's music videos.

Max himself stepped away from the drawing table early on to concentrate on the mechanics of the cartoon craft. Frustrated by the limitations of cel animation, he was driven by a dream of a more lifelike product. After extensive experiments with live-action films, he struck upon the idea of filming actors in motion, then projecting the images onto paper and tracing them. The process, known as Rotoscoping, created smooth, realistic action that allowed illustrators to duplicate subtle human behaviors and predated the best efforts of Walt Disney by fifteen years. First displayed in Koko cartoons of 1916, the process is still used today in such animated films as *Beauty and the Beast* (1991) and *Pocahontas* (1995) and in video game production. Bray would call the process "super-animation," but Fleischer simply explained it as the greatest achievement in pen-and-ink production.

Next Max dreamed up the Rotograph, a system by which live-action film is projected to the underside of the artist's table one frame at a time, which allowed animators to draw Koko among real New York skylines. The real world and the India-ink clown were then brought together in a single exposure. This ingenious method was a precursor to techniques used in *Mary Poppins* (1964) and *Who Framed Roger Rabbit?* (1988).

Fleischer was also an innovator in color animated films. He beat Disney to a three-color process with *Somewhere in Dreamland* (1936) but suffered when Walt signed an exclusive contract with Technicolor merchant Natalie Kalmus. With Technicolor tied up, Fleischer adapted a two-color process to compete. He also forged into the world of three dimensions, developing 3-D processes for films *Popeye the Sailor Meets Ali Baba's 40 Thieves* (1937) and *Gulliver's Travels* (1939) that were state-of-the-art and forced others to adjust their methods again.

A tireless tinkerer, Fleischer presented a steady stream of optical tricks of color innovations, and sound curiosities that baffled and delighted his peers. Had he focused on any one technology, his studio might have become more famous than Disney's. Absent a distinctive style, the ever-changing look of a Fleischer cartoon became a symbol for the restless mind of Max. What his films lacked in consistent quality, they made up for in unexpected zaniness; he kept audiences entertained and competitors fearful. He had more genius than Disney but lacked the showmanship, the discipline, and, most important, the vision. Both men forged clear paths toward realism in animated films, but while Disney built upon each success, Max left behind yesterday's innovations for the wonders of tomorrow.

30

JOHN FORD

Born: February 1, 1895, Cape Elizabeth, ME
Died: August 31, 1973, Palm Desert, CA

*He kept calling me a clumsy bastard and a big oaf and kept
telling me that I moved like an ox.*

—JOHN WAYNE

In 1914, director Francis Ford encouraged his younger brother Seamus to leave Ireland for Hollywood. Seamus got work as an extra, playing a hooded Ku Klux Klan member on horseback in D. W. Griffith's *Birth of a Nation* (1917), before working his way onto the production crew, first as a propman and soon as assistant director on serial westerns. Cashing in on Francis's success, he changed his name to John Ford and landed a position at the William Fox studio, in 1921.

Now a full-fledged director, he created silent western epics, including *The Iron Horse* (1924), and became well known for his skill at telling a story straight. Ford's early films may have settled the West, but the westerns he made after World War II added depth to the genre. His breakthrough *Stagecoach* (1939) was the most influential western made since Edwin S. Porter's *The Great Train Robbery* (1903). The shining performance of a handsome young John Wayne was complemented by a remarkable cast of character actors. Along with the daring stunt work of Yakima Canutt, the film presented horse falls and stagecoach leaps that had never before been captured on film; this facet of *Stagecoach* alone raised the bar for serial action pictures. The final sequence, an Indian attack, was a masterstroke of tension and timing that became the template for climactic horseback battles in all westerns that followed. *Stagecoach* has been referred to as the greatest all-around western ever, a milestone in American film and in the genre itself.

Ford also got the chance to film back home in Ireland, making *The Informer* (1935) and *The Quiet Man* (1952), both Oscar winners. But it was on American soil with American subjects that Ford built his reputation, illuminating the country's most cherished values in such dramas as *Young Mr. Lincoln* (1939) and *The Grapes of Wrath* (1940).

My Darling Clementine (1946) revealed a darker side of Ford's work and required a nastier turn from Henry Fonda, a member of Ford's stock troupe of performers. The stark, isolated story of a famous shootout was filmed against the landscapes of Monument Valley, a favorite Ford location. The Arizona desert would become his personal playground, and his best work is remembered for the towering pillars of red rock as much as for the spectacular open-space vistas. The romantic feeling of his films owes much to the untouched beauty of these settings.

Ford's traditional values and sentimental stories were best suited for actors like Fonda, Jimmy Stewart, Ward Bond, and Ben Johnson, but it was Wayne who became most closely associated with the Ford western after the war. Their collaboration on *She Wore a Yellow Ribbon* (1949) was accentuated by the special Technicolor hues developed especially for Ford by Natalie Kalmus. The film set the look and feel of the modern western in the age of color films. Wayne and Ford also blazed trails in the genre with *Fort Apache* (1948) and *Rio Grande* (1950). These films, often referred to as a trilogy, helped define the code of the cowboy that Wayne embodied best.

Clearly in control of his medium, Ford was a temperamental man who would cut entire scenes from a script if an actor's pomposity or a producer's skepticism irritated him in the slightest. Despite bringing in most of his films under budget and on time, he was not an easy collaborator. Hollywood stayed out of his way, and he delivered reliable grosses without fail. His films are undeniably the product of a solitary creative spirit, and a slow maturation can be seen throughout his body of work. His early efforts were more personal and reflective, filled with social comment, but his films took on a darker mood as his art developed.

Most critics consider Ford's *The Searchers* (1956) the darkest western ever made—a Wayne vehicle that rubbed the luster from cowboy stories. It was followed by *The Man Who Shot Liberty Valance* (1962), shot in black and white. These two films showed that Ford was unafraid to erase the good-versus-evil stereotypes and challenge the notions of heroism. They represented the last of his films with the "Duke" character, an icon he had spent fifty years molding. After his final western, *Cheyenne Autumn* (1964), Ford saddled up and rode off into retirement.

Technically and ideologically, all westerns are framed by John Ford's influence. As a man who shunned introspective discussion about technique or meaning in his films, Ford had a no-nonsense manner that was reflected on the screen in the simple, consistent choices he made as a director. This shoot-from-the-hip attitude rubbed off on the productions, and soon the genre had become an extension of the man. In this way, John Ford was to westerns what Alfred Hitchcock was to suspense films.

WILLIAM FOX

Born: January 1, 1879, Tulchva, Hungary
Died: May 8, 1952, New York, NY

*No second of twenty-four hours passed that the name William Fox
was not on a screen in some part of the world.*

—WILLIAM FOX

A look at the life of William Fox is a look into the balance sheets of Holly-wood. A successful garment broker, Fox took over a nickelodeon in 1904 and turned it into a chain of fifteen movie theaters, introducing organ accompa-niment to silent films and pioneering other amenities for the comfort of patrons long before Sam Rothafel opened his famous palatial Roxy theaters. When profits in projection were small, Fox tackled distribution. In 1912, he started his own film rental company, which meant leasing pictures to many of the theater owners he had competed with for years. As he approached full capacity in the rental market, he decided to venture into film production. Slowly and methodically, Fox built the solid business that has today become a leading television network, an expansive cable giant, and a blockbuster movie studio. He is a hero who saved motion pictures from the greedy clutches of Thomas Edison and transformed the first group of unknown actors into bankable stars.

As a trailblazing independent producer at the turn of the century, Fox began showing some success at playing all fields; he made movies from scenarios his wife had written, rented them to theaters, and showed them in his own venues. But by 1913, Thomas Edison's Motion Picture Patents

Company had formed a trust to keep a monopoly on the equipment used in making motion pictures. Edison's group was willing to use violence to ensure compliance with their rules, even threatening to dynamite the Fox offices. Fox played a fundamental role in the dissolution of the Edison Trust. He resolutely fought the group in court, almost entirely without support, and his victory cast him as a hero in the young industry. From that time, his leadership would spread to every corner of the film world.

By 1915, Fox had a monopoly himself: his empire included strong production, leasing, and exhibition units that merged into Fox Film Corporation, a forerunner of 20th Century–Fox studios. Soon, Fox was a multimillionaire with tremendous influence during the studio heyday of the silent era. He showed only Fox films in Fox theaters, and by the end of the 1920s, his story factories pumped out fifty films a year, bringing in over $200 million worth of ticket grosses. Success, however, did not bank Fox's fiercely competitive fires.

A host of ambitious Fox firsts followed. He was the first to nurture the careers of his top talent through clever publicity stunts; and his efforts made stars of silent actors Theda Bara, Betty Blythe, William Farnum, and Tom Mix. He was first with the newsreel, premiering the series Movietone News in 1927. He was the first to attempt sound films. He was also the first to import features from overseas, the most notable being the famous F. W. Murnau film *Sunrise* (1927).

On the heels of *Sunrise,* Fox sought to acquire more theaters and more production facilities. He bought a major stake in MGM and secured 45 percent of Britian's most productive studio, Gaumont. His appetite for companies continued, and he attempted a takeover of Marcus Loew's studio. With an eye on the next craze in film, he invested heavily in early wide-screen processes of the twenties and ramped up for sound films by retrofitting more than eleven hundred theaters at the height of the Depression.

In 1929, independent studios lobbied for antitrust legislation against Fox. Seeking to prohibit the lockout of their films from Fox theaters, they successfully broke the stranglehold he had on the majority of theaters nationwide. Fox fought various court battles with all of his resources, until his bankruptcy in 1936. For attempting to bribe the judge at his bankruptcy hearing, he was sentenced to a Pennsylvania prison, where he served six months. He then retired from the industry forever.

With his reputation blemished, he encouraged novelist Upton Sinclair to conduct a survey of the movie industry and determine whether Fox was a hero or goat. In 1933, Sinclair wrote a book about the case called *Upton Sinclair Presents William Fox* and paid for its publication. The dour piece on Hollywood, which attacked the executives who had targeted Fox, restored the luster of the theater magnate's fascinating accomplishments and remains a fitting testament to his contributions.

32

GEORGE LUCAS

Born: May 14, 1944, Modesto, CA

*Speed stirs the beast. Fast-paced action and a hustling camera
suck the thrill seeker in us into the scene.*

—JOHN BOORSTIN

Ironically, the unique filmmaking gifts of George Lucas were first revealed in
a slow, methodical futuristic story he made into a student film in 1965.
THX1138, later remade as Lucas's first feature in 1971, showcases the director's early attempts to experiment with pacing. He would use this knowledge
to a different effect in his Skywalker trilogy, whose dogfight scenes would
have an earth-shattering influence on films to come. Lucas increased the
speed of films through editing and exhilarated audiences by overloading their
senses. Through the experimental pace of *Star Wars* (1977), Lucas discovered that the human eye was able to distinguish nearly twice as many shots
as traditional films used at the time. Movies suddenly got much faster.

After leaving the USC film school in 1968, Lucas found work with fellow
alumnus Francis Ford Coppola on *Finian's Rainbow* (1968) and *The Rain
People* (1969) before getting an opportunity to direct his own features.

The breakthrough film for Lucas was the mainstream *American Graffiti*
(1973), a fond rememberance of the director's adolescence shot in just
twenty-nine days outside his hometown north of San Francisco. Lucas used
a large collection of vintage hotrods and period costumes to re-create the
life of 1962 teens. Editing the film in close collaboration with editor Verna
Fields and his wife Marcia, Lucas created what started as a frivolous romp

through yesteryear and turned into a comment on the fleeting innocence of American youth. Hailed as a truly original work, *American Graffiti* was Oscar-nominated for Best Picture, Best Film Editing, Best Screenplay, and Best Director, and actress Candy Clark received a Best Supporting Actress bid. The film ushered in a nostalgia craze of fifties rehash and eventually a sequel, *More American Graffiti* (1979).

Most significant was the film's soundtrack, a collection of sock-hop oldies that was released as an album and sold well throughout the decade. Its success spawned literally thousands of soundtrack recordings that are now a staple of the industry. The heavy reliance on recordings of popular music would spark a dramatic shift in movies away from original compositions. Martin Scorsese, Robert Zemeckis, Oliver Stone, Barry Levinson, and many more directors would fill their subsequent soundtracks with rock 'n' roll classics; Woody Allen, Robert Altman, Peter Bogdanovich, and others would use jazz, rhythm and blues, and country standards to establish mood and period. The Lucas soundtrack influenced the majority of films made since the release of *American Graffiti,* and its solid success as a hit record, particularly its consistent sales over the years, served as a valuable lesson to Lucas about the importance of merchandising.

Lucas's next project was based on a 1976 science fiction novel. Seeking to restore some of the drama missing in Stanley Kubrick's *2001* (1969), Lucas consulted with literary expert Joseph Campbell to arrive at a script that used timeless elements of myth and religion. Lucas added traditional symbols of good and evil and pitched the story to various studios as a western set in space. The strange characters and ambitious sets would require expensive costumes and labor; most studios rejected the film, but 20th Century–Fox proposed a strict budget and agreed to go ahead.

The production of *Star Wars* (1977) was troubled by union stonewalling, casting disputes, and delays with set construction. Unsure that they had made a sound investment, Fox executives asked special effects pioneer Linwood Dunn to tour the Lucas project under the guise of a friendly visit and closely examine the working methods of the extremely young and inexperienced staff of model makers, animators, and student filmmakers. Dunn was shown outlandish monster creations and was taken step-by-step through the special effects of the starfighter sequences. When he reported back to Fox, Dunn assured the studio that the wunderkinds seemed to have their hands on something new and remarkable.

Star Wars became a phenomenal hit, shattering all previous box office records. Produced for under $10 million, it grossed more than $400 million worldwide. Fans of the film boasted about seeing it hundreds of times, and sequels *The Empire Strikes Back* (1980) and *Return of the Jedi* (1983) reaffirmed the mysterious lure of the original. In 1997, the entire trilogy was re-released in a special edition with some minor new sequences edited into the story with the benefit of computer-generated images. Again, the series excelled at the theaters, breaking records twenty years after its initial release and introducing the films to a new generation of moviegoers. The unwavering popularity of *Star Wars* is still central to the sales of video games and merchandise today.

But the success of *Star Wars* was about more than special effects. The breathtaking pace of the scenes, edited by Lucas in a hands-on collaboration with his wife, resulted in a major advancement in the understanding of film. Lucas increased frame rates and used optical zooms to create lightspeed space flight. To avoid the graininess of these effects on 35mm film, Lucas switched to the 70mm format. He researched the cowboy-and-Indian battle sequences in John Ford westerns and mimicked their mixing of raw action with character vignettes. Lucas raised the expectation of action and effects in all genres, not simply space epics. Today's editors are constantly challenged by the pace of *Star Wars* and its imitators.

A wildcat mentality followed the success of *Star Wars* in 1977. The combined successes of Steven Spielberg's *Jaws* (1976) and Lucas's films established the era of the blockbuster. Industry pundits felt that special effects and fantasy were the key in convincing consumers that rising ticket prices were justified. To strike it rich, producers searched for stories that lent themselves to explosions, spaceships, and monsters. Lucas developed a cottage industry by offering his Industrial Light & Magic company's visual effects services to other filmmakers for such spectacles as *Poltergeist* (1982), *Terminator 2: Judgment Day* (1991), *Jurassic Park* (1993), *Jumanji* (1995), and *Twister* (1996), as well as most of the *Back to the Future* comedies, *Indiana Jones* adventures, and *Star Trek* features.

33

LINWOOD GALE DUNN

Born: December 27, 1904, Brooklyn NY

Since 1934, there has not been a single production that did not utilize the services of the optical printer.

—LINWOOD DUNN

As a cameraman for RKO in 1928, Linwood Gale Dunn toyed with the idea of automating the transitions between scenes in a film. In the days of legendary cameraman Billy Bitzer, wipes, fades, and other transitions were done "in the camera," meaning the cinematographer would hold an opaque piece of paper in front of the camera and slowly cover the lens. Dunn altered RKO's crude optical printers so they could effect the transitions. This singular contribution would make him "the father of special effects."

The optical printer is essentially a camera aimed straight at a projector. The projector runs in precise synchronization with the camera, casting images directly onto unexposed film. To this simple apparatus, Dunn added controls to automate the fades, dissolves, and wipes seen in practically every film. He skipped every other frame to speed up action, or exposed a frame twice to give the appearance of slow motion. By filming the same image repeatedly, he made scenes freeze. His optical printers could combine shots by masking off portions of a single frame, rewinding the negatives, and replacing them with others.

An additional innovation that Dunn brought to the optical printer is the use of glass cels between the camera and projector. These sheets of glass allowed Dunn to place mattes, painted sections of scenery or opaque areas to block out parts of the projected film. A typical matte shot involved projecting a scene of a car driving down a street while masking the buildings and background from the exposure. Then, Dunn would stop the camera, rewind the film, set up a reverse matte that blocked out the areas of the frame where the car traveled, and project a scene of an oversized monster coming over the buildings in the background. When the film was developed, the combination of the shots would create a devastatingly realistic scene of a beast chasing fleeing motorists.

Within a few years, Linwood Dunn was the undisputed master of the optical printer and these tricky matte shots. For twenty-eight years at RKO, he honed his skills on such films as Willis O'Brien's *King Kong* (1933) and Orson Welles's *Citizen Kane* (1941). In fact, many of *Kane's* deep-focus scenes attributed to Gregg Toland were actually created with the optical trickery of Linwood Dunn. The famous campaign scene is, in actuality, four separate shots of a crowd, a stage, a balcony, and the large poster of Kane, combined under the painstaking care of Dunn and his magical equipment. Another scene required Dunn to make a shot of a nurse attending to Kane at his bedside appear as if it were reflected in the broken pieces of a fallen snow globe. Welles took to the concept of the optical printer quickly after Dunn explained its untapped artistic capabilities, and *Kane* has some of the finest uses of its scope.

Safety was another reason for using the special effects of the optical printer. In the film *Ace of Aces* (1933), Dunn combined footage of a real explosion with location shots of an aviator crawling from the cockpit of a wrecked fuselage. Through the magic of special effects, the result looked as if the pilot had made a daring last-minute escape from a burning plane. Stars Cary Grant and Katharine Hepburn couldn't be put at risk of a leopard attack on the set of *Bringing Up Baby* (1938), so Dunn filmed the wild cat separately from the actors. In the final scenes, it appears that Grant and Hepburn are intimately involved with the "domesticated" feline.

When RKO folded in 1957, Dunn leased the studio's special effect division and founded his own company, Film Effects of Hollywood, where he manufactured the Acme-Dunn, the first commercially available optical printer. Linwood Dunn offered his expertise as a consulting service to the filmmakers using his equipment. He helped establish his invention in television, actually filming the opening sequences of the space series *Star Trek,* in which the *Enterprise* ship passes quickly through space.

His expertise was instrumental in creating matte scenes for famous movie settings that never really existed. The remarkable title sequences of Robert Wise's *West Side Story* (1960) were the result of collaboration between Dunn and celebrated graphic designer Saul Bass. Working together for nearly five months, they devised a 70mm print of the classic overture effects. The last scene of Stanley Kramer's *It's a Mad, Mad, Mad, Mad World* (1963) was a collection of twelve different shots, including detailed paintings of buildings, documentary footage of a busy boulevard, a burning roof, and a stop-motion sequence by master animator Willis O'Brien. As the scene unfolds, there is no visible clue that it is a mixture of such disparate elements.

Dunn also freelanced for all of the major studios as Hollywood's most celebrated fix-it man. In hundreds of movies, the optical printer saved studios costly reshoots. Martin Scorsese asked Dunn to alter the bloody shootout scene near the end of *Taxi Driver* (1976) to get an acceptable rating for general viewers. The scene featured a mohawked Robert De Niro executing a pimp played by Harvey Keitel. Scorsese didn't have time or money to shoot the scene over; Dunn washed the film negative in sepia tones that muted the harsher shades of the blood, and ran the film through the optical print to lighten certain areas. The changes passed the ratings board, and Scorsese kept the sepia-toned sequence when he restored the film for a re-release.

Dunn's lengthy career yielded two Oscars for service and dedication to the industry. His impressive list of credits includes *The Hunchback of Notre Dame* (1939), *The Cat People* (1942), *The Thing* (1951), *The Narrow Margin* (1953), *My Fair Lady* (1964), *The Great Race* (1965), *The Bible* (1966) *Hawaii* (1966), and *Airport* (1970). Dunn also campaigned for a special branch of the Academy of Motion Picture Arts and Sciences to include the visual effects expert. He became their first representative and served three terms on the Academy's board of governors. Now in his nineties, Linwood Dunn is still consulted by top directors for advice. He keeps abreast of the latest trends in technology and has played a significant role in the development of 3-D special effects, IMAX projection devices, and digital video distribution.

Blue-screen photography was added to the features of the optical printer, and many of its principles are now accomplished with computer technology. But these new processes don't begin to undermine the important contributions Dunn's innovations have made to the spectacular realism of such films as *Star Wars* (1977). Special effects professionals thoroughly understand the incalculable value of Dunn's formative work. Still in use today, the optical printer has evolved into an indispensable tool. It is the most vital piece of equipment ever developed for the creation of special effects.

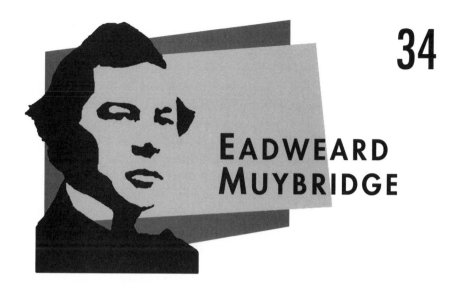

34

EADWEARD MUYBRIDGE

Born: April 9, 1830, Kingston upon Thames, England
Died: May 8, 1904, Kingston upon Thames, England

Edison, Muybridge, Lumière, are all monomaniacs, men driven by an impulse, do-it-yourself men.

—ANDRÉ BAZIN

The story is legend: California governor Leland Stanford makes a bet with Dr. John D. Isaac, in 1872. Stanford wagers $25,000 that at a certain point during a fast trot a racehorse will have all four legs off the ground simultaneously. After commissioning the services of experimental photographer Eadweard Muybridge, Stanford wins the bet and sparks a motion picture revolution. A nice story, but unfortunately it's not entirely true.

Stanford was not the state's governor at the time. Isaac did not take the bet. And Eadweard Muybridge wasn't actually Eadweard Muybridge. His real name was Edward James Muggeridge; he was a well-respected photographer whose stills of the Yosemite Valley in 1869 and advances in camera shutter design had made him famous in the growing circles of amateur photography. Muybridge was perhaps the perfect candidate to solve the dispute; he was a relentless, pragmatic thinker who addressed each task with laborious attention to detail but worked quickly as well. His first successes were widely praised landscapes of the Yosemite Valley and detailed, panoramic compilations of early San Francisco, but these lacked any creativity. Muybridge's interest in the emerging craft seemed more scientifically experimental than artistically expressive. His approach to photography was straightforward, and what remains of his extensive collection of humans and animals photos are cold, clinical examinations of forms in motion, completely devoid of any dramatic lighting effects or unusual point-of-view angles.

In appearance, he was an odd figure of a man, with gangly limbs and gaunt features. His bizarre mannerisms and long-winded rhetoric, rumored to be the result of a head injury he sustained in his youth, made him a source of social ridicule and further contributed to his reputation for eccentricity. Muybridge was infamous in the San Francisco Bay area of the 1870s, having been the defendant in a well-publicized murder trial, at which he was exonerated. After the lengthy and expensive trial, Muybridge approached Leland Stanford about conducting experiments in exchange for room and board, and the two men struck a deal.

Stanford's real interest was in studying horses closely enough to understand their behavior in motion. By doing this, he hoped to improve the breeding and training methods he used for his racehorses. What Stanford needed was the shutter technology that only Muybridge had. Muybridge had pioneered several key developments in the area of automated mechanisms for cameras. Previously, film exposure was achieved by hand; as a subject posed perfectly still, the photographer would carefully remove the lens covering, then quickly replace it after the right amount of light was captured. The trouble most photographers had was estimating the right amount of exposure time for different situations. But the sophisticated Muybridge devices could be triggered to open and close a shutter quickly, allowing multiple exposures. This technology was explained to Stanford by Muybridge, who had aspired to solve the burning question of the equestrian by galloping a horse in front of a row of twelve cameras while the shutters captured consecutive positions in the horse's gait. In May of 1872, Muybridge was successful in securing a sequence of still images, darkly lit silhouettes revealing that the horse's hooves were all airborne at once.

Because the typical shutters that Muybridge had originally designed were a bit slow for capturing successive phases in the horse's motion, he made improvements. He looked for a trip mechanism that would time the shutters with the horse's legs. Borrowing principles used in the production of railway telegraphs, Mubridge devised a system that opened the shutters much faster. Finally, Muybridge rigged his equipment on a deserted Sacramento racecourse with several cameras placed low to the ground and triggered by a trip wire. The new contraption was tested in 1877, when Stanford's favorite horse, Occident, tripped the tiny wires at full speed. Muybridge continued his series photography, expanding the number of cameras to twenty-four and improving shutter speed with a system of magnetic releases that gave an exposure every two-thousandths of a second. He then proceeded to capture the stride of many different animals. Soon, these photos would reach all corners of the world.

In 1879, Muybridge adapted these images to a popular children's toy called the "wheel of life," or Zoetrope. The Zoetrope was an optical illusion toy, very much in vogue at the time, that worked on a scientific principle to create a phenomenon dubbed "persistence of vision," the ability of the human brain to blend a series of still pictures into a continuous stream that emulated life-like movement. Muybridge had something unique. The Zoopraxiscope, first demonstrated in Stanford's home, became the forerunner to early projection devices like the turn-of-the-century nickleodeons.

Meanwhile, his pictures were widely published as still photographs; they might have remained no more than interesting oddities if they had not caught the attention of Laurie Dickson, the laboratory assistant Thomas Edison had assigned to study Muybridge's work. Seeing the Zoopraxiscope in operation gave him definite ideas of how to best apply its principles to moving images. These demonstrations strongly impressed Edison, and he agreed to let Dickson incorporate the shutter mechanism into motion picture equipment. High-speed shutters became an integral part of the first motion picture camera.

Muybridge became an instant celebrity from the event, recognized for his vital achievement. In 1887, he returned to his native England and set out to publish an astounding eleven volumes of his experimental still photographs, methodically recording the natural movements of hundreds of animals as well as a diverse collection of humans involved in various activities. These books became the authoritative guide for animators, who still study the photos for anatomical acccuracy. Toward the end of his life, Muybridge tinkered with new technologies and continued to lecture well into his seventies. Ironically, he was not fond of the early motion pictures he saw and could barely sit through a seven-minute short.

Muybridge's ranking may seem rather low considering his seminal work in shutter technology and his vast dissemination of his findings through extensive lectures worldwide. However, several significant technologies were required to integrate the principles that Muybridge discovered into a usable film camera-and-projection system. Furthermore, the other producers, directors, performers, and technicians that precede Muybridge here were all vital contributors to filmmaking's evolution into the art form it is today. Fittingly, Muybridge falls just behind special effects pioneer Linwood Dunn, who shared with this legendary man a curious, persistent spirit that wrestled with a basic limitation in photography, finally uncovering a revolutionary new way of bringing images together to create something quite magical.

35

KATHARINE HEPBURN

Born: May 12, 1907, Hartford, CT

You never pull up a chair for Kate. You tell her, 'Kate, pull me up a chair, willya, and while you're at it get one for yourself.'

—HUMPHREY BOGART

Katharine Hepburn broke the glass ceiling in Hollywood long before anyone had even heard of the glass ceiling; her determination and intelligence kept her on course through a glorious career, devoid of compromise. Her screen performances enabled men and women to be seen on an equal footing, and she deliberately shunned roles that required her to play women in conventional situations. Perenially listed among the most admired women in the world, Hepburn is the very essence of the cosmopolitan woman, a scrapper who took charge of her own career for more than six decades and led an exceptionally liberated lifestyle that both offended and inspired women in the modern age.

Her own influences were highlighted by an upbringing in a wealthy New England home, where her mother was an early crusader for women's rights. The young, tomboyish Kathy preferred to wear her brother's clothes and was often sent home from school to change into a dress. By the time she appeared in her first film, strong female roles had come to Hollywood. Inspired by several of the outspoken women in her own family, Hepburn created a number of feminist characterizations in such early films as *A Bill of Divorcement* (1932), *Little Women* (1933), and *Stage Door* (1937). Perhaps no film foreshadows Hepburn's career more than *Christopher Strong* (1933).

Directed by the pioneering female director Dorothy Arzner, the film featured Hepburn as a daredevil aviatrix who falls in love with a married man and begins a love affair that threatens to destroy his family.

Hepburn's early movie roles, under the guidance of such forward-thinking directors as George Cukor and George Stevens, were groundbreaking characters that challenged the accepted gender norms of society. Cukor's *Morning Glory* (1933) earned Hepburn her first Best Actress Oscar, and *Alice Adams* (1934) secured another nomination. But by *Sylvia Scarlett* (1935), her smart, spirited woman-in-trousers performances upset conservative theater owners, who canceled many of her films rather than answer to their Middle American constituencies. Despite work in comedy classics such as *Bringing Up Baby* (1938), Hepburn had turned into a public relations nightmare for studios.

She suffered through five straight box office failures, leading many theater exhibitors to assume her favor with moviegoers was permanently gone. Gossip columnists smelled the scent of a dying actress and began digging around her personal life, reporting on her footloose and fleeting romantic relationships with famous directors, producers, publicists, and leading men. Her brief affairs with John Ford and Howard Hughes kept her in the midst of scandalous rumors. Reported to have been dismissed as a candidate for Scarlett O'Hara in the upcoming *Gone With the Wind* (1939), she refused to audition for the role and left Hollywood for New York.

Starring in a successful Broadway play, she used her salary from the show to purchase the screen rights and returned to the Hollywood ranks triumphantly in *The Philadelphia Story* (1940). The film proved to be a rewarding comeback, bringing her exceptional praise, record-breaking ticket sales, a third Best Actress nomination, and eventually the Oscar. The stage became a lifelong passion; throughout her long career, Hepburn would return to Broadway frequently, usually in roles that reinforced her image as an individualist. In the 1970 smash hit *Coco*, she played the eccentric Parisian fashion designer Coco Chanel to rave reviews.

Despite her growing acceptance among audiences, her long adulterous relationship with actor Spencer Tracy dominated the headlines and polarized her admirers. Despite the fact that Tracy was Catholic and married, he pursued Hepburn until an eventual divorce exposed the depth of their affections to the public. But by that time, most moviegoers already felt privy to their mutual attraction when watching the two performers work together in *Woman of the Year* (1942), *Adam's Rib* (1949), and *Pat and Mike* (1952). The pair seemed a perfect match; Tracy's masculine smugness often found a worthy adversary in Hepburn's feline strength. Their on-screen battles spanned ten films, and their off-screen romance lasted twenty-seven years, until Tracy's death in 1967.

Though unorthodox characters turned out to be one of Hepburn's trademarks, she stumbled into a surprisingly offbeat role in John Huston's *The African Queen* (1951) that aided her transistion from youthful ingenue to strong matriarch. Hepburn took on the role of Rose Sayer, a spinster who tells a battered Humphrey Bogart after a trip down whitewater rapids, "I never dreamed that any mere physical experience could be so stimulating!" While the romantic overtones of *African Queen,* and subsequently *Summertime* (1955) and *The Rainmaker* (1956), softened Hepburn's image and gave her several chances at Academy Awards during the fifties, her maturing features and air of experience left her well suited to tackle the serious subjects presented by the unsettling civil strife of America in the 1960s. She accepted challenging roles in *Long Day's Journey Into Night* (1962), *Guess Who's Coming to Dinner* (1967), and *The Lion in Winter* (1968), and her powerful monologues on such issues as alcoholism, homosexuality, and bigotry established her as the personification of the nation's social conscience.

At the height of feminism in the 1970s, she was finally seen as someone years ahead of her time, a woman whose career goals had superseded a need for a marriage and children. The qualities that had been labeled as too masculine for the attractive Hepburn—her stubborn determination, her imperious and competitive spirit, her political activism, her industriousness—were now the very characteristics espoused by outspoken women's advocates who saw the actress as the embodiment of their movement. This formidable persona made her the perfect choice to play a foil to a chauvinistic John Wayne in *Rooster Cogburn* (1975).

She settled quickly and comfortably into more mature roles. After a bout with illness, she returned in *On Golden Pond* (1981), which boosted her Oscar nomination count to an unprecedented twelve and her number of wins to an equally unprecedented four, three awarded after she was into her sixties. A near-fatal car accident in 1984 slowed her again, but she rebounded to make a brief, bittersweet appearance in the romantic *Love Affair* (1994) and published several memoirs, including a recollection of *The African Queen.*

Hepburn's contributions to the cinema were unique. Her portrayals of fiercely independent women with strong feminist dispositions paved the way for actresses like Barbara Stanwyck, Audrey Hepburn, Faye Dunaway, and Jane Fonda. As a performer who actively forged her own image and exercised a producer's control over her own career, Hepburn's commanding presence in the film industry can only be compared to that of Mary Pickford. And though Greta Garbo and Anita Loos deserve slightly higher praise—and ranking—for their substantial influences in other areas, Hepburn's efforts to advance the roles of women in film have since been unequaled.

36

WINSOR McCAY

Born: Sept. 26, 1867, Spring Lake, MI
Died: July 26, 1934, New York, NY

McCay had no one to consult for guidance in the art of animation.
—LEONARD MALTIN

The advent of motion pictures offered unique opportunities to Winsor McCay. A product of traveling sideshows and a legend of the newspaper trade, McCay was better prepared to use the medium of film than any other American artist of the age. He was a conceptual thinker with a rare work ethic, and he was gifted with strong public-speaking skills. He found the wonders of animation a challenging diversion from his daily drawing, and the film industry found itself the perfect pitchman.

Without much training in art, McCay started his career painting circus signs and fantasy posters for theatrical productions. In 1897, his work as an illustration artist for a carnival promoter caught the attention of the *Cincinnati Times Star* and he was hired to illustrate criminal trials and sporting events, working his way up to better jobs until he became an editorial cartoonist for the *New York Evening Telegram* in 1903. He first earned fame in 1905 with his meticulously rendered Little Nemo comic strip, a fantastical adventure strip based on the dreams of an imaginative boy.

In 1906, pioneer director Edwin S. Porter was experimenting with trick photography, and he approached McCay with the intention of using another comic strip as the basis for a short film, *Dreams of a Rarebit Fiend* (1906) which attempted to turn a McCay series of wicked, surreal nightmares into entertainment. To promote the strange film, Porter put McCay in front of national audiences. McCay began making occasional public appearances as the film's presenter in vaudeville houses. He toured the country with several other productions as well, telling anecdotes about his life as a cartoonist while drawing caricatures of audience members. He was a popular performer, and offers continued to pour in from other venues.

During this time he met Stuart Blackton, another animation pioneer, who experimented with stop-motion techniques on a blackboard. Blackton had developed a reputation for himself in film circles as an important innovator, and McCay was inspired by some of their conversations about the possibilities of animation. Combining Blackton's crude examples with an idea he got from a child's flip book, McCay produced a Little Nemo short in 1908 from more than four thousand drawings, each of which was shot onto a roll of 35mm negative film, then developed and hand-colored one frame at a time by the patient and meticulous illustrator. Another attempt at animation was McCay's *The Story of a Mosquito*, (1912), a hand-drawn flea circus he presented with the Little Nemo film to vaudeville audiences.

Audiences were puzzled; they thought McCay's mesmerizing drawings were tricks put on with wires and mirrors. An amateur magician, McCay often used sleight-of-hand when introducing these films, which left the audience skeptical that perhaps more than drawing talent was involved in making the characters move. Disappointed by this first attempt and feeling cheated by the reaction, McCay set himself on a mission to demonstrate the power of his moving drawings.

He took a brief hiatus from newspaper drawing and immersed himself in a third film. The production of *Gertie the Dinosaur,* which began in 1909, was a mammoth undertaking of ten thousand drawings, each inked on thin rice paper. Working with an assistant, McCay conceived many primitive devices to keep the illustrations of his brontosaurus in register, using the corner of a shoebox to align the translucent drawings. Every line in the film's background—mountain, trees, clouds, and a nearby lake—was carefully traced onto each slight variation of the dinosaur's movement. Within two years, McCay was back on stage.

Gertie was a cultural breakthrough; suddenly audiences realized they were not being fooled. Appearing in person, McCay displayed tall stacks of the original drawings before making the extinct reptile come to life on a screen behind him. His live performances consisted of a dialogue between the animator and his creation. The audience stared in amazement as they realized no magical wires or mirrors could create a moving dinosaur before their eyes. Although Gertie did not speak, she responded instantly to every one of McCay's commands. She charmed audiences with a distinctly demure personality. She was comic and coy. She was alive. She was the first true animated cartoon character.

Gertie was originally shown to fellow journalists and cartoonists from the newspaper business at Reisenweber's restaurant in New York before McCay was willing to introduce her to audiences. Present among the group that night was Mighty Mouse creator Paul Terry, who would go on to make nearly fourteen hundred cartoon shorts after the inspiration of the film struck him like a bolt. McCay's success prompted hundreds of other artists to create cartoon creatures.

Winsor McCay took the exhibition clip he used in vaudeville houses and combined it with a live-action re-creation of the Reisenweber gathering to open the film. This included a comprehensive explanation of the drawings required to make Gertie move. The country's finest theaters showed the offical filmed version of *Gertie the Dinosaur* (1914) and other shorts to their uppercrust patrons. Theaters made animated films a staple of their daily bill. McCay's sales pitch was over, and the fledgling film industry had already opened a new frontier.

McCay's next attempt, *The Sinking of the Lusitania* (1918), was further proof of his prodigious talent. This film had even more drawings than *Gertie,* boasting the first attempt at twenty-five thousand frames, unheard of in animation circles up to that time and for years to come. McCay produced six more films, but he became disenchanted with the quality of other animators' efforts and felt that the cartoon industry was not following his lead in the spirit of his original desire for an animated art form. McCay dropped his newfound hobby and returned to newspapers exclusively around 1920. His comic strips waned in popularity, and when he died in 1934, his films went into obscurity until other animators came along to take over in his mold. Major steps in character development and technical advances would later spark new interest in cartoons, but Winsor McCay's first steps remain among the largest in film history.

37

STANLEY KUBRICK

Born: July 26, 1928, Bronx, NY

2001 was a small step for Stanley Kubrick, but it was a giant leap for special effects.

—JOHN CULHANE

The celebrated career of director Stanley Kubrick is also one of the most enigmatic in cinema. A gifted artist and a tireless craftsman, Kubrick has accumulated a body of work that is nearly impossible to compare to any other director's in the history of the movies. His films defy categorization, and their elusive meanings often send the most articulate film buffs into rambling conjecture. Fans will speculate about the hidden messages in dialogue, the symmetrical construction of his scenes, and the obscure references to the director's personal life tucked away in the subtext of the films. These curiosities are fueled by the mysterious behavior of this reclusive man. Kubrick shuns all discussion of his own pictures, preferring to let them communicate unencumbered by explanation. His strikingly powerful images are indelible, and his greatest contribution to film is the grand vision he consistently brings to the screen.

Stanley Kubrick spent his adolescence hauling around a copy of Vsevolod Pudovkin's *Film Technique* and analyzing every shot and sequence of the classic films available for study at the Museum of Modern Art. His position as a staff photographer for *Look* magazine in 1950 afforded him the spare time and access to equipment that he needed to make a documentary film. *Day of the Fight* (1951), his first effort, was an interesting boxing picture, which

Kubrick sold to RKO for a profit of $100. In 1955, while still an independent filmmaker, Kubrick made the highly stylized racetrack heist film *The Killing* (1956). Despite the presence of the controversial actor Sterling Hayden, who had appeared before a congressional hearing to "name names" of fellow actors who were sympathetic to Communist causes, the film received a positive critical reception, and Kubrick acquired enough financial backing for another project, *Paths of Glory* (1957), an antiwar film that started a career of intensely personal projects.

Paths of Glory, written by Kubrick and pulp-fiction novelist Jim Thompson, was a biting World War I drama about a French army commander forced by his egocentric superior to send his men into a futile battle situation. Early signs of the absurd and ironic narrative that Kubrick favors were already present. The notable casting of rebellious maverick Kirk Douglas continued a Kubrick trend of working with Hollywood "radicals." A tense, tightly woven film of tremendous impact, *Paths of Glory* was the first step in the growth of the director's unique vision.

Ironically, his next directorial effort was the sprawling *Spartacus* (1960), a film assigned to Kubrick by studio executives when it was already halfway through production. Kirk Douglas, the film's star, clashed with director Anthony Mann and demanded that Kubrick take the helm. The script, by blacklisted screenwriter Dalton Trumbo from the bestselling novel by Howard Fast, lacked the characteristic Kubrick touches. Although the film would ambitiously tackle the subjects of homosexuality and religious persecution, it remains a slick and incongruous reminder that this was Kubrick's first Hollywood assignment. Still, it was immensely popular and brought Kubrick offers for other films with unlimited creative freedom. But he turned his back on many of the prospects, choosing instead to make films on his own terms.

Leaving the United States for England, Kubrick began his next film at the Shepperton Studios in 1961. *Dr. Strangelove or: How I Learned to Stop Worrying and Love the Bomb* (1964), perhaps the most famous black comedy ever made, was taken from the novel *Red Alert* by Peter George. Kubrick and irreverent writer Terry Southern (who later coscripted the 1960s counterculture films *Barbarella* and *Easy Rider*) crafted a serious film about nuclear Armageddon, but after reading the first draft of the script, they found themselves laughing at the heavy irony and humor of the straightforward dialogue. With minor adjustments, they turned the film into a masterpiece of Cold War inanity. Timeless performances by Peter Sellers, George C. Scott, Sterling Hayden, Peter Sellers, Slim Pickens, Keenan Wynn, and Peter Sellers made the film an instant success. It became a cult classic and—fueled by the rumors of Kubrick's permanent status as an expatriate—was viewed as an American's condemnation of his country's military policies, specifically the anti-Communist witch-hunts and accelerated nuclear escalation.

For *2001: A Space Odyssey* (1968), Kubrick became obsessed with nearly every B-movie adaptation of science fiction stories and began consulting a wide collection of scientists, computer experts, astronomers, and engineers about their conceptions and philosophies regarding issues of space travel, technological progress, and existentialism. He swore artists to the strictest secrecy before commissioning the $10.5 million worth of sets, costumes, music, and scale models of futuristic spaceships for wide-screen Cinema-Scope presentation of the film. With its startling special effects and hypnotic visuals, *2001: A Space Odyssey* updated the space exploration genre by light years. It was startling in so many ways. More than half of the film's running time has no dialogue. Form takes precedent over plot. A deliberate tedium reinforces the main theme. Stark landscapes and lengthy establishing shots required unprecedented intellectual fortitude from the audience. The public and critical opinions of *2001* were extremely polarized.

But the film survived the initial reaction and was soon hailed as an extremely important cornerstone of modern filmmaking. Kubrick's concepts of time and technology have remained influential to sci-fi movies for thirty years. The standards for visual special effects in the genre were raised incrementally. Thematically, it echoed our fears of technology's pace, yet fueled our desires to learn more about artificial intelligence and planetary colonization. The frighteningly straightforward HAL computer revived the Frankenstein motif of a man-made creation run amok. The film simultaneously made all preceding science fiction films unsophisticated and ensured that all that followed had to live up to the technical and scientific expectations created by *2001*, including the genre's best efforts: *THX 1138, Alien, Star Wars, War Games,* and *Star Trek.*

His other futuristic vision, *A Clockwork Orange* (1971), was more controversial but equally conceptual. Adapted from a novel by Anthony Burgess, the film's grim and disturbing study in violence and governmental control not only challenged contemporary ideas but offered graphic metaphors that renewed the tremendous respect filmmakers have for Kubrick as a visual stylist.

Kubrick became more methodical and calculating with each project, producing just a handful of films over the next twenty-five years. His working methods are slow and painfully meticulous, and his legendary perfectionism frequently reaches a level of absurdity that cast and crew find intolerable. The shooting schedule for *The Shining* (1980) ran past two hundred days; for his recent *Eyes Wide Shut* (1998), well beyond three hundred. His actors cite extreme emotional stress when Kubrick insists on lengthy retakes to match a visual picture that resides in his head. Tom Cruise was asked by Kubrick to repeat a scene ninety-three times before the director settled for a take he deemed adequate.

Questions remain as to whether Kubrick's loyal fans have benefited from the large degree of creative freedom he has arranged for himself. Since *Clockwork Orange,* the subsequent releases of the expatriate director have been uneven and infrequent. The overlong *Barry Lyndon* (1975) was followed five years later by an adaptation of Stephen King's novel *The Shining.* Between the wartime *Full Metal Jacket* (1987) and the most recent, *Eyes Wide Shut,* there was a span of more than ten years, during which Kubrick reportedly abandoned several films that were deep into production. His leisurely production pace may be catching up with him; he is perenially rumored to be making a film about artificial intelligence but has experienced dramatic setbacks when the advances of new technology render his scripted material outdated.

Eccentricities aside, Stanley Kubrick has proven himself a unique talent in film history. He ranks with the few directors who can claim to have redefined an entire genre, and his vision of space exploration is still the pervasive one, both in theme and execution. George Lucas brought a number of interesting elements to the *2001* legacy (and ranks higher than Kubrick because of his substantial influence on film editing), but not since William Cameron Menzies's *Things to Come* (1936) has an artist skillfully turned a series of fantastic images into an enduring worldview of the future.

38

BUSTER KEATON

Born: October 4, 1895, Piqua, KS
Died: February 1, 1966, Woodland Hills, CA

*Keaton, even more than Chaplin, knew how to create
a tragedy of the Object.*

—ANDRÉ BAZIN

Joseph Frank Keaton's stony perfectionism is deeply rooted in his parents' vaudeville act. The Three Keatons were regular faces performing with W. C. Fields, Bill "Bojangles" Robinson, Eddie Cantor, and master entertainer Al Jolson in theater houses at the turn of the century. From the age of four, he was trained in low comedy, mastering a routine with his father in which Buster would wait for a grievance to be inflicted upon him, retain his position with a businesslike countenance, and proceed to hold this stolid expression while pummeling his father for laughs. Another physical routine had Keaton's father disciplining the mischievous child by throwing him all over the stage, prompting the visiting magician Harry Houdini to nickname the kid "Buster."

His mastery of the deadpan would get him plenty of work in Roscoe "Fatty" Arbuckle shorts from 1917 to 1920, beginning with *The Butcher Boy* (1917), the first of fifteen two-reelers with Arbuckle. His first starring role came in the feature-length *The Saphead* (1920). After Arbuckle was lured to another studio, Keaton was handed the camera and his first chance to direct without interference. Keaton took straight to the task, making his directorial debut with *One Week* (1920), a do-it-yourself homebuilder's course performed in a twelve-minute one-reeler. After he slipped into a theater and saw people breaking up with laughter, Keaton was hooked on the movie business.

In the next eighteen months, he would produce the most amazing sequences of any comedian in film history. His inventive collection of silent classics, including *Our Hospitality* (1923), *Sherlock, Jr.* (1924) and *The Navigator* (1924), stands today as a record of his ability to mix trick photography, unprecedented stunt work, and elaborate prop gags in a way never again matched on film.

While Keaton lacked the magical charm of Charlie Chaplin, he compensated with acrobatic stunts and wildly imaginative scenarios that entertained and stupefied audiences. Doing all of the hair-raising feats himself, Keaton framed himself against hostile landscapes of falling rocks, cars, boats, policemen, and armies. He opted for simple camera setups and long takes that make visible everything that happens. Keaton also established himself as an icon—the unwitting simpleton overrun by the modern mechanized world—repeatedly using his physical dexterity to overcome intractable machines. His pragmatic approach to solving his dilemmas was always understated by his stoic glance, and the effect was hilarious.

Keaton's masterpiece, *The General* (1927), set during the Civil War, is best remembered for an elaborate chase involving a runaway train that set the pace of action thrillers for generations. Through ten features for United Artists, Keaton kept the innovations coming. *Steamboat Bill, Jr.* (1928) includes the famous scene in which a collapsing building narrowly misses Keaton; throughout the high-speed action of a twister attack on a small town, Keaton elevated his comedy beyond the sight gags of Chaplin and into the surreal world of dreams. His final self-produced film, *The Cameraman* (1928), was consistently used by major studios to train new cameramen and second-unit crews in the standards of comedic moviemaking.

In 1928, he signed a deal with MGM, but his fame dwindled. By 1932, he was divorced, reduced to costarring, and alcoholic. Forced to direct films from other's scripts rather than his own ideas, stifled and confused by the studio system, he lost the imagination of the early years, and his films amounted to nothing more than sappy and sentimental love stories. Because of his drinking, he was committed to a mental hospital in 1935; that same year MGM rehired him at a meager $100 a week to write gags on comedies like the Marx Brothers' *A Night at the Opera*.

A brief tour with a live performance group called the Cirque Medrano put Keaton back on the stage in Paris in 1947. His career was considered washed up until small turns in Billy Wilder's *Sunset Boulevard* (1950) and Chaplin's *Limelight* (1952) rekindled interest in him as an artist. A bizarre turn of events salvaged films that were thought lost; after actor James Mason purchased Keaton's palatial mansion in the Hollywood hills, a secret stash of old films was discovered; the nitrate stock was preserved, and the films were shown to students and in festivals throughout the world. Keaton was hailed as a genius, a term he despised, and he received a special Oscar for his achievement in comedy films in 1954. Until his death at age seventy, he made cameo appearances in such star vehicles as *Around the World in 80 Days* (1956) and *It's a Mad, Mad, Mad, Mad World* (1963).

His immortal comedies served as a model for cartoon animators—the Pink Panther was created in Keaton's likeness—and contemporary filmmakers as diverse as Woody Allen and Hong Kong's Jackie Chan have taken inspiration from Keaton, but no one has captured the impeccable timing and precise choreography of this comic artist, who was hopelessly ahead of his time.

39

JAMES AGEE

Born: November 27, 1909, Knoxville, TN
Died: May 16, 1955, New York, NY

*I am of the Agee-an school of criticism, considering it a
conversation between moviegoers.*

—JUDITH CRIST

Though remembered as the most influential film critic of all time, James Agee was originally a poet. He grew up in Tennessee's Cumberland Mountains but was sent to various Appalachian boarding schools and seminaries following the untimely, accidental death of his father. In an effort to deal with feelings of isolation and abandonment, Agee channeled his emotions through a rigorous writing habit, which developed his rare gift for penetrating prose. His intelligent, passionate views later found a place in critical essays throughout the 1940s, and his reviews of contemporary films made him famous among moviegoers. He developed a loyal readership, and his deeply personal and insightful opinions forged a solid vocabulary for a new generation of film buffs. His aesthetic standards later became the basis for European film criticism, and echoes of his colorful style surfaced again and again in film-related newspaper columns and television shows of the 1960s and 1970s. His poetic language produced the finest examples of film criticism and inspired other writers, including Pauline Kael, Rex Reed, Roger Ebert, and Janet Maslin, to devote themselves to the appreciation of film.

Agee's writing showed promise from an early age. While still a boy in Tennessee, he developed a close relationship with a Jesuit priest, Father Flye,

127

who served as a mentor and guided the intellectually curious and creative young pupil toward poetry. Flye helped Agee gain entrance to the prestigious Exeter Academy and eventually to Harvard University. After graduating in 1932, Agee was recommended to publishing magnate Henry Luce by a Harvard colleague; he hitchhiked his way to Luce's New York offices and was hired to write for *Time* magazine. Throughout the rest of the 1930s, he wrote feature articles, poetry, and occasional anonymous film criticism for a number of Luce's ventures, including *Fortune* magazine.

Agee's empathetic nature often undermined his objectivity as a feature writer. In 1936, while assigned to a *Fortune* feature about small businesses in America's heartland, Agee turned in an overlong report about the plight of poverty-stricken sharecroppers throughout Tennessee and Alabama. However, the story assignment resulted in a collaboration with photographer Walker Evans about the poor working conditions in the South. Agee and Walker traveled the backroads of America, sleeping in the homes of their subjects and documenting their family histories in words and pictures. These reports for *Fortune* led to a book, *Let Us Now Praise Famous Men* (1941), a compilation of Evans's photographs accompanied by Agee's reactions in text. The book became a milestone of photojournalism and one of Agee's best-known works; it also launched a close friendship between Walker and Agee that would last throughout their lives. Shortly thereafter, Agee wrote "Knoxville: Summer of 1915," a brief essay for the fledgling publication *Partisan Review* about his childhood experiences; it became the precursor to a novel, *A Death in the Family* (1957), that garnered huge acclaim and is widely considered a literary gem.

In 1938, the *Nation* published his first movie critiques, which were immediately noticed as something quite different from standard theatrical reviews. Agee judged film as art, taking exception to the idea that it was a commercial product and therefore understandably compromised by the whims of its public. He considered film a serious medium and held its directors up to praise and ridicule in his eloquent criticisms. The beauty of his prose and the fierce convictions behind his writing won over fans who were looking for a rigorous, academic approach to studying the "art" of filmmaking. He encouraged film lovers to patronize only those movies that aspired to the highest standards and to view their favorite directors with a discerning eye. When he wrote the famous line "There are few men whose eyes I would trust as I do my own," he coined the catchphrase of film buffs who looked at film through a critical lens.

Some felt his deep love of the movies compromised his objectivity; Agee often suggested his own creative fixes for films, and he defended his favorite directors to a fault. Charlie Chaplin's *Monsieur Verdoux* failed to bring in the box office receipts usually associated with a Tramp picture, but Agee praised the film for years after its disappointing release. At other times, his words dripped with sentiment; in describing Buster Keaton's stone-faced mug, Agee gushed: "Almost with Lincoln's as an early American archetype, it was haunting, handsome, almost beautiful." In a 1949 essay, "Comedy's Greatest Era," Agee presented the argument that silent funnymen Harry Langdon and Harold Lloyd deserved equal placement with Chaplin and Keaton as the four cornerstones of screen comedies. The article did much to encourage the revival of both men's films in art houses around the world. Constantly surprised by his eclectic cinematic tastes, readers responded to Agee's refreshing approach to reviewing everything from animated shorts to historic newsreel films. One particularly inspired Agee essay looked at cartoon director Friz Freleng's *Rhapsody Rabbit* (1946), comparing the Carl Stalling musical score to the jazz antics of comedian Spike Jones.

Throughout most of the 1940s, he continued to write movie reviews, but in 1948, he became restless at his journalistic posts and quit the magazine business to cowrite John Huston's *The African Queen* (1951). It wasn't his first attempt at a screenplay—he had penned several documentary films in the 1940s—but *African Queen* inspired Agee to focus his efforts on screenwriting. His biggest success came with a script for first-time director Charles Laughton, *The Night of the Hunter* (1955). The powerful story of a psychotic preacher, played wickedly by Robert Mitchum, became an instant cult classic.

Agee became a permanent fixture of Greenwich Village art circles and was highly respected as an artist, but his troubled personal life prevented him from enjoying the little success he achieved while he was alive. Thirty years of heavy drinking made him violent and abusive toward family and friends. Two of his marriages dissolved, and a third wife remained estranged until his death. His outspoken, radical political views made others uncomfortable in social settings. Jealousy, contempt, and fits of rage marked a self-destructive personality that fueled his excessive smoking and his alcoholism. On May 16, 1955, the anniversary of his father's death, Agee suffered a fatal heart attack in a taxicab en route to a doctor's appointment. He was just forty-five years old.

Though he is revered by thousands of film critics today, Agee saw little effect of his popularity in his own lifetime. However, upon his death, it was discovered that he had left behind several books and screenplays that were nearly finished. His body of criticism was gathered into the acclaimed *Agee on Film*, published in 1958. Still considered to be the seminal work of film criticism, it won him the Pulitzer Prize, awarded posthumously. Its success bolstered his status as a mythic literary romantic and prompted the publication of another book, *Agee on Film II* (1960), consisting of his five film screenplays. These books are the legacy of James Agee; in the 1970s, a new generation of film critics seeking to redefine the standards of the motion picture art form used Agee's insights as their springboard.

Agee's high place among film critics is indisputable; while the mainly academic writings of André Bazin and Sergei Eisenstein rank higher because of their illuminating analysis of film language, Agee's contributions to the study of cinema transcend the simple deconstruction of themes, plots, techniques, and performances. He taught moviegoers how to appreciate films and, in many cases, how to enjoy the very experience of watching a movie.

FRITZ LANG

Born: December 5, 1890, Vienna, Austria
Died: August 2, 1976, Los Angeles, CA

Hitler was probably the only man who could intimidate him.
—JOAN BENNETT

Paranoid, vengeful, obsessed, and twisted are a few of the nicest things ever said about Fritz Lang's movies. As a director who explored the outermost reaches of humanity, he placed himself and his characters in a variety of desperate situations. Because of a rich visual style that ran through his entire body of work, his films remain fascinating to watch. Because of their troubling themes, they have become the finest examples of film noir. The term "film noir" refers to movies whose subject matter contains overtones of obsession, despair, loneliness, and isolation—the darker side of human existence. Defining the person responsible for the genesis of film noir is impossible; the term was coined almost twenty years after the creation of films that critics cite as examples of the style. But Fritz Lang can be considered its most consistent practitioner. His films have given shape to the fuzzy term.

As a young artist, Fritz Lang ditched his architectural classes in 1916 for a chance to write screenplays for the large number of companies just entering Germany's explosive film industry. Most of Lang's scenarios were thrillers or horror stories. He set a precedent with a two-part crime story called *Spiders* (1919), which featured themes of world domination. The film's success brought Lang a small fortune and prospects of his own production. Joining with Carl Mayer, Hans Janowitz, and Robert Wiene, he worked on a script

131

for a psychological thriller based on stories the group had heard about insane asylums; it was their shared suspicion that many of the people walking the streets of Hamburg were in fact criminally insane and uncaptured felons. The result of these discussions was the schizophrenic and bizarre screenplay for *The Cabinet of Dr. Caligari* (1919).

Caligari might have been the first feature film directed by Lang. He had begun developing the film with Wiene, who would eventually direct when Lang stepped aside to finish another project. But Lang made a significant contribution to the preproduction of *Caligari,* and his key addition to the story, a framing device in which the story is revealed to be a dream, is arguably the most widely emulated structural technique among fantasy and horror films. It can be seen today in hundreds of dramatizations, usually as a convenient way out of sticky plot entanglements. When it opened, *The Cabinet of Dr. Caligari* became a landmark of the German expressionist movement and drew international attention to the country's finest filmmakers.

Fritz Lang stepped to the forefront of the German film industry with dynamic and striking frame compositions. His early films, among them the dark noir *Destiny* (1921), had tremendous influence over directors Alfred Hitchcock and Raoul Walsh. His folk fantasies, *Siegfried* and *Kriemhild's Revenge,* made in 1924, were intended to be seen on consecutive nights, a popular gimmick in theater houses of the day. Lang's other notable German films included the silent classics *Dr. Mabuse* (1922) and *Spies* (1928), both of which received enormous praise.

His stylized, futuristic *Metropolis* (1926) became another landmark in film history—a science fiction film that has endured as perhaps the finest example of a paranoia film. Capitalizing on the combined fears of rising socialism and growing industrialization, Lang created a world where the individual workers of an underground community are reduced to mechanical cogs in a machine that fuels a rich, sophisticated modern city situated far above. The film established trends in set design, and it predated concepts of a computerized society by thirty years. It remains a seminal influence on every science fiction film made today.

Lang's next film, *Woman in the Moon* (1928), gained notoriety when Hitler ordered all prints and negatives of it destroyed. Lang speculated that his movie rockets too closely resembled the weapons that were being built by the German forces. His fear of Hitler became more acute after his transition to sound films. *M* (1931), starring Peter Lorre, was a film noir masterpiece about a child murderer who confesses to his compulsive criminal behavior. *M* became Lang's most famous film to date and drew the attention of Nazi chief propagandist Joseph Goebbels. Looking for a director who could match the effectiveness of Leni Riefenstahl, Goebbels approached Lang in 1934 and asked him to make a series of propaganda films for Hitler. Lang left the country that evening. He stayed in Paris briefly before going to America. Producer David O. Selznick, who had met him on the set of *Liliom* (1934), signed him to a contract with MGM.

In Hollywood, Lang quickly assimilated the American way of life. He scoured popular magazines to pick up the nuances of the language; he went to parties to improve his English and to develop an ear for the slang and patterns of American speech; he traveled throughout the United States to familarize himself with the history and the geography of his new country. Upon returning to work, he was assigned a series of B movies at MGM and slowly earned the respect of the studio. Soon, he was writing his own scripts again and went back to exploring dark themes in his stories.

Lang's working methods were rather unorthodox. He was a fastidious daily reader of newspapers and magazines and frequently clipped out small pieces of news or an interesting advertisement for inclusion in a scrapbook. These scraps became the source for much of his material. When reports of a mob lynching in San Jose, California, appeared in newspapers throughout the state, Lang became fixated on the case, using the clippings as the basis for *Fury* (1936). The finished film, turned into a Spencer Tracy vehicle by MGM executives, received huge praise for its realism and contemporary feel. It started a buzz throughout town about the talents of the studio's newest director.

Lang remained an offbeat director, resisting big-budget assignment and big stars. Although he was sought after by such leading actors as Marlene Dietrich, Henry Fonda, and Glenn Ford, he preferred to develop smaller "no-name" pictures that allowed him room for creative growth. As meddling producers pressed him to make his films more mainstream, Lang seemed determined to explore even darker territory. For the next twenty years, he directed a variety of bleak thrillers that laid the foundation for film noir: *Man Hunt* (1941), *Ministry of Fear* (1944), *House by the River* (1950), *The Big Heat* (1953), and *While the City Sleeps* (1956). Lang's hypnotic visuals also found a natural home among the westerns of the day, most notably *Rancho Notorious* (1952). Never has another director collected a group of such jaded, shady, desperate characters and wrapped them around plots involving prostitution, blackmail, and drug dealing. Murder almost seems a tolerable habit in a Lang film. Visually stunning, these movies achieve rare moments of artistry that represent the very best of film noir. A typical frame: a femme fatale sits in front of a three-panel mirror while a detective and a thug talk behind her, each panel reflecting a different character to reinforce the triangle of deception that has bound them together.

Lang's influence was felt immediately. He had tremendous impact on contemporary directors who specialized in thrillers: Alfred Hitchcock, Jacques Tournier, Tod Browning, and Otto Preminger. The multitalented Orson Welles confessed to studying the compositions of Lang's films before making his own debut and relied heavily on the way Lang's sets architecturally imprisoned the actors for *Citizen Kane* (1941). A perfectionist who demanded total control over his projects, Lang was fed up with Hollywood in the mid-fifties. When studio interference became unbearable, he suddenly returned to Germany and retired.

As a creative force who was integral in the success of two separate film industries in the prime of their productive output, Fritz Lang is a towering figure in cinema. His collective accomplishments in art direction—the development of the German expressionist aesthetic, the creation of the futuristic look of science fiction films, and the introduction of shadowy westerns that dominated the 1940s—are substantial enough to warrant inclusion on a list of influencers. But his prodigious body of film noir standards is clearly the greatest contribution to that genre.

MARCUS LOEW

Born: May 7, 1870, New York, NY
Died: September 5, 1927, New York, NY

You must want a big success and beat it into submission.

—MARCUS LOEW

Peep-show purveyor Marcus Loew had already failed in business twice before acquiring a penny arcade in 1905. His third attempt would be blessed by smart partnerships, good fortune, and old-fashioned tenacity. Loew was bolstered by the savvy purchases of small vaudeville venues and theatrical halls in Manhattan and Cincinnati with partner Adolph Zukor. With a strong interest in the future of motion pictures, he converted every building to exhibit them. Zukor left the company to concentrate on distribution, and by 1907, Loew owned some forty theaters all over the country. In a short time, he would be the king of a new empire. As one of the only movie barons to focus on theaters early, Loew would hold the keys to the cinematic kingdom and rule the industry for a lifetime.

He wisely moved to Hollywood to keep close to the people who made films. As the new center of movie production, Southern California was plagued by threats from the Edison Trust. The tense situation called for wisdom, and Loew decided to steer clear of all conflict by simply displaying the films of Thomas Ince and Jesse Lasky without making any of his own. He would leave the independents to fight the battles while he raked in the grosses.

As he added theaters, he began to differentiate them by their names, Loew's Chinese Theater being the most famous. The clout Marcus Loew carried was remarkable, and his Chinese Theater and other marquee establishments became the places to premiere prestigious films. He then went to Europe looking to expand his empire overseas. But by 1912, Loew realized that to control the destiny of his four hundred movie houses, which represented more than half of all theaters nationwide, he would need to control the production of films as well. Other theaters owned by production companies were able to provide a frequent stream of popular stars. They could supply double-billed features and add serials to the showings.

Looking to protect his investments with a steady flow of exhibits, Loew absorbed small independent studios over the next few years. The largest purchase was Metro Pictures, which had contracted directors like Erich von Stroheim and young producers like Irving Thalberg and David O. Selznick. A small man of incredible business acumen, Loew demanded long hours and the utmost loyalty of his staff, and he received it. Most studio executives stayed with him for the duration of their careers.

Both feared and respected, he was able to fend off attempts by William Fox and Adolph Zukor to force theatre owners to purchase packages of features, cartoons, and shorts in order to get films starring big names like Mary Pickford. Loew held steadfast against monopolistic practices. He also refused to fix his admission prices or participate in pooling practices that affected smaller theater owners. These ethical decisions were rewarded years later when government regulation required Loew to relinquish many of his theaters. He sold large portions to old competitors and placed Metro talkies in the theaters of others.

In 1924, after Loew bought Sam Goldwyn's corporation, he struck an agreement with Louis B. Mayer to consolidate under the name Metro-Goldwyn-Mayer, or MGM, with Loew's, Inc., being the parent company. With the strong support of theaters and deep resources, Loew became the most powerful man in the industry. He plotted a new course for MGM by scouting the biggest names and concentrated on quality productions, quickly molding the new studio into the largest maker of motion pictures in the world.

A heart attack in 1923 forced him to retire from the business before theaters became widespread around the world. With the benefit of better health, he would have been among the richest men in the world in a few more years. Still, at his death in 1927, his personal fortune was well over $30 million. Among people who have dominated and influenced the exhibition of movies, he is outranked only by William Fox, and the great film exhibitors who would mold the way audiences watch movies, such pioneers as Samuel Rothafel and Richard Hollingshead, never came close to exerting the power over movie theaters that Marcus Loew exercised throughout his long career.

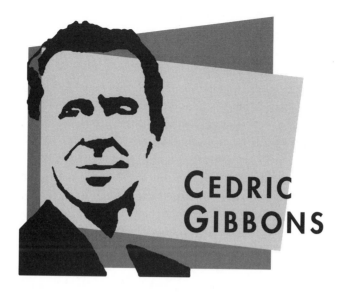

42

CEDRIC GIBBONS

Born: March 23, 1893, New York, NY
Died: July 26, 1960, Westwood, CA

*MGM was not run, oddly, by L. B. Mayer, but by the
head of the art department.*

—ELIA KAZAN

Cedric Gibbons was appointed head of the art department at the newly formed MGM in 1924, following short stints with the Thomas Edison studio and the independent Goldwyn company. While negotiating his contract, he had a clause inserted that stated his name was to be listed as art director on every MGM film during his tenure. This gave Gibbons's name the greatest exposure on screens for thirty-two years, and to this day he has accumulated more credits than any other single person in film history; listed on more than fifteen hundred films as "art director," Gibbons worked on only a handful. But if Gibbons was not "the" art director on every film, he was the key architect of the glitzy look that shimmered across nearly all MGM films.

The son of two architects, Gibbons was born to high style. He was a vain man who loved to have his photograph taken, especially since he was seen wearing the latest fashions. He lived a life filled with expensive cars, beautiful wives, and exotic food. His personal fashion sense inspired those around him, and even costume designers sought his advice.

As the head of a collective of studio art directors and set designers, Gibbons introduced three-dimensional furnishings to replace the flat, painted backdrops of previous films. His characteristic flair and his art deco–style sets distinguished the golden era of Hollywood films and sparked a trend in interior decorating across America. Gibbons is also responsible for lighting innovations in MGM films that made the other studios follow suit. These significant changes would make him one of the most influential figures in the years following the sound era, and Gibbons's talent for supervision and training would mark hundreds of MGM films.

His team of top production designers reads like a who's who of important design figures in film: Preston Ames, Jack Martin Smith, Lyle Wheeler, Raoul Dufy, Vincent Minnelli, and William Cameron Menzies. He had available to him all of the industry's top special effects men, including A. Arnold Gillespie. The consistent design work of Gibbons's team easily passed Irving Thalberg's standards of excellence in *The Big Parade* (1925) and was prominent in *Our Dancing Daughter* (1928) and *The Bridge of San Luis Rey* (1929). His personal sense of artistic excellence was the very essence of MGM quality.

Gibbons's design sense was critical to another Hollywood standard: in 1927, he was asked by Louis B. Mayer to design a statuette that was to be awarded to selected artists by the newly formed Academy of Motion Picture Arts and Sciences. The famous sculpture took shape as a man holding a sword by the hilt and standing on a film canister. It became known as the "Oscar" several years later; there is some mystery as to the nickname's origin. Gibbons's artists were eventually nominated for thirty-seven of the awards, winning eleven, one for a film that Gibbons designed alone.

Though indoor sets most exemplify his influence, Gibbons also worked on adventure films, including *Ben-Hur* (1926), *Mutiny on the Bounty* (1935), and *Captains Courageous* (1937). Gibbons himself directed only one film, *Tarzan and His Mate* (1934), and the highly praised visuals spawned a popular series. Given Gibbons' guidance, the MGM musicals and comedies of the thirties and forties stayed on top: *Grand Hotel* (1932), *The Thin Man* (1934), *A Night at the Opera* (1935), and *Ninotchka* (1939) remain best of their respective classes.

The Wizard of Oz (1939) represented the apogee of Gibbons's career. He adopted Natalie Kalmus's Technicolor processes for the film, which is rivaled by only *Gone With the Wind* of the same year for beauty. But his personal stamp was present on hundreds of films, passed along by a team of designers that carried out his exacting standards. In later years, Gibbons would be nothing more than a figurehead, but his regal taste lingered throughout MGM's lengthy heyday, and his work still serves as a reference of high style in set design among Hollywood's finest production specialists.

43

JAMES CAGNEY

Born: July 17, 1899, New York, NY
Died: March 30, 1986, Stanfordville, NY

He came on in the movies as though he were playing to the gallery in an opera house.

—ORSON WELLES

The product of New York City's tough Lower East Side, James Cagney escaped to settlement-house vaudeville revues as a song-and-dance man in the 1920s. By 1930, he was a veteran of Broadway and ripe for a career in motion pictures.

Cagney's first film was a repeat performance of his 1929 Broadway success *Penny Arcade,* called *Sinner's Holiday* (1930), with actress Joan Blondell. His roots were evident when he was cast as a rough-hewn scrapper in *The Public Enemy* (1931), his most memorable role in the minds of Depression audiences. The angry, seething criminals he played in thirty-eight films, including *The Roaring Twenties* (1939), *Angels With Dirty Faces* (1938), and *White Heat* (1949), lifted a troubled Warners studio in the early sound era.

In fact, Cagney came to exemplify the first generation of sound stars. His choppy delivery and knowing sneer made audiences feel as if he were letting them in on a joke. Moviegoers easily impersonated his jerky shoulders, tiptoe stance, and teeth-gritting lines like "You dirty rat." His apparent comfort in criminal situations added a carefree swagger to his characterizations that translated to a deeper strength than his slight five-feet-six stature first suggested. His on-screen demeanor was so natural, in fact that other actors seemed somewhat false and theatrical next to him. This naturalness heightened his appeal, and Cagney came to own the American gangster genre for an entire decade, despite the constant attempts by George Raft, Humphrey Bogart, and Edward G. Robinson to unseat him.

The stubborn edge of Cagney's persona was often softened by the Irish sensibility of fellow actor Pat O'Brien. Through films spanning four decades, the two brash actors fought side by side in *Here Comes the Navy* (1934), *Devil Dogs of the Air* (1935), *The Irish in Us* (1935), *Ceiling Zero* (1935), *The Fighting 69th* (1940), and *Torrid Zone* (1940). The cool logic of the fast-talking O'Brien was an excellent counter to the hotheaded impulsiveness of Cagney in the popular wartime dramas. After a twenty-year hiatus from acting, the two costars were reunited for the last time in *Ragtime* (1981). It would be the final screen appearance for both, and Cagney was hailed for getting back to rugged form as the wiley curmudgeon Sheriff Rheinlander Waldo.

But Cagney won greatest critical praise for musicals like *The Seven Little Foys* (1955). He put his jittery gait to work as showman George M. Cohan in *Yankee Doodle Dandy* (1942) and won the Best Actor Oscar. Displaying a bravura unusual among sound film stars, he was a song-and-dance man of the highest order and embodied the American ideal of the tireless entertainer. Comic turns in *A Midsummer Night's Dream* (1935) and *Never Steal Anything Small* (1959) further established his versatility.

Like Humphrey Bogart and Bette Davis, Cagney had signed an exclusive long-term contract with Warners that left him unhappy after his value skyrocketed. And like his predecessors, he battled to have his deal renegotiated; a sweeter deal in the 1950s afforded him an unprecedented share of decision making and profits. Later, Cagney would independently produce and distribute his own vehicles, including a tribute to Lon Chaney entitled *Man of a Thousand Faces* (1957).

Following comedic performances in *Mister Roberts* (1955) and Billy Wilder's *One, Two, Three* (1961), Cagney retired for twenty years until director Milos Forman enticed him with *Ragtime* (1981), after he had already been honored with a 1974 American Film Institute Life Achievement Award.

The first international star of the talkies, James Cagney smirked his way into the hearts of Depression audiences to become one of the most respected and beloved actors in cinema history. Moviegoers found his explosive temper, quick fists, and grapefruit-squeezing boldness refreshing while they sat waiting for prosperity; Cagney seemed to offer cathartic escape through machine-gun justice that took him to the "Top of the world!"

44

BEN HECHT

Born: February 28, 1894, New York, NY
Died: April 18, 1964, New York, NY

With the advent of sound, studios scrambled to recruit 'real' writers.

—PETER HAY

Ben Hecht began his writing career in 1914 as a WWI reporter for the *Chicago Daily News*, stationed in Berlin. He was the first foreign correspondent there after Germany's military defeat, and his insightful observations were delivered in a choppy, smart style that came to exemplify Chicago journalism. Upon his return from the war, he started a daily human interest column for the *Daily News* and developed a reputation as one of the trade's best writers. He was intensely passionate about politics and wrote opinion pieces on all international matters.

Hecht's close association with radical novelists and poets made him a key figure on the Chicago literary scene of 1922. He began writing pieces that espoused socialist views, and his first novel was deemed "obscene" and "dangerous" by the U.S. government; the entire printing was seized and burned. Under a cloud of suspicion among his colleagues and employers, Hecht was discharged from his position on the *Daily News.* He packed up and moved to New York, intent on becoming a playwright.

Hecht became a regular face at the Algonquin Hotel, a hangout for famous *New Yorker* magazine contributors and figures of the publishing and theater districts. His close friend Herman Mankiewicz suggested Hecht try his hand at screenwriting and enticed him to Hollywood in 1925.

Director Joseph von Sternberg shared the cynical attitude Hecht had toward America's values and Hollywood's decadence, and together they worked on a story that would become the first gangster drama, *Underworld* (1927). The film would boost Sternberg's sagging career and win Hecht the first Oscar ever awarded for an original story.

Hecht had the perfect disposition for a writer working within the studio system of the sound era; he liked anonymity and actually disdained screenwriting, making it clear that he did it only for the money. Of the sixty movies he wrote, he claimed to have written more than half in two weeks or less. When he wasn't required to be in Hollywood, he retreated to New York. This improved his image in the eyes of the writer-snobs of the Algonquin Round Table, who counted Hecht among their extended family. Their respect for Hecht had far-reaching implications. When Hecht dragged Charles MacArthur to Hollywood in 1928 to write the film version of their Broadway smash *The Front Page* (1931), he sparked an exodus of New York's finest writers. Soon, the top literary talent on the East Coast headed west: Dorothy Parker, Robert Benchley, Marc Connelly, George S. Kaufman, Robert Sherwood, and Moss Hart, and others were close behind them.

For the next forty-two years, Hecht wrote scripts for classic pictures, including *Queen Christina* (1933), *Gunga Din* (1938), *Wuthering Heights* (1939), and *Duel in the Sun* (1946). He worked easily in any genre, tackling them all, but his gift for satire made for a strong series of outlandish farces and screwball comedies, among them *Twentieth Century* (1934), and the Marx Brothers' *At the Circus* (1939).

Besides *The Front Page* and *Foreign Correspondent* (1940), directed by Alfred Hitchcock, Hecht wrote another cult favorite among budding journalists, *Nothing Sacred* (1937), starring Fredric March and Carole Lombard. The screwball plot provided a biting look at the ethical responsibility of the media.

Film noir thrillers were another speciality of Hecht's. He and MacArthur wrote *Crime Without Passion* (1934), a powerful crime horror film starring Claude Rains as a demonic lawyer on a killing spree that is still a late-night classic, and *Kiss of Death* (1947), in which a psychopathic hitman (Richard Widmark) hunts a small-time jewel thief about to inform on the mob, left a permanent impression. Widmark's crazy delivery of Hecht's lines sparkles as he interrogates the crook's mother: "I'm askin' ya, where's that squealin' son of yours? You think a squealer can get away from me? Huh? You know what I do to squealers? I let 'em have it in the belly, so they can roll around for a long time thinkin' it over."

He also became Hollywood's busiest script doctor. David O. Selznick trusted his judgment implicitly, once calling him in desperation and offering $15,000 for some anonymous fixes to *Gone With the Wind* (1939), including the classic "frankly, my dear" addition. Hitchcock religiously passed scenarios under Hecht's nose and used him to script *Spellbound* (1945), *Notorious* (1946), and *The Paradine Case* (1947). As a favored writer of Irving Thalberg, Hecht facetiously coined the term "treatment" for the way the young producer doctored his scripts.

Hecht was seldom concerned about receiving screen credit and often worked without recognition. The top directors of the age consulted him discreetly for his much-needed help on their scripts: Howard Hawks, Rouben Mamoulian, Otto Preminger, William Wellman, Howard Hughes, Orson Welles, and John Ford are just a few. In fact, Hecht was a ghostwriter on the memorable lines of Rita Hayworth in *Gilda* (1946), Danny Kaye in *The Inspector General* (1949), Gregory Peck in *Roman Holiday* (1953), and Frank Sinatra in *The Man With the Golden Arm* (1955).

Ben Hecht legitimized screenwriting to the entire literary world. His success, both financially and artistically, made it comfortable for other writers to come to Hollywood, and his skill put screenwriters on an equal ground with directors as the architects of motion picture storytelling. He rests comfortably in the ranking between Anita Loos and Dalton Trumbo, and together their influences can be felt in the vast majority of screenplays written today.

45

INGMAR BERGMAN

Born: July 14, 1918, Uppsala, Sweden

For Bergman, to be alone means to ask questions. And to make films
means to answer them. Nothing could be more classically romantic.

—JEAN-LUC GODARD

The magical films of director Ingmar Bergman are purely autobiographical. Woven from strands of family, love, tragedy, and death, his body of work represents a completed tapestry of a single life. No other filmmaker has come closer than Bergman to articulating personal fears and dreams through compelling storytelling devices. His use of huddled spaces, visual metaphors, flashbacks, and rhythmic dance created the language of feelings. Focusing on the exploration of the self, his ideas meshed easily with Freudian psychoanalytical thinking, and college students studying his films found ways to express their own inner emotions.

Bergman made tremendous strides in modernizing cinema in the 1950s. After entering the Swedish film commmunity as a screenwriter for director Alf Sjoberg, Bergman was assigned to direct his own films and released *The Devil's Wanton* (1949). Already present in his stories was the strong use of religious symbols and a preoccupation with death. This fatalism, which stemmed from a deeply troubled childhood, became at first a thread throughout his films, then a stigma as many fans playfully joked about the depressing nature of his themes.

His next films, *Summer Interlude* (1951) and *Summer With Monika* (1953), revolved around feelings of ill-fated love that reflected Bergman's

144

eternal questions about marriage, a theme he would return to time and time again. These early films established strong roles for women. In *Interlude,* a restless ballerina reexamines a first love as a means of infusing her career with new enthusiasm. The wit and energy reflected by the females are set against the lethargy and cynicism of their male counterparts.

His *Sawdust and Tinsel* (1953), in which traveling circus performers stumble through poor villages in nineteenth-century Sweden, saw the beginning of a visual approach that strongly marked his later films. He used ancient settings to explore classical themes, but with a modern theatrical feel reminiscent of experimental stage plays. Beautiful black-and-white photography echoes the past, but the striking costumes and contrasting makeup give the characters the stylized appearance of kabuki players. This allowed Bergman to express his thoughts on jealousy, despair, and sexuality through metaphors. The culmination of his newfound style and age-old ethics was a medieval morality play, *The Seventh Seal* (1956), in which a battle-weary knight fresh from the Crusades confronts his own fears of mortality. A pensive performance by actor Max von Sydow is highlighted by scenes in which he must play a game of chess with the Grim Reaper. Through the long struggle for his life, the knight balances his will to live with the harshness he sees around him. Bergman managed an almost Shakespearean mix of complexity and humor, filled with comic characterizations and excellent dialogue. He suddenly found himself an internationally famous filmmaker.

Following *The Seventh Seal* with a mature study of the elderly in *Wild Strawberries* (1957), Bergman was making a name for himself in art houses and among intellectual audiences. His signature scenes usually included elements of fantasy that visualized his characters' meditations on their own existence: an old man facing death sees the hands of his watch disappear or views his own body lying in a coffin. Another stamp of the Bergman style was open sexuality expressed as a reflection of his feelings of vulnerability and insecurity; scenes of characters undressing or engaging in sex often evoke feelings of awkwardness or emotional distance.

Bergman's so-called chamber style of photography was essentially a tendency to use extreme close-ups to highlight subtle nuances of an actor's face. Using light to suggest the passing of time and shifting of moods became a new and revelatory technique. Bergman's longtime collaborater in these efforts was Sven Nykvist, highly regarded as the most significant cinematographer in films since Gregg Tolland and Karl Struss had made their contributions. Bergman's favorite subjects—religion, suicide, love, and sexuality—revealed themselves in his stark, quiet trilogy made up of *Through a Glass, Darkly* (1962) *Winter Light* (1962), and *The Silence* (1963).

The visual experimentation of Bergman's work is evident in the films of Woody Allen, Paul Mazursky, and John Cassavetes, but the films of Bergman's later period—*Persona* (1966), *Cries and Whispers* (1972), *Face to Face* (1976), and *Autumn Sonata* (1978)—are most imitated, though often without the same effectiveness. These explorations of family taboos and secrets were highlighted by the emotional reconciliations and epiphanies that have become the standard fare for movie-of-the-week specials on television and cable presentations. His final film, the celebrated *Fanny and Alexander* (1983), became a poignant end to Bergman's unequaled career.

Ingmar Bergman holds a unique position among influential directors. His cinema is the cinema of feelings. While his films may not be uniformly appreciated, they each contain extremely personal insights into the spiritual and psychological struggles that Bergman himself encountered in his life—a powerful body of work that reads like a blueprint of an unusual artist's emotional development.

HUMPHREY BOGART

46

Born: December 25, 1899, New York, NY
Died: January 14, 1957, Hollywood, CA

He is quite unreplaceable. There will never be anybody like him.

—JOHN HUSTON

During World War I, a young navy gunner had an accident. While rough-housing on a wooden stairway, he slipped and took a wood splinter in his upper lip. Once the injury healed, it left a stiffness that became one of the trademark features of Humphrey Bogart's unforgettable face. This tight-lipped loner would climb through the Hollywood ranks the hard way—scraping by in dismal action films and box office disasters. When his face took on a harder edge, he started building a reputation as a tough guy and struggled through bouts of typecasting as a second-rate gangster. In the prime of life, his mug would be one of the most recognizable in the film noir genre. And with age, his hangdog visage would become the icon of a generation—war-weary and weathered.

After his discharge from the navy, Bogart got in touch with a family friend, William A. Brady, who was turning small profits as a Broadway theatrical producer. Brady gave Bogart acting work, but the young sailor didn't shine in any of his roles. In fact, most reviews were quite discouraging. So he followed some friends to Hollywood in the early thirties, where it was rumored that the film studios were searching out stage actors with strong voices to capitalize on the rage for talkies. Immediately, Bogart landed a picture deal with Fox for *The Devil With Women* (1930), his first feature film. When the movie performed dismally at the box office, and two other failures followed, Fox tore up Bogart's contract and put him out on the streets.

He landed jobs at Columbia, Universal, and Warner Bros., making forgettable appearances in a string of B-movie westerns alongside another awkward cowboy actor, James Cagney. However, Bogart's ability to portray gritty characters soon emerged as a clear speciality, and his role as a prison inmate opposite Spencer Tracy in *Up the River* (1930) showed signs of promise. But after several years of supporting roles, Bogart's name still eluded the attention of executives; defeated, he returned to New York in 1934.

Determined to make it on Broadway, he approached playwright Robert E. Sherwood for a chance to play killer Duke Mantee in *The Petrified Forest*. This time, Bogart got raves from cosmopolitan theater critics and film scouts alike. Warner acquired the film rights to the play and turned it into a smash on-screen adaptation (1936), starring Leslie Howard, Bette Davis, and Bogart. Warners offered Bogart a $550-a-week contract, and over the next five years he served his apprenticeship as a heavy in gangster stories and prison dramas, usually backing up the tough talk of Edward G. Robinson, Paul Muni, George Raft, or his old friend Cagney in such films as *The Roaring Twenties* (1939), *Invisible Stripes* (1939), and *They Drive by Night* (1940)—twenty-eight features in all. Among Bogart's early financial successes were *Dead End* (1937) and *Angels With Dirty Faces* (1938), in which he gave a memorable performance beside the Dead End Kids.

Gangster roles would turn out to be a blessing in disguise; although Bogart disliked being typecast as a tough guy, he often was the first actor under consideration when Cagney or Raft turned down a role. Luckily, this was the case when director Raoul Walsh was casting *High Sierra* (1941), about a criminal making a last attempt at a new life. The script, by John Huston, called for the death of leading character Roy Earle. Raft simply refused to die, so Bogart stepped into history. The tense direction and supporting performance of Ida Lupino helped turn the film into a huge hit.

Suddenly, Bogart was able to break away from underworld figures and show himself as a leading man. *Casablanca* (1942), his first romantic role, would provide further proof that Bogart was star material. Based on an unproduced play called *Everybody Goes to Rick's,* the film places nightclub owner Rick Blaine in the middle of a love triangle between an old flame and her freedom-fighting husband, who is escaping from Hitler by way of Morocco. Bogart's haunting portrayal was at the heart of one of the screen's greatest love stories. The lingering piano, the bizarre cast of characters, the classic farewell at the airport, and the memorable pledge of friendship at the close of the film made *Casablanca* irresistible. At Oscar time, Bogart was nominated for Best Actor, and the movie won for Best Picture.

Teaming again with John Huston in his directorial debut, *The Maltese*

Falcon (1941), Bogart returned to darker themes. The film featured Bogart as detective Sam Spade in what became the first of a long collaboration between the unconventional director and the established movie star. Under Huston's guiding hand, in *The Treasure of the Sierra Madre* (1948) and *Beat the Devil* (1954), a deeper sentiment replaced the cynical, self-reliant exterior. Huston helped carefully nurse Bogart's reputation by casting him against type, and often these offbeat characters revealed an unexplored side of the aging tough, breathing new life into his career. This lasting legacy would inspire Jean-Luc Godard and Woody Allen, among others, to elect Bogart the patron saint of sensitive-but-manly males.

In 1944, Warner offered Bogart the unprecedented sum of $15 million for a fifteen-year agreement, signaling a significant change in Hollywood's preferences for leading men. Bogart's trademark performances were far from the glamorous swashbucklers and macho leaders that had long gained favor with audiences. In fact, Bogart was the antithesis of these men—his successes were almost exclusively based on roles that required him to play the sullen outcast who shuns responsibility or romantic involvement. Throughout his performances in *High Sierra, Casablanca, The Maltese Falcon,* and *The Treasure of the Sierra Madre,* Bogart carved a niche as the quintessential loner, a character type that would become the dominant choice for protagonists in thousands of scripts to come. In casting the mold for the outsider, Bogart became a forerunner of Robert Mitchum, Marlon Brando, James Dean, Jack Nicholson, and Robert De Niro.

Bogart's love life flourished when a sexy, young femme fatale in *To Have and Have Not* (1944) taught him to whistle. The sharp, witty twenty-year-old fashion model named Lauren Bacall married Bogart in 1945. Their May-December romance generated sparks, both on camera in smoldering dramas and behind the scenes of political battles, where they vocally supported the blacklisted Hollywood screenwriters during the witchhunts of the McCarthy era. With Bacall as his costar, Bogart went on to make *The Big Sleep* (1946), *Dark Passage* (1947), and *Key Largo* (1948)—films that permanently marked Bogart as the epitome of the film noir actor. He continued in several memorable roles in the dark and moody *Dead Reckoning* (1947) and *The Desperate Hours* (1955).

Bogart's skyrocketing salary led to another important development in 1947; he became the first major actor from the studio system to set up his own independent production company, Santana Productions. Although still under contract with Warner, Bogart's company would produce several films for exclusive distribution through a different studio, Columbia. This trailblazing move was envied by his peers and soon became the ideal sought for by such actors as James Cagney, Clark Gable, John Wayne, and Bette Davis. (Today, hundreds of stars form their own production companies to develop scripts into movies.) Although many of the Santana productions did not feature Bogart, he did eventually wind up in four, notably the gritty *Knock on Any Door* (1949) and the cult favorite *In a Lonely Place* (1950). His turns in *Tokyo Joe* (1949) and *Sirocco* (1951) were forgettable Santana productions that didn't perform well at the ticket counters, further proving that audiences weren't interested in seeing Bogart in action-adventures.

The African Queen (1951) was the film that explored most deeply the inner complexity of the "Bogie" persona. Depending heavily on Huston for the proper sense of comic vulnerability and romantic quibbling, Bogart played a seafaring drunkard compelled to help a spinster missionary, elegantly performed by Katharine Hepburn. The simple, charming script won over audiences and the Academy. Bogart was awarded a Best Actor Oscar, beating out Marlon Brando in the landmark film *A Streetcar Named Desire*. The film also proved to be the launch of Bogart's final period, marked by an oddball and complex turn as the unbalanced Captain Queeg in *The Caine Mutiny* (1954), for which he received another Best Actor nomination. Bogart's other roles, as a wily film director in *The Barefoot Contessa* (1956), a wealthy stuffed-shirt in Billy Wilder's *Sabrina* (1956), and the unscrupulous sportswriter of *The Harder They Fall* (1956), rounded out a stellar final year that showed the diverse sides of the aging actor.

Bogart's influential role in film history coincides with a sweeping change in the types of scripts Hollywood selected after World War II. During the heyday of large-scale epics and high-adventure films, Bogart was an actor out of sync with the tastes of moviegoers and studio heads. But as money became scarce in postwar America, producers turned to smaller settings and more intimate stories. The camera got closer than ever to actors, and directors began examining the pysche of characters. Suddenly, the darker themes of film noir were popular, and the weathered face of Humphrey Bogart grew on audiences. In fact, his image became an indelible screen icon—often listed with Buster Keaton and Charlie Chaplin as one of the greatest faces in cinema. Like many high-ranking actors on this list, he stood for an entire genre. True, his image is not as closely associated with film noir as John Wayne's is with the western. Nevertheless, he forged a new identity for the modern movie male that was distinctly different from the decisive man of action that preceeded him—Bogart's screen portrayals allowed audiences to examine the complexity of characters who weren't heroic. The enduring popularity of the antihero, a type that has dominated scriptwriting since Bogart's memorable performances, is a testament to his lasting influence on films.

LEON SCHLESINGER

Born: September 9, 1884, Philadelphia, PA
Died: December 25, 1949, Los Angeles, CA

Schlesinger was no artist, he was a moneyman.

—LEONARD MALTIN

In 1929, when financial woes threatened the Warner Bros. studio, executive Sam Warner put a tremendous amount of faith in two men—Hal Wallis and Leon Schlesinger. Wallis, one of the industry's most respected figures, would eventually oversee more than four hundred of the most popular features in the history of Hollywood (most notably gangster films) that collectively scooped up thirty-two Academy Awards and 121 Oscar nominations from the late 1920s to the mid-1970s. Schlesinger, on the other hand, was in charge of Porky Pig.

Leon Schlesinger had been a financial backer of Warner Bros.' gamble on sound films, bankrolling *The Jazz Singer* (1927) and profiting handsomely from its success. A producer of several early John Wayne westerns, Schlesinger also owned a title effects company in Hollywood called Pacific Arts and Titles, which had a long-standing contract to provide dialogue cards for most of Warners' silent feature films. This production experience, combined with the excellent facilities Schlesinger possessed, gave Warner an idea.

Sam Warner had a problem he thought Schlesinger could solve. Owning more than seventeen thousand theaters in roughly seventy-five hundred towns throughout the nation, Warner Bros. had more than 10.5 million seats to fill with paying customers. To attract patrons on a regular basis, he needed a steady stream of new features, serials, and animated shorts. He proposed a deal with Schlesinger that would give Warners a fresh cartoon every two weeks. Schlesinger could handle production any way he liked; Warner would take care of distribution.

To complete twenty-six cartoons a year, Schlesinger would require several established animators, preferably those with proven characters. He had heard that artists Rudy Ising and Hugh Harman had developed a few shorts featuring the antics of a character named Bosko, so he hired them, along with animator Friz Freleng, at $200 a week each and began a series of cartoons in 1930 based loosely on Disney's Silly Symphonies, called Looney Tunes.

The success of their first short starring Bosko, *Sinking in the Bathtub* (1930), launched a second series, called Merrie Melodies, and put pressure on Schlesinger to make one cartoon a month for the next three years. A typical seven-minute cartoon required 5,040 drawings and cost nearly $30,000. Since cartoon shorts often take up to twelve months from conception to delivery, Schlesinger devised a system whereby each animator would have to be the lead "director" on several projects simultaneously to complete two shorts a month.

Immediately, Harman and Ising wanted out of the hectic pace, and they took Bosko with them. A desperate Schlesinger corralled the talents of Robert McKimson, Bob Clampett, Chuck Jones, and Tex Avery and refocused these men away from melody-based cartoons to character-driven plots. He was forced to compete with new cartoon personalities being introduced by MGM and others. Schlesinger conceived of the idea of developing an "Our Gang" of cartoon characters modeled on the comedies of the Hal Roach studio. He handed the task to his young animators, and soon Bob Clampett had an idea. Clampett showed the group drawings of a curly-tailed pig and black cat, named Pork and Beans. It was the first sketch of Porky Pig, and Leon knew the perfect voiceman for bringing him to life—stuttering contract actor Joe Dougherty. Warners had a new star, and Schlesinger was back on schedule.

He then focused on cartoons that would win Academy Award recognition, and Friz Freleng became the first Warners director to win an Oscar nomination, with *It's Got Me Again* (1931). Tex Avery, however, would create cartoons that showered the Warners division with more Oscars and more respect. MGM began to notice the up-and-coming young Warners team, and Schlesinger used the attention to recruit more talent. He lured Ub Iwerks, Frank Tashlin, and movie theater organist Carl Stalling (who had been behind Disney's Silly Symphonies) into his own cartoon stable. Another prize acquisition was radio personality Mel Blanc, who provided more than four hundred distinct voices for three thousand shorts—a whopping 90 percent of all WB cartoons. In 1937, Blanc took over the dialogue of Porky Pig and

Daffy Duck; in 1940, he introduced "Happy Rabbit," the Brooklyn Bunny later known as Bugs.

At the height of competition for animated shorts, Leon let the young cartoonists loose. His hands-off approach resulted in the wackiest collection of classics ever assembled, including such celebrated films as *The Daffy Doc* (1938), *A Wild Hare* (1940), and *Inki and the Minah Bird* (1943), as well as a legacy of interchangeable antagonists like Sylvester, Foghorn Leghorn, Speedy Gonzales, Pepe LePew, and Yosemite Sam.

Much has been made of the free rein the animators had at Warners. It has been suggested that Leon was an absent manager who cared little for the product, a criticism that lacks foundation. He oversaw story ideas, movitated the animators with contests and bonuses, brainstormed new characters, hired and fired, handled the day-to-day management of the talent by promoting and developing his employees, and devised long-term plans for Clampett, Jones, and Freleng specifically. To keep harmony among his temperamental artists, he often lent out animators, giving them a chance to work for Walt Disney, MGM, or the Walter Lantz studios. If animators left his studio for other commissions, Schlesinger never hestitated hiring those same employees back years later when they became available. But the animators did have contempt for their boss. The voice of Daffy Duck was a pointed jab at Leon's lisp. They presented the voice to him and snickered when he didn't see the obvious parody.

Schlesinger struggled to keep his animators happy. Tex Avery, who had dreamed up a series of talking animal shorts, asked Schlesinger to retool the studio for live-action shorts or stop-motion experiments. The dispute turned sour, and Avery was punished with a lengthy suspension, returning only to resign from Warners. After the incident, Clampett asked to develop a hand-puppet series and was allowed his Cecil and Beany shorts, which eventually became a television show. Others, like Freleng, were lured to MGM by the sheer prospect of more money, but came back to Warners on Leon's initiative.

In 1944, Schlesinger sold his interest in the animation venture to Warners, but he stayed on until 1946 to run the operation. He handled the merchandising of characters created during his reign, and he negotiated television rights and promotional tie-ins on behalf of the Warners Bros. studio. By then, the key players were permanently rooted; Freleng continued as head animator on more than three hundred projects, Chuck Jones would hone his timing and become a legendary master through an association with Warners that spanned sixty years, and Robert McKimson remained for thirty-two years until the studio shut its doors.

Schlesinger left just in time; the conditions of the industry had changed since Sam Warner first approached him. A historic 1948 Supreme Court ruling, stating that Hollywood was monopolizing the entertainment field, ordered all production companies to sell any movie theaters they owned. Studios were forced to become independent distributors and convince theater owners to run their cartoons. But theater owners didn't want to pay for seven-minute cartoons that cost roughly the same as ninety-minute features. With annual costs of close to $1 million, the frugal boss of the Warners studio, Jack Warner, felt, "There is no money in short subjects."

Furthermore, when Schlesinger left, the relationship between the studio and the renegade department became strained. Schlesinger had permitted only a minimum of interference from Warners when he was in charge: Jack Warner claimed never to have set foot inside the animation building. Once Schlesinger departed, Warner appointed Eddie Selzer to run things. His mission was clear: find a more economical way to make cartoons. Selzer instituted cost-cutting measures and demanded that every animated short be scripted, something the animators only did loosely in storyboards. Clearly, Selzer wasn't the man to change the ways of the free-wheeling Loonies. Warner grew impatient and closed the studio briefly in 1955, giving animators a hiatus. Upon their return, things hadn't changed, and Jack Warner was resolute.

The demise of the famous studio came in 1963, relegating Looney Tunes to television reruns. Today, these cartoons still enjoy the popular vote among millions of aficionados, many of whom are unaware of Schlesinger's role.

LOUELLA PARSONS

Born: August 6, 1881, Freeport, IL
Died: December 9, 1972, Santa Monica, CA

Nowadays, nearly five hundred ladies and gentlemen of the press cover Hollywood, but in those rip-roaring twenties, I had a monopoly on the news.

—LOUELLA PARSONS

Louella Parsons's love affair with the typewriter began in 1910 when she worked for nine dollars a week at the *Chicago Tribune*, in the syndication department. At night she wrote film scenarios; through her cousin, she sold her first screen story to the Essanay Movie Company in Chicago. She subsequently took a position at Essanay as a scriptreader for twenty-five dollars a week. Within a few short years, Parsons's tenacity and bravura would secure her a ticket to Hollywood, but not as screenwriter. She became a gossip columnist who used the power of the press to command the attention of the industry, eventually instituting a rumor mill that forced movie studios to counter her published opinions with their own publicity campaigns. Before her retirement, Louella Parsons became one of the most feared and respected women in Hollywood. In her more gracious moments, she single-handedly dominated public opinion to such an extent that she sent her vast and loyal readership racing to the pictures she recommended. In her more unscrupulous moods, she was known to fuel the most salacious scandals in the history of cinema.

In 1919, she approached two major newspapers in Chicago and New York about reporting from California on lifestyle issues. The *Chicago Record-Herald* bit, and later she moved her reports to the *New York Morning Telegraph*. The job led to a full-time column exclusively about Hollywood, and a year later Parsons was popular enough to warrant an offer from William Randolph Hearst. By writing kind words in her columns about Hearst's mistress, starlet Marion Davies, Parsons attracted his attention, and he offered Parsons a job reporting on movie news. She demanded and received $250 a week.

Coincidentally, a bizarre incident on Hearst's own yacht—the death of pioneer producer Thomas Ince in 1924—resulted in Parsons's most famous assignment. According to her initial reports, an oceangoing celebration of Ince's appointment as head of a new production company took a fatal turn when Hearst shot Ince in the abdomen during a moment of jealous rage. In the fabricated story, the newspaper tycoon allegedly believed Ince was actually comedian Charlie Chaplin, caught in a romantic embrace with Marion Davies. In truth, no bullet was ever fired and Ince's death was determined to be the result of chronic liver and stomach ailments, exacerbated by alcohol use. But truth left little room for the mystery and excitement of Parsons's reports, and she used the nationwide interest in the fatal evening to further her career. Parsons claimed to have been on board the yacht and her reports of the "actual events" had two important motives: to make Parsons herself appear to be a frequent guest at Hollywood's most exclusive functions and, more important, to steer controversy away from her employer. Many of her unfounded speculations of the night have remained a permanent part of urban legend, and readers around the country eagerly awaited her daily wire reports for any detail of the investigation. The rumors were later debunked, but the tragic event hoisted Parsons into the limelight, and she took on celebrity status that overshadowed many of the famous actors and studio heads involved in the scandal.

As her enormous popularity grew, Hearst had little choice but to make her the first nationally syndicated gossip columnist, the position she practically invented. By March of 1926, Parsons's columns were syndicated across the country, and within a few years roughly 375 papers were carrying her gossip. Soon, the scope of her influence was international. Among the cafeterias and nightclubs of Culver City, young Louella rubbed elbows with as many industry people as she could, building an intricate web of friends and adversaries that would last a lifetime. Mary Pickford, Gloria Swanson, and Joan Crawford would confide in her and conversely benefit from glowing notices in the news. With each new scoop, Parsons muscled her salary up another notch.

Parsons's column burgeoned into an entire gossip industry. Every rival paper hired its own Hollywood insider, the most notable contender being

Hedda Hopper, another old-timer from the studio backlots. Hopper and Parsons began a scoop war that left casualties in the form of reports on fallen stars, broken marriages, lost libidos, fatherless children, and the infidelities of everyone remotely connected to Tinseltown. Discretion was not an issue. Getting tips from her infamous collection of informants—hairdressers, hospital orderlies, doctors' wives, and studio assistants—Parsons revealed pregnancies, predicted divorces, and offered sympathy directly through her columns in the press. To a gossip-hungry public, she announced the marriage of Chaplin to eighteen-year-old Oona O'Neill, revealed Grace Kelly's and Ingrid Bergman's lovers, and exposed Joseph Cotten's adulterous affair.

Parsons was truly feared by stars and studios alike; they thought she was capable of swinging Oscar nominations and wins through public support, and they knew she was prone to vengeful acts against stars she deemed even slightly uncooperative. She insisted on interviews from the latest stars, demanded advance screenings of highly anticipated films, and bullied studio executives with threats of negative press when she didn't get her way. Her wrath was especially felt by those actors who refused a dinner invitation or skipped out early on one of Parsons's parties. "If you were part of the movie business, you could not ignore her," actress Jane Greer remembered. "The recurring nightmare among actors in Hollywood was to be invited to Hedda's and Louella's on the same night."

The most famous object of her retribution was *Citizen Kane* (1941). When Parsons heard a rumor that her employer was the subject of the film's satire, she demanded that Orson Welles give her a private screening. When he refused, she leaked vicious tirades in print against the young director until he relented and showed her the film. Hearst never had a more devoted ally than Parsons, and her efforts were instrumental in sinking *Kane*. She threatened RKO studio heads with nasty and salacious exaggerations in print, and called Radio City Music Hall in an attempt to convince theater owner Van Schmus to cancel *Kane's* premiere on the threat of no newspaper support. RKO and Welles outsmarted her, however, by using the blackout to their advantage in the now famous Welles exclamation: "The film Hollywood doesn't want you to see."

Another sign of her enormous influence was the sheer number of people who took her advice. A survey outside some New York theaters found that 80 percent of moviegoers were standing in line waiting for a film simply because of Louella's favorable notices in broadcasts. A 1949 poll ranked her as America's best-loved woman commentator, and Parsons cashed in on her fame quickly. She toured with a stage show called *Louella Parsons' Stars of Tomorrow,* published a scandal-riddled autobiography, and made regular radio broadcasts of her columns. The radio program, *Hollywood Hotel,* included advance notices of upcoming films and celebrity interviews. Later, her gossip columns were a staple of *Photoplay, Modern Screen,* and *Motion Picture* magazines. Eventually her name drew such a loyal following to these publications that, overwhelmed, she had the articles ghostwritten.

Louella Parsons's effect on Hollywood was significant; she forced studios to rethink the way they packaged their films and stars before presenting them to the public. Almost single-handedly, she initiated a lucrative market for entertainment news that has existed ever since. By the 1950s, studios had learned to counter gossip reporters by establishing huge publicity departments to "handle" the press. Still, Parsons's legendary tenacity enabled her to capitalize on public interest and keep Hollywood firmly under her thumb for thirty years. As teenagers became an increasingly dominant market segment in the sixties, Parsons's appeal faded, and her failing health eventually forced her to retire. She ranks among a handful of journalists powerful enough to make studios take notice and change the way in which they market their films. The "queen of the trades," she was a self-styled propangandist who wielded her considerable influence on movies through the role she alone invented—the Hollywood gossip.

ROGER CORMAN

Born: April 5, 1926, Los Angeles, CA

He gave me and a lot of others a chance.
—Francis Ford Coppola

Stanford graduate Roger Corman went to Hollywood in 1947 and endured a menial job as a messenger boy until his script for *The Monster From the Ocean Floor* (1954) came to life under his own direction and under a distribution deal that gave Corman a solid start; American International Pictures loaned him the money to make movies that he felt were marketable. This advantageous agreement was perfect for Roger Corman, who would use his intuition and business prowess to become a powerful producer in Hollywood by specializing in B movies. Throughout his illustrious career, Corman has been responsible for bringing some of the worst films and the finest talent to the big screen.

By 1955, Corman had a method that countered Hollywood's traditional principles: take chances on new actors, unusual stories, and cheesy special effects. While others were praying for huge profits on a few blockbusters, he was content to nurture hundreds of thin budgets of less than $100,000 into highly successful films with lurid titles like *Swamp Women* (1955), *Attack of the Crab Monsters* (1957), *She Gods of Shark Reef* (1958), and *Teenage Caveman* (1958). These exploitation films found a home in one of the only areas where Hollywood was seeing substantial growth—the drive-in movie theaters.

Though Hollywood has a long history of manufacturing B movies—the name given to cinematic retreads that are released close on the heels of popular Hollywood blockbusters—these films thrived in the age of drive-in theaters, when teenage audiences were more interested in cheap thrills than in art films. Throughout the fifties, Corman developed an assembly-line process for churning out B thrillers that blatantly leveraged the leftover costumes, props, sets, plotlines, and dialogue of established successes. Releasing an average of seven pictures a year, Corman learned to shoot extremely fast; several of his films were made in less than a week. *Little Shop of Horrors* (1960) reportedly took only two days and a night from original script to final print.

Coming off the financial success of *The Wasp Woman* (1960), Corman secured the services of veteran horror actor Vincent Price and produced a series of fantastic adaptations from the classic works of Edgar Allan Poe, among them *The Pit and the Pendulum* (1961), *The Raven* (1963), and *The Masque of the Red Death* (1964), which have become favorites among horror fans. These projects were more ambitious, and Corman increased his spending on them, but the low-budget discipline was ever-present: while filming *House of Usher* (1960), Corman heard a report of a burning house and quickly gathered a camera crew to shoot some footage.

As the viewing habits of filmlovers ebbed and flowed, so did Corman themes. In the sixties, he focused on young hippies with a string of films featuring graphic violence and drug references. Some attempts—*The Wild Angels* (1966) and *The Trip* (1967), for instance—were more original than most. (He was offered a chance to produce the phenomenal hit *Easy Rider* (1969) but turned it down.)

The discovery of bright young talent became a Corman trademark. He scouted a fresh crop of college students with his keen eye for talent and gave early opportunities to a stellar group of today's top filmmakers: Francis Ford Coppola, Peter Bogdanovich, Jonathan Kaplan, Jonathan Demme, Paul Bartel, John Sayles, James Cameron, Joe Dante, Ron Howard, and Martin Scorsese. The actors he took chances on included eventual superstars as well. Jack Nicholson made his debut in *Little Shop of Horrors* (1960); stars like Robert De Niro, Charles Bronson, Sylvester Stallone, Dennis Hopper, Peter Fonda, Barbara Hershey, and Bill Paxton also graduated from the "the Roger Corman School of Film." Even more impressive is the distinguished list of directors whose films the dynamic Corman imported and distributed in art houses: François Truffaut, Ingmar Bergman, and Federico Fellini found the "king of the B's" willing to distribute their films in the United States.

Another important contribution to the industry was Corman's success with overseas distribution. As second-run theaters and drive-ins diminished in number, he discovered that the revenue of his B films could be greatly increased by selling them internationally. In many cases, he made arrangements to sell the rights to distribute a film before shooting had commenced—an incredible testament to the track record of the legendary producer. Corman's deft understanding of foreign markets and videocassette sales continues to perpetuate his legendary success in the film industry. He claims he has never lost money on a film, and his method was the subject of his book *How I Made a Hundred Movies in Hollywood and Never Lost a Dime* (1990). In fact, fewer than half of Roger Corman's movies actually turned a profit, but the receipts do nothing to dim a sparkling career.

Corman stopped directing in 1971 and gave his full attention to production and distribution through his companies, variously named over the years but most recognized as New World. He sold his independent studio in 1983 for nearly $17 million and founded a new one immediately. Operating outside the studio system, Corman has become a legendary financier and a master of distribution. He follows a sound business model, making twenty films a year, which collect roughly $94 million worldwide.

Corman is perenially listed among the most powerful influencers in Hollywood despite his reputation as a schlock broker. He possesses a keen sense of which stories will entice film fans, a talent that has become vital for the contemporary producer. His mastery of the low-budget production has had a tremendous impact on independent filmmakers, documentarians, and studios alike. His creative approach to marketing films has illuminated the lucrative opportunities for B movies in foreign markets and videocassette sales; one result has been the massive influx of films that circumvent traditional theater distribution and head straight to video stores. Finally, he has provided an alternative industry of films where fledgling directors and actors can break into mainstream moviemaking. Roger Corman has established himself as a savvy film producer whose secondhand films continue to give audiences a first look at fresh faces of tomorrow.

50

EDITH HEAD

Born: October 28, 1898, San Bernardino, CA
Died: October 24, 1981, Hollywood, CA

She raised costume design to the level of high art.

—ALLY ACKER

To find temporary work in the summer of 1923, Stanford alumna Edith Head wiggled her way into Paramount's wardrobe department by falsely stating that she had experience as a sketch artist. She wound up staying at the studio for forty-four years. Her eight Oscars, from a record-setting thirty-four nominations, highlighted one of Hollywood's most illustrious careers, and her remarkable influence carried over into the fashion world.

In the 1920s, Head became thoroughly acclimated to the politics of the studio system, often battling with the Production Code censors over the suggestive costumes she created for sex goddesses Clara Bow and Jean Harlow. Head still managed to emphasize the best assets of these "bad girls" by creating gowns that hinted at the famous forms that lay beneath them. Her clever use of loose folds around the drooping neckline of Harlow's dresses playfully moved with the actresses' buxom physique. After several years assisting others and gaining notice in early sound features, Edith Head's first shot as a credited costume designer was *She Done Him Wrong* (1933), a Mae West vehicle that became an overnight sensation and topped the box office at the height of the Great Depression. Although Head was forced to incorporate the diamond necklaces and velvet bustiers that West favored from earlier vaudeville performances, she soon began to break with the practice of adopting gaudy stage accoutrement for the screen.

Throughout her long career, Edith Head would repeatedly set style through movies. The sarong she designed for beauty Dorothy Lamour in *The Jungle Princess* (1936) created a nationwide fashion trend. She continued to dress Lamour for several years, handling the traveling apparel in most of her *Road* pictures with Bob Hope and Bing Crosby. Head's tailored suits, worn by top actresses Bette Davis in *All About Eve* (1950) and Elizabeth Taylor in *A Place in the Sun* (1951), did for women's wear what Max Factor did for makeup.

The conservative-but-sexy Grace Kelly of Alfred Hitchcock's *Rear Window* (1954) and *To Catch a Thief* (1955) is the trademark look of Edith Head. Her prep-school aesthetic dominated fifties moviemaking, seen best in the sleek sweaters and stretch stirrup pants of the decade. Hitchcock provided her more opportunities in the outfitting of Shirley MacLaine, Doris Day, and Kim Novak in *The Trouble With Harry* (1955), *The Man Who Knew Too Much* (1956), and *Vertigo* (1958), respectively. She would work for the Master of Suspense again in *Marnie* (1964), *Torn Curtain* (1966), *Topaz* (1969), and his final film, *Family Plot* (1976). In fact, Head clashed and collaborated with some of Hollywood's most skillful and particular directors: Billy Wilder, John Ford, Cecil B. DeMille, and Bob Fosse. She moved from genre to genre easily, draping the characters of classic film noir thrillers, westerns, and period dramas.

Edith Head was also the driving force behind the glamour of the Academy Award ceremonies. She was a special adviser for the first televised Academy Awards, then dressed hundreds of stars for the event for nearly twenty-five years. According to a famous anecdote, Joan Crawford commissioned Head to prepare two identical gowns from the same pattern, one in black and one in beige. Upon seeing the preceding presenter appear in ebony, Crawford opted for the beige, and changed dresses while waiting in the wings.

As the first woman to head a design department in a major studio, Head often got screen credit for gowns that were designed by others, and her name was attached to many films she had little influence over. Audrey Hepburn dragged her own outfits to the set of *Sabrina* (1954), and the Givenchy dresses were mistaken as Head's own creations. Nevertheless, she was the rare production specialist known to women by name, and her credits became more prominent as her successes multiplied.

The name on the screen soon became the name on the label, as Head was recognized in every home. She won work outside of Hollywood, designing uniforms for international airlines, creating Vogue patterns that rivaled the latest Paris fashions, appearing on Art Linkletter's television show to give hints to American housewives, and writing columns in many of the day's top fashion magazines. She also authored self-help books for those without her gifts for color coordination.

With so many book deals and TV appearances, many studio executives felt she was hogging the spotlight and demoralizing the hundreds of other production crew members. Her extreme popularity inflated her ego, and during the 1960s she was a feisty collaborator. Paramount punished her in 1967, by allowing her contract to expire without offering a renewal. At her departure, she had been a Paramount employee longer than anyone else in the studio's history except its founder, Adolph Zukor.

Head's undeniable talent was quickly employed by others. Her work for *The Sting* (1973) launched male fashion trends in the early 1970s. On more than 750 films, spanning six decades, Head's work endured. The proof: her final designs, for Steve Martin's *Dead Men Don't Wear Plaid* (1982), utilized styles she had created for many of the thirties and forties clips featured in the movie.

BERNARD HERRMANN

Born: June 29, 1911, New York, NY
Died: December 24, 1975, Universal City, CA

Herrmann's works introduce a new dimension of dancing light and sound.

—GORDANA VITALIANO

Bernard Herrmann's radio experience was instrumental in developing the skills to become a modern movie composer. His ability to pull together short, catchy melodies and borrowed pieces of historical ballads was a trick born of the time constraints of live broadcasting. It would help him succeed on a grand scale in Hollywood, where he became the preeminent film musician, an innovative master of the small arrangement. At first unorthodox, his use of brief pieces of music systematically replaced the traditional melodies of the silver screen with short, lively themes.

Herrman started in music early. In 1924, at age thirteen, his first-prize composition in a neighborhood (Queens, NY) contest was followed by an audition to the famed Juilliard School of Music in New York. By the time he was twenty, he had formed his own orchestra; a few years later, he was writing the radio score for Orson Welles's 1938 *War of the Worlds* broadcast. When the panic of that famous show subsided and Welles was offered a job directing films in Los Angeles, Herrman went west as well. His first work on a musical score was for *Citizen Kane* (1941), and after the phenomenal success of that film, Hollywood quickly made Herrmann's musical style its own. At the time offers started to roll in for other movies, he was not yet thirty years old.

For the score of *Kane,* he took elements of Mexican marches, operettas, and children's rhymes to match many of the juxtapositions Welles had developed in the story. He liked to be intimately involved with the production, and after viewing the daily rushes, he would discuss his ideas with Welles, talking over musical approaches to the ambitious scenes of the film. For a compressed vignette examining the first marriage of Charles Foster Kane, Herrmann used violin strings that became increasingly agitated as the couple's relationship became strained. He attempted to create two basic themes for *Kane:* the one he called "Power" served to reinforce the aggressive, dominating spirit of the lead character, and the other, called "Rosebud," echoed the lost innocence of the man's childhood. Herrmann even wrote a Strauss-like opera for the film. The *Kane* score was nominated for an Oscar that year but was beat out by another Herrmann score, *The Devil and Daniel Webster* (1941). Welles would continue to recommend Herrmann for projects he was involved in, including *The Magnificent Ambersons* (1942) and *Jane Eyre* (1944).

For *Hangover Square* (1945), in which a tortured musician creates a piano piece through the course of the film, Herrmann composed an entire concerto, which he later recorded himself. His diversity also garnered praise for *The Ghost and Mrs. Muir* (1947). Already present in his work was the trademark use of horns, styled in a variety of ways to match the need of a film, but nevertheless an unmistakable Herrmann signature. His scores were an eclectic mix of traditional orchestral sounds and hip urban riffs, combining the incongruent booms, eerie strums, high harmonics, hysterical strings, and sudden shrieks of a variety of instruments. Though he preferred to compose on the piano, and used it extensively, he incorporated instruments as diverse as castanets, timpani, harps, woodwinds, organs, and guitars. In fact, Herrmann was the first Hollywood composer to give the bluesy style of an electric guitar a prominent place in a feature film score.

The creepy whine of *The Day the Earth Stood Still* (1951) features more of the early electric sounds that defined the fifties science fiction/fantasy genre. His strange ensemble of electronic instruments was accompanied by the ever-present brassy sound. Herrmann also lent his suspenseful sounds to other sci-fi films, including the stop-motion skeleton swordplay in Ray Harryhausen's *The 7th Voyage of Sinbad* (1958) and the thrills of *Journey to the Center of the Earth* (1959), *The Three Worlds of Gulliver* (1960), and *Fahrenheit 451* (1966).

Working closely with Hollywood's top directors, Herrmann built a reputation as a stubborn perfectionist who insisted on developing a film's score in tandem with the director's shooting schedule. During his association with Alfred Hitchcock, which lasted over eight films including *The Man Who Knew Too Much* (1956), *Vertigo* (1958), and *North by Northwest* (1959), he drew inspiration from watching the Master of Suspense prepare. These films demonstrated the effective use of short melodic pieces of music. The soundtrack for *North by Northwest,* includes more than fifty tracks that heighten the story for just minutes at a time. As Herrmann put it, "Hitchcock only finishes a picture 60 percent; I have to finish the rest for him."

The two talents would clash frequently on the set. Herrmann resisted Hitchcock's suggestion that jazz music be played over the title sequence in *Psycho* (1960) and instead developed the slashing strings that became immortalized as the shrilling accompaniment to the violent attack of the film's famous shower scene. More violins, synchronized with the windshield wipers of Janet Leigh's car, were used as a simple rhythmic pattern to underscore the tension of the getaway scene at the film's beginning. Herrmann's skillful work is apparent throughout *Vertigo* and *Psycho,* and these themes have been used repeatedly in such films as *High Anxiety* (1977), *Twelve Monkeys* (1996), and *Reality Bites* (1994). On the set of *Torn Curtain* (1966), the artistic relationship between Herrmann and Hitchcock ended abruptly. When Herrmann completely ignored the director's demands, Hitchcock replaced the famous film composer and threw out the entire soundtrack for the film.

Retreating to London to write more classical compositions, Herrmann remained an expatriate until the 1970s, when student filmmakers revived interest in his work. Herrmann was "rediscovered" by the likes of François Truffaut, Brian De Palma, and Martin Scorsese, who commissioned new scores that contributed to many of their finest films. A fitting end to Herrmann's career is captured in the haunting saxophone solos of *Taxi Driver* (1976), his fiftieth score. He died three days after finishing it. Scorsese paid homage to the musical genius by reusing Herrmann's original score of *Cape Fear* (1962) in the 1991 remake of the same name.

Today's film scores use an increasingly large proportion of original popular music from hit songs, but these rock 'n' roll clips are cut together into sophisticated soundtracks that use the kind of specially created sound effects and short set pieces Herrmann instituted. The longer themes of 1940s Hollywood are rarely heard in contemporary films, largely due to the dramatic power Herrmann demonstrated in his unique approach, which has inspired nearly every film composer working today. His soundtracks continue to be sought by collectors and film buffs.

52

GARY COOPER

Born: May 7, 1901, Helena, MT
Died: May 13, 1961, Los Angeles, CA

Cooper took a cut in salary and got, in compensation,
what is now called a 'participation.'

—KENNETH MACGOWAN

As a weekend guide at Yellowstone National Park, Gary Cooper spent his idle time dreaming of a job on a big newspaper, drawing cartoons for a living. But a trip to California in 1924 landed him work as a movie extra, where he utilized his horseback skills in a number of westerns as a cowboy heavy and stunt rider. A two-year string of two-reelers brought him to the attention of Sam Goldwyn, and he was cast in *The Winning of Barbara Worth* (1926), a big box office hit. By the time talking pictures like the *The Virginian* (1929) rolled into town, Cooper was building a following among audiences. His plain features and unaffected manner made him a natural hero in other adventures—*Morocco* (1930), *The Plainsman* (1937), and *Beau Geste* (1939)—and his role as the soldier in Hemingway's *A Farewell to Arms* (1932) cemented him as a romantic lead.

To millions of men and women, Cooper embodied honor and decency. This type was particularly effective when directors put him into sophisticated settings and let his awkward charm win over hearts, as Frank Capra did in *Meet John Doe* (1941). Years before Jimmy Stewart became Capra's golden boy, Gary Cooper was filling the role nicely. Capra is often credited with the creation of Cooper's man-of-few-words character, but the "Yup" fellow of several early Cooper pictures was more the creation of pulp writer Clarence Budington Kelland, a prolific writer of extremely popular dime novels and serialized magazine stories. Kelland's tales reflected a small-town philosophy and patriotic bent that inspired these films. One of Kelland's bestsellers became *Mr. Deeds Goes to Town* (1936), and Cooper's portrayal of a simple, plain-speaking man owes more to Kelland's writing than it does to Capra's direction. The laconic acting style of these films became a Cooper legacy that has had a tremendous influence on hundreds of actors. The tight-lipped, understated performances of Clint Eastwood hail directly from Cooper, whose unpolished and hesitant do-gooders only moved when they felt compelled to take action.

In 1941, Cooper starred in *Sergeant York;* along with an Oscar for the role came huge paychecks. The U.S. Treasury Department released a report that year showing Cooper as the nation's highest-paid wage-earner. Earning $482,819 he sent a signal to America that movie stars were the nouveau riche. He made a much-publicized trip to Europe, where he was greeted like a king and became romantically involved with a real-life princess. To his fans worldwide, his skyrocketing fame crystallized the idea of the rags-to-riches dream.

Another significant development would make Cooper even wealthier. His contracts were rewritten to allow him a percentage of the ticket grosses in exchange for a lower wage. Soon, the homespun park ranger would be a multimillionaire, and dozens of the top stars in Hollywood would take notice and gamble their futures on the financial success of their films. Jimmy Stewart, James Cagney, Bette Davis, Katharine Hepburn, and Humphrey Bogart were just some of the stars who changed their compensation packages to include the "percentage" clauses.

Cooper stayed on top at the box office by partnering with many of the day's leading ladies—including the immeasurably talented Shirley Temple. His aptitude for strong, silent acting continued to be displayed in such roles as ballplayer Lou Gehrig in *The Pride of the Yankees* (1942), Robert Jordan in the adaptation of Ernest Hemingway's *For Whom the Bell Tolls* (1943), and Howard Roark in *The Fountainhead* (1949), based on Ayn Rand's bestselling novel. His weathered looks cost him some roles until a script for a western provided Cooper with the perfect part for a return to the saddle. *High Noon* (1952) clinched him another Oscar for his definitive performance of an aging gunslinger, a role that would foreshadow the memorable turns of William Holden in *The Wild Bunch* (1973), John Wayne in *The Shootist* (1976), and Clint Eastwood in his haunting *Unforgiven* (1992).

Cooper received a special Academy Award in 1960, accepted on his behalf by a tearful James Stewart, who had moments earlier learned of Cooper's bout with incurable cancer. One month later, Gary Cooper died at age sixty.

He is remembered as a straightforward actor who embodied a plain truth, and the influence of his restrained style on today's actors is notable enough to earn him a ranking on this list. His high placement here also takes into account the way in which he changed the business of acting. While many contemporary actors enjoy large portions of a film's sales receipts, it's important to acknowledge Cooper as the first person to get royalties for actors and to turn actors into royalty.

53

MIKE TODD

Born: June 22, 1907, Minneapolis, MN
Died: March 22, 1958, Grants, NM

*The American public has always responded to the novel, the bigger,
and, perhaps, the better.*

—MIKE TODD

In response to the inroads made by television in the decade after World War II, Hollywood studios scrambled to provide moviegoers with a compelling reason to leave the comfort of their own homes. To lure the public back into the theaters, new experiments with 3-D movies, color processes, and stereo sound were launched, but they failed to establish a regular following. A Broadway producer named Mike Todd, however, saw an Achilles heel in television's bid for viewers: television pioneers had made a big mistake in duplicating the proportion of height to width of early films. Todd had invested much of his personal fortune in a new motion picture technology that would give film studios the competitive edge they desired—movies especially made to be projected on screens in a wider format. Wide-screen processes had previously been tried, in the late 1890s and again in the late 1920s, without much success, but Todd maintained that his new perfected process would present the theater patron with a larger and grander and more overwhelming experience. The threat of television was believed to be over; the rush to wide-screen was on.

Mike Todd was as feared in the entertainment industry as he was respected. A renaissance man with diverse talents, he was best at raising money for new ventures, and those skills led to a role as a producer of plays in 1936. His success on the stage eventually took him to Broadway, and after a rocky fourteen years, he went on to make nearly $18 million from more than sixteen shows. However, heavy borrowing and a gambling compulsion kept Todd close to bankruptcy.

A fateful visit to the 1939 World's Fair in New York introduced Todd to Fred Waller, formerly head of the special effects department at Paramount, and inventor of a new film projection system that simultaneously cast eleven different images onto a screen curved to a 165-degree angle. The idea was to simulate peripheral vision by engulfing an audience with screen images from ear to ear. The much-heralded exhibit fired a passion in Todd that would consume the rest of his life and bring him his greatest financial success. After starting Michael Todd Productions in 1945, he put his business savvy to work by financing a variety of film projects with some success. He formed a number of limited partnerships to finance his quest of a wide-screen process for more than ten years.

Finally, Waller tried to make a system he called Cinerama more commercially viable by reducing the number of 35mm projectors to three and enlisting the help of a sound engineer, Hazard E. Reeves, to develop a multichannel, directional sound system to go with the wider pictures. To support the experiments, Todd raised money for Cinerama by attracting both the wealth of the Rockefeller and the Luce empires. But as time passed, the investors remained unconvinced, and in 1950 they pulled out of the venture. Unable to attract a major studio, the Cinerama group, under Todd's direction, set out to demonstrate the potential of the process by producing and exhibiting their own independently financed films. The first of these, *This Is Cinerama,* was introduced on September 30, 1952, at the Broadway Theater. It opened to huge publicity, and crowds lined up around the block for more than two years after the debut.

Cinerama had its shortcomings. Todd was disappointed with the travelogues that were the sole features shown; they were simply simulated experiences of exotic locations without the benefit of a story or characters. Furthermore, the projection of three images created two distracting seams on the screen. Many of the stereo sound processes designed to enhance the experience were poorly implemented, and theater owners were reluctant to install new sound equipment that had not been perfected. To further add to the confusion, Walt Disney and several other studio heads announced widescreen processes of their own: Circarama, Quadravision, Wonderama, and Cinemiracle, to name a few.

In 1952, Mike Todd convinced 20th Century–Fox president Spyros Skouras and former Universal chief Joseph Schenck that wide-screen movies would give their studios a competitive advantage against the increasing popularity of television. That year, the three men formed a new Cinerama corporation, and their first act was to purchase the manufacturing rights to the patented work of Henri Chrétien, a French optics inventor. Chrétien had originally applied his ideas to World War I submarines, extending the view of periscopes to 180 degrees wide by developing special convex lenses. He had been adapting these lenses to film cameras as early as the 1920s, working out two distinct parts to the process called anamorphic optics. During the shooting of a film, an anamorphic camera lens squeezes an image onto a film negative. When the film is projected, another anamorphic lens stretches the image and displays the picture in its wide view. It had taken Chrétien more than thirty years to draw Hollywood's attention to the process that eventually was dubbed CinemaScope.

To improve CinemaScope even more, Todd switched to the wider 70mm film stock, which could hold an elongated 65mm picture while keeping five sound tracks (of 1mm each) available for many of the experimental sound processes of the day. In June of 1954, Todd asked optics maker Brian O'Brien and the American Optical Company to help with prototypes; for their contribution, he named the venture Todd-AO, for American Optical. Ultimately, it would take the expertise of the Bausch & Lomb company to perfect a lens that would reduce distortion, but finally his 70mm process was a complete picture-and-sound system synchronized from a single projector. The first CinemaScope film to display the new process was *The Robe* (1953), for which Chrétien received a special Oscar for technical achievement.

Todd sold his portion of Cinerama in 1953 to fund other wide-screen spectacles. His Todd-AO company purchased a proven Broadway success and planned to make *Oklahoma!* (1955) his first solo project, but studio backers wrested it from his control, after paying Todd a $7 million settlement. With the proceeds, he began a mammoth production of *Around the World in 80 Days* (1956), an adaptation of the Jules Verne novel originally drafted by Orson Welles. *Around the World* reportedly used seventy-five thousand costumes, 680,000 feet of film, a cast of sixty-eight thousand extras and logged fourteen million air miles of travel. The film marks the origin of the term "cameo," a small part played by a famous person, in this case such established stars as Frank Sinatra, Marlene Dietrich, and Buster Keaton. The film cost $6 million to make, grossed $100 million, and won Todd a Best Picture Oscar for 1956.

In 1958, while he was traveling to collect Showman of the Year honors in New York, Mike Todd was killed in a plane crash, leaving his wife, actress Elizabeth Taylor, a widow. Todd was remembered at his funeral as a pivotal figure in the formation of wide-screen, but his lasting contribution would not become evident for years to come. He would change movies in ways he probably never anticipated. The daring showman who championed wide-screen and new sound processes may not have staved off television's encroachments on movie profits, but he did spark some interesting developments.

When Stanley Kubrick's *2001: A Space Odyssey* came out in Cinescope, the 70mm format was found to be critical to the awe-inspiring special effects. Almost all subsequent space epics, including *Star Wars,* used the larger 70mm film to retain image quality during the multiple exposures of matte photography. Television shows like *Star Trek* adopted the film stock for special effects. Blue-screen photography and digital computer effects benefit from the higher resolution as well.

Wide-screen images have now became so popular with moviegoing audiences that 35mm films, which feature a square aspect ratio of 1.33:1, achieve the illusion of wide-screen's of 1.85:1 aspect ratio by a masking process that is created during the projection of most films. When visiting a movie theater, today's audiences may not be aware that opaque horizontal bars across the top and bottom of the film projector actually prevent the rest of the original film image from making it to the big screen. When these faux-wide-screen movies make it to television, they are again trimmed through a pan-and-scan method before being broadcast to homes. Ironically, nearly 90 percent of all contemporary films projected in today's movie theaters are still showing 35mm prints, which must be cropped to fill Todd's popular wide-screen format. And television is finally catching up to the concept of wide-screen; now that letterbox versions of movies are becoming increasingly popular, the proposed HDTV (high-definition television) sets should all but resolve an incompatibility that has existed between television and films since 1952, the year Mike Todd first showed the entertainment industry the shape of the future.

ERNST LUBITSCH

Born: January 28, 1892, Berlin, Germany
Died: November 30, 1947, Hollywood, CA

Lubitsch invented the modern Hollywood.
—JEAN RENOIR

Behind the greatest productions of the German cinema of the 1920s was Ernst Lubitsch. Lubitsch had not only directed some of the decade's most artistic and influential costume spectacles, including *Passion* (1919), and *Deception* (1920), but he had demonstrated a keen sense of dialogue that imparted a very warm and human quality to otherwise stiff plots. His films were instrumental in securing a commercial film market for Germany before the country's famed expressionist era started. Already present in Lubitsch films was a mastery of the close-up, and this made him attractive to a young producer named Adolph Zukor, who had one of the world's most famous faces under contract, international star Mary Pickford.

Adolph Zukor brought Lubitsch to Hollywood to make "Little Mary" vehicles. The first assignment was the troubled production of *Rosita* (1923). A temperamental Pickford insisted on giving Lubitsch her constant advice, and their relationship immediately turned adversarial. Pickford and Lubitsch would never work together again, and she would call the film the worst in her career. Unimpressed by his foreign import, Adolph Zukor sent Lubitsch off to make a series of films for which there were no great expectations. Freed of the domineering Pickford, however, the young director would surprise everyone with *The Marriage Circle* (1924), *The Love Parade* (1929), *Monte*

Carlo (1930), and *Trouble in Paradise* (1932). Lubitsch's eventual successes in America would later lead other European emigrés, notably film noir director Fritz Lang, to come to Hollywood.

Soon, Lubitsch established a filmic style that came to be known as the "Lubitsch touch," a graceful mix of refined dialogue, understated wit, and polished camera work arrived at through careful planning and rehearsal. Lubitsch's urbane style marked him as a cosmopolitan director who could handle drama, comedy, and musicals with equal panache. He enjoyed an impressive string of hits as he made the transition from silent films to talkies, owing much to scripts that poked fun at the sexual mores and affectations of high society. As a European director introduced suddenly into a pretentious Hollywood clique, he had an outsider's vantage point that resulted in an insightful mocking of American values during the Roaring Twenties. A trademark of the Lubitsch films of the 1930s was the use of subtle sexual innuendo, coyly disguised in clever banter to elude the censors who enforced Hollywood's Production Code.

Lubitsch also gained regard for his significant innovations in the use of sound. He preferred the feeling of an intimate scene, but the noise of the film winding through the camera interfered with the hushed words of cuddled lovers. To get the extreme close-ups he desired without set noise, Lubitsch simply filmed without recording any sound, then dubbed entire scenes in postproduction. This allowed for greater dynamic camera movement and also gave Lubitsch an opportunity to shout directions to the actors while filming. When shooting was complete, his actors would record their lines by quietly whispering into a microphone in a soundproof booth while watching themselves projected on a nearby screen. This technique was used extensively by Orson Welles, Alfred Hitchcock, and Otto Preminger, and the practice is still widespread in studios today. The Lubitsch musical also created sound innovations. Though most of the song-and-dance films of 1930s were primarily revues, Lubitsch found ways to incorporate musical numbers into a tightly woven plot, allowing his characters to sing only during appropriate places in the storyline. The songs were carefully selected to echo the themes of the film. This integration made the Lubitsch musicals far superior and revolutionized the structure of the entire genre, making the chorus-line spectacles of Busby Berkeley virtually obsolete. Nearly all musicals filmed in the last forty years owe a debt to this underlying influence.

By 1935, Lubitsch had been elevated to head of production at Paramount, but his continued stints at directing overshadowed his managerial skills, and he resigned his duties after only a year to focus on comedies. With a final output of *The Merry Widow* (1934), *Ninotchka* (1939), *To Be or Not to Be* (1942), and *Heaven Can Wait* (1943), Lubitsch put an unmistakable signature on light comedies that has remained the standard ever since.

The career of Ernst Lubitsch was blessed with both consistent commercial success and a solid standard of artistry—a rare blend in Hollywood. In his lifetime, he was respected by every director, most of whom styled their work on his. Among the other great directors on the list, Lubitsch trails in ranking because he did not affect a single genre in the same way as John Ford, Fritz Lang, Alfred Hitchcock, or Buster Keaton did. Lubitsch floated from genre to genre with ease, carrying with him an instinct for economical storytelling and wry humor. However, no other romantic comedies have been imitated more than Lubitsch's, and no other films ever approached his in elegance.

55

SIDNEY POITIER

Born: February 20, 1924, Miami, FL

I worked at Columbia Pictures when there wasn't another black person to be seen.

—SIDNEY POITIER

Sidney Poitier grew up in the British West Indies but served in the U.S. Army during World War II as a medical assistant. Relieved of his duties and released to New York City, he took work doing light janitorial chores backstage at the American Negro Theatre. His handsome features and athletic build were attractive enough to get him small parts in several stage productions, but his thick Bahamian accent kept him from getting any speaking roles. To remove his accent, he spent his nights reading books aloud and practiced enunciating the routines he heard on the radio. After his vocal lessons had finally flowered into better stage appearances, Poitier began to receive critical attention. He was making a name for himself as a black actor who exuded confidence, intelligence, and self-respect. He opted for a career in movies in 1950, moved to Hollywood, and landed a part in *No Way Out* (1950). His memorable turn in that film, combined with the recognition he received for *The Blackboard Jungle* (1955), brought him roles that were quite unconventional.

Many of the black actors of the 1950s continued to appear in stereotypical parts. While veterans like Woody Strode were taking token parts as slaves or kitchen cooks in action adventures or westerns, Poitier was offered the thinking man's role. His Oscar-nominated appearance in *The Defiant Ones* (1958) was clearly a breakthrough. The simple plot about a prison breakout was accentuated by racial issues that established Poitier as a torchbearer for a nation in the midst of the civil rights movement.

A reprise of his Broadway role in *A Raisin in the Sun* (1959) led to better and better scripts, including *Lilies of the Field* (1963), which won him an Academy Award as Best Actor. It was the first time the award had been given to a man of color. The mainstream appeal of Poitier was evident after roles in *To Sir With Love* (1964) and *A Patch of Blue* (1965) attracted large white audiences and made him a bona fide Hollywood star. Despite his success, his roles continued to center on issues of race in *In the Heat of the Night* (1967), and in *Guess Who's Coming to Dinner* (1967) opposite Spencer Tracy and Katharine Hepburn.

Generally acknowledged as single-handedly breaking the Hollywood color barrier, Poitier did it by making a series of films that showed a black man coping in a society dominated by whites. These films were made for first-run theaters owned and operated by whites but were also screened in many of the segregated theaters that usually presented only black films. Poitier's true crossover appeal ushered in the first movies that blacks and whites were seeing at the same time, albeit in separate venues. He had reached a status that even the great entertainer Paul Robeson or the prolific director Oscar Micheaux had never attained.

Poitier founded First Artists Production Company in 1969 and made atypical screen roles available to black actors and directors. He was also instrumental in producing black films for white audiences—films like *Buck and the Preacher* (1972), in which he costarred with Harry Belafonte, and *Stir Crazy* (1980), which starred Gene Wilder and Richard Pryor. When the black cinema of the early seventies brought new opportunities, Poitier was a natural choice for directorial duties. *Uptown Saturday Night* (1974), *Let's Do It Again* (1975), and *A Piece of the Action* (1977), all with Bill Cosby, were tame versions of the genre films made by other blacks at the time, but the blaxploitation movement that was greatly attributed to Melvin Van Peebles is still considered a direct result of Poitier's groundbreaking sixties films.

Ironically, in the 1980s, a decade that made huge leaps in the advancement of blacks in filmmaking, Sidney Poitier was rarely seen. After a ten-year absence from acting, he resumed his career with his usual prominence and majestic power, returning to action-oriented roles in *Shoot to Kill* (1988) and *Sneakers* (1992). These films performed well at the box office, but neither focused on issues of race. Poitier's great strides have changed the position of blacks in cinema, however, and his placement on this list will likely climb as the number of black filmmakers continues to rise.

56

SAUL BASS

Born: May 8, 1920, New York, NY
Died: April 25, 1996, Los Angeles, CA

His animated titles often suggest the theme and the mood of a film,
functioning more like a prologue.

—EPHRAIM KATZ

The two most influential events in the development of opening titles are their absence in Orson Welles's *Citizen Kane* and their presence in Otto Preminger's *Carmen Jones* (1954). The *Jones* titles were the work of graphic designer Saul Bass. Bass was an extremely gifted designer with a flair for austere design solutions, which he applied to many of the most memorable product packages and corporate logos; he is responsible for the classic look of Wesson Oil, Dixie Cups, Quaker Oats, United Airlines, and AT&T.

While working for Hollywood studios in the 1950s, Bass had noticed how moviegoers tended to linger in the lobby well past the beginning of a film, assuming they had time to purchase candy and soft drinks until the credits passed. Bass got the idea to integrate the titles with the story experience and set out to captivate an audience from the moment the curtain opened. Inspired by the title work of John Hubley in *The Four Poster* (1952), with its imaginative use of animated text and colors, he created a preface to *Jones* that hinted at the tension and excitement of the film. Bass had shattered all previous concepts of title sequences in films. As Hollywood began featuring these clever introductions on nearly every film, audiences soon learned to claim a seat well before the movie started.

His stylized cartoon overture for Mike Todd's *Around the World in 80 Days* (1956) further secured his international reputation, and soon his art direction was sought for such major productions as *Spartacus* (1960) and the Cinerama thriller *Grand Prix* (1966). The long, complicated sequence he designed for Robert Wise's *West Side Story* (1961) was shot with the assistance of optical printer pioneer Linwood Dunn. Its incredible number of subtle camera moves had to be succinctly timed and captured in one continuous shooting session. The stunning result was the film credits that appear on the brick wall and buildings of the film's set.

Alfred Hitchcock's own interest in graphic design drew him to Bass's stylish sequences. Hitchcock first used him as a multifaceted visual consultant on *Vertigo* (1958). Bass's execution of a spiraling camera, red swirling vortex designs, and an extreme close-up of a woman's face in the titles for *Vertigo* so impressed Hitchcock that he borrowed the swirl imagery for many touches throughout the film. For *North by Northwest* (1959), Bass animated a series of lines that move vertically up and down until they eventually fade into a picture of elevator doors that open to reveal Cary Grant in the film's opening shot. The Master of Suspense also used Saul Bass for help with *Psycho* (1960). His fragmented typography, slashing lines, and swiping bars created helter-skelter patterns that symbolize the personality of Norman Bates and foreshadow the film's landmark shower scene.

There is a long-standing debate in film circles over the extent of Bass's involvement with *Psycho*. In addition to titles for the film, Bass was commissioned to create storyboards for the shower scene, the staircase murder of a private detective, and the film's finale. Apparently, Hitchcock was enamored with the use of shock cuts and montage in the Orson Welles film *Touch of Evil* (1958) and asked Bass to sketch a series of drawings to suggest how the scenes might be shot. These storyboards are at the heart of a dispute as to who is ultimately responsible for the famous bathroom sequence. The storyboards were recovered by film historians and shot in sequence so that a side-by-side comparison could be made against the Hitchcock scene. Clearly, the similarities between Bass's drawings and Hitchcock's final cut show that Bass was instrumental in the visual planning of the sequence; Bass later claimed that the director even let him perform some camera work on the set of the shower scene. Crew members and actors, however, especially the film's star Janet Leigh, adamantly insist that Bass was not around when Hitchcock ordered the cameras to roll. The dispute was aggravated after Hitchcock's death by assertions from Bass that the shadowy scene of a light bulb dangling over a decomposing body was also taken from an idea he had conceived.

Hitchcock and Preminger involved Saul Bass in many stages of filmmaking, and Bass offered his expertise in every facet of the movie production process. His designs for movie posters, beginning with *The Man With the*

Golden Arm (1955), instituted another sweeping change in the industry. He urged Preminger to approve a design that featured nothing but a single abstract arm jutting from the edge of the paper. The cast and crew were listed in two minuscule sentences along the bottom of the poster. The shocking simplicity was in direct contrast to the traditional movie poster, a cluttered mess of vignettes and headlines. Saul Bass's clean, bold designs have influenced movie advertising ever since.

After a decade of little impact, Bass's career was revived when he collaborated with director Martin Scorsese on *Goodfellas* (1990). His title sequences and special effects in *Cape Fear* (1991), coupled with the classic track of Bernard Herrmann's eerie score, showed that Bass still possessed creative judgment unmatched after forty years in films. He created a more graceful look in the flowery images of *The Age of Innocence* (1993) and finished his last assignment with his finest title sequence, a rousing mix of Las Vegas glitz with fire-and-brimstone dissolves in *Casino* (1995).

Few film fans are aware of how penetrating the influence of Saul Bass has been. He bucked all conventions to apply his exceptional insight in graphic design to another visual medium. His revolutionary title sequences are a permanent legacy to films. His advertising poster designs are masterpieces that have become sought-after collectibles. His work with the elite directors of cinema has produced images of unforgettable power. Saul Bass was a talented commerical artist who wandered into moviemaking and changed the look of films suddenly and forever.

57

BILLY WILDER

Born: June 22, 1906, Sucha, Austria

Wilder created the sort of richly sophisticated and acerbic movies
that helped give Paramount its distinction.

—RON BASE

The colorful career of Austrian director Samuel "Billy" Wilder began when
he was given a job as a screenwriter on several German films in 1929. Immediately, his talent for cynicism surfaced in the intricately woven narratives he
came to master. The Wilder trademark was most evident in films that had a
seemingly impossible premise; one such script inspired the American film
D.O.A. (1949), in which a poisoned man has just enough time left to track
down his own murderer.

These ambitious scripts marked Wilder as a valuable commodity, and when
he escaped Hitler's reign in 1933 and came to Hollywood, he was courted by
almost every major studio. His outsider's view of American culture mixed
well with the talents of other German immigrants, including director Ernst
Lubitsch. The two men worked together on the screenplay of *Ninotchka*
(1939). But it was a creative partnership with Charles Brackett that gave life
to a sophisticated writing style on *Midnight* (1939) and *Ball of Fire* (1941).
Wilder would be closely associated with Brackett over several films, which
demonstrated his ability to collaborate with top talent.

In the Brackett/Wilder days, Billy assumed a more prominent role as
director in some of the 1940s' most controversial films, including the mur-
derous film noir breakthrough *Double Indemnity* (1944) and a social and

psychological indictment of alcoholism in *The Lost Weekend* (1945). The two films would become landmark cases of Hollywood resistance to the Production Code of 1934, instituted by the film industry's puppet dictator Will Hays.

Double Indemnity was a crafty telling of an adulterous affair that leads to murder. The script called for several violations of the Code, and the film's steamy sexual overtones drove the censors to madness. Integral to the plot was the success of the crime—the murderer had to go unpunished. This violated a strictly enforced taboo in filmmaking, but Wilder's sophisticated script was based on a popular dime novel, and Wilder was willing to make small concessions on other plot points. The film passed the censors and went on to become a film noir classic. Incredibly daring for the times, *Indemnity* eluded the stifling Hays Production Code and put Wilder in the forefront of a volatile debate.

Lost Weekend showed the grim reality of alcoholism, the self-loathing, the pattern of isolation, the details of detoxification. Originally, homosexuality was behind the torment of the lead character in the novel by Charles R. Jackson. But Wilder tackled one taboo at a time. *Weekend* was hailed as another Wilder masterpiece, exposing the dangers of drink and breaking down the walls of silence in motion pictures. The result was a flood of films that openly dealt with alcoholism beyond the comic characterizations previously tolerated by the Hays office—*Come Back, Little Sheba* (1952), *The Country Girl* (1954), and *Days of Wine and Roses* (1960).

In 1946, Wilder returned from wartime duties to film the underappreciated *A Foreign Affair* (1948) and the nostalgic *Sunset Boulevard* (1950), his final collaboration with Brackett. By the time *Stalag 17* (1953), *Sabrina* (1954), and *The Seven Year Itch* (1955) were reaping critical acclaim, it was obvious that Wilder was no accidental success. He was equally at ease with all subjects and genres, and his ability to combine visual beauty with intelligent dialogue made him the quintessential writer-director.

Another longtime association, with writer I. A. L. Diamond, brought out a wit in Wilder that highlighted his skill as a director of comedies and poked fun at his place in smashing taboo subjects. Cross-dressing was the focus of the classic *Some Like It Hot* (1959), starring Jack Lemmon, Tony Curtis, and Marilyn Monroe; two other Lemmon vehicles, *The Apartment* (1960) and *Irma la Douce* (1963), tackled adultery and prostitution, respectively, and an insurance scam brought Lemmon together with Walter Matthau for the first time in *The Fortune Cookie* (1966). The team of Wilder and Diamond produced eleven films, tackling contemporary themes that made their work fresh well into the 1960s.

In 1986 the American Film Institute honored Wilder with a Life Achievement Award, and at the 1988 Academy Awards ceremony he was presented with the Irving G. Thalberg Award. A maverick in Hollywood, Wilder built an enviable collection of films that illuminated the dark manners and sexual mores of Americans through clever and groundbreaking scripts.

58

BETTE DAVIS

Born: April 5, 1908, Lowell, MA
Died: October 6, 1989, Neuilly-sur-Seine, France

There is something elemental about Bette—a demon which
threatens to break out and eat everybody alive.

—JOHN HUSTON

Unsuspecting director George Cukor had no idea what tenacity he instilled in a young actress in 1928. As head of a theater company in Rochester, New York, he dismissed a girlish Bette Davis and sent her home after an awkward audition. Davis's mother, furious that Cukor would overlook such genius, marched Bette straight to Broadway, where good reviews in Virgil Geddes's *The Earth Between* in 1929 led to her first hit, *Broken Dishes*, in 1930. Her first Hollywood film, *Bad Sister* (1931), failed at the ticket office despite a smoldering performance by costar Humphrey Bogart, and her next five films flopped as well. It looked as though Bette Davis would be sent home again. But a Warner Bros. executive felt encouraged by her apparent determination and cast her in the breakthrough *The Man Who Played God* (1932). She was hailed as a rare screen talent with magnetic eyes and a deep understanding of acting. Warners immediately drafted a long-term contract that made her a lifetime featured player.

After small roles throughout the 1930s, Davis felt Warners was not honoring their agreement; she wasn't given opportunities in films that showcased her unique gifts. She went to court to break her contract, but in a series of hard-fought, precedent-setting cases, Warners maintained control of the temperamental star. By then, however, much of the damage was already done. Davis was furious with the court's decision and became unmanageable during filming, her moods on the set turning bitter and despondent. Quite uncharacteristically, the bosses at Warners relented and allowed her to make a picture that had been offered to her by RKO: *Of Human Bondage* (1934), based on the popular novel by W. Somerset Maugham. Starring opposite leading man Leslie Howard, Davis delivered a riveting performance that again established her prominence as an actress. It also formed her reputation as a woman who could steal attention from popular male leads.

Her performance in *Of Human Bondage* was universally regarded as the best by any actor of the year. But the studios, not eager to reward Davis for her rebellious behavior, conspired to lock her out of the Academy Award nominations that year. Before 1934, all nominations for Academy Awards were offered by a hand-picked thirty-five-member team of Louis B. Mayer's liking. He controlled the nominations, exercised veto power over choices he disliked, and doled out special recognition awards. The final ballots went out to roughly fourteen hundred voters, representatives of each trade union in the industry. But when Bette Davis did not appear on the year's selection, members of the Screen Actors Guild cried foul and threatened to wrest the Oscar ballot procedures from Mayer's control. SAG president Frank Capra encouraged a write-in campaign, and thousands of voters jotted her name at the bottom of their ballots. Getting wind of the grass-roots movement, Mayer quickly changed the Oscar rules to prevent write-ins, and Bette Davis was passed over completely. A furious Capra would commit to a long struggle to democratize the process and by 1941, the envelopes were sealed by independent consultants.

With better parts in *Dangerous* (1935), *Jezebel* (1938), *Dark Victory* (1939), and *The Little Foxes* (1941), Davis delivered Oscar-winning portrayals and big profits. Her persistent defiance of directors prompted heated battles on many of her sets, and Davis became a prima donna of outlandish proportion. Warners, however, tolerated its genuine institution. Never had Hollywood seen an actress who exuded such feminine strength and masculine aggressiveness on screen. She led the way for Barbara Stanwyck, Jane Fonda, and Faye Dunaway, actresses of independent spirit. Her tough-willed stature got her elected as the first female president of the Motion Picture Academy of Arts and Sciences.

The hypnotic Davis eyes, choppy speech, and affected mannerisms created a unique persona. The mercurial Joan Crawford enjoyed a similar longevity, both women's careers spanning five decades, but the Davis legend seemed to accumulate with each fiery role. Her perfectly tempestuous Margo Channing in *All About Eve* (1950) launched worldwide parodies of her lines and gestures. She would become a singular personality, mocked in animated cartoons and lionized in popular songs.

During the 1960s, she starred in a series of macabre films, notably *What Ever Happened to Baby Jane?* (1962) and *Hush . . . Hush, Sweet Charlotte* (1964); her last appearance was with Lillian Gish in *The Whales of August* (1987). In 1977, she became the first woman to receive the American Film Institute Life Achievement Award. In all, her hundred film roles reaped ten Academy Award nominations and two Oscars for Best Actress. Her career made her a true role model for women in the film industry, and her incomparable performances left the sharpest images of forthrightness ever presented on screen.

59

ERICH
VON STROHEIM

Born: September 22, 1885, Vienna, Austria
Died: May 12, 1957, Maurepas, France

Hollywood killed me.
—ERICH VON STROHEIM

The love/hate relationship between Erich von Stroheim and filmmaking touched every level of the industry. Audiences marveled at his immeasurable talent, both as an actor and director. They rushed to see the ultrarealistic settings he created and cowered in the face of his convincing portrayals of frighteningly cruel characters. Studio heads raved over his repeated commercial successes but cursed his indulgent production expenses. Fellow performers thrilled at a chance to work with him, then quit when subjected to his arrogant ways.

The strangest figure in movie history, Stroheim adopted the "von" before leaving a European military academy in 1914 for America. Stints as a newspaperman, vaudeville trouper, and playwright led him to Hollywood, where he informed D. W. Griffith, Allan Dwan, and other directors of his uniformed past and signed on as a costume consultant for such battle epics as *The Birth of a Nation* (1915) and *Panthea* (1917).

Wanting his own directing assignment, he hustled deals for his first three films—*Blind Husbands* (1918), *The Devil's Passkey* (1919), and *Foolish Wives* (1922), a trilogy of sexual fantasies that kept Hollywood gossip mills busy with rumors of debauchery on the set. Stroheim would round up enough actors and crew members to film an orgy scene, then lock them all in a warehouse together over a weekend to capture candid moments he felt would enhance the believability of the material. What went on behind those closed doors made Stroheim a worldwide curiosity.

His first great gift to the art of film was detail. Whereas many early silent films tended to use any prop or painted stage flat that happened to be lying around, Stroheim's lavish sets were immaculate, featuring ornate furniture, authentic costumes, and carefully crafted accessories. Audiences viewing a simple dinner party scene in one of his films were stunned by the beveled windows, patterned carpets, hand-carved chairs, lace tablecloths, painted dishes, polished silverware, and a complete meal, always prepared correctly, accompanied by condiments, and served with the proper utensils. Each detail was supervised by Stroheim, who wanted audiences to inspect every frame. This emphasis on realism would precede other directors' by more than twenty years and strongly influence the cinema verité school of directors.

Unfortunately, *Foolish Wives* also earned him another sort of reputation; its lengthy running time and overbudget costs annoyed studio executives. Stroheim had been allowed his indulgences while he continued to bring in profits, but when Universal production chief Irving Thalberg was placed in charge of Stroheim's production, the two men began a long and difficult battle of wills. When Thalberg argued over questionable expenses, Stroheim quickly whipped himself into a frenzy of delicious insults and playful hand gestures. Thalberg then issued warnings, which Stroheim flatly ignored. When weeks passed and the budget overages continued, Thalberg closed the production and cut two-thirds of the finished footage out of the film. *Foolish Wives* still did brisk business and added to the legend of Stroheim, with its images of women smoking cigars and other shameful practices of the day, but the feud between Thalberg and Stroheim escalated. Their differences helped to perpetuate the idea of directors as "difficult"—a term that surfaced years later with Orson Welles, Sam Peckinpah, and Francis Ford Coppola, although the outlandish exploits of these successors to Stroheim paled in comparison to his own. The stigma would cast a dark shadow over the rest of Stroheim's career.

He proved unmanageable again on *Merry-Go-Round* (1922), purchasing hand-embroidered silk underwear for all the extras to wear, even though the garments would never appear on film. Thalberg fumed, but Stroheim insisted the underwear was necessary to create a sense of realism in their portrayals. Thalberg had little choice but to replace the headstrong director.

When the two men were later reunited at MGM, Thalberg decided to go ahead with another one of Stroheim's grand spectacles. The tragic novel *McTeague* was the source for ninety-one hours of footage, shot without aid of a formal script. The final film would become the mythic *Greed* (1924), considered by all who saw it the most awe-inspiring piece of entertainment ever captured on celluloid. But as production got underway and costs mounted, Thalberg was at Stroheim's heels again. He wanted to see a rough-cut version of the film before approving additional shooting. Stroheim showed him a print that ran ten hours. Stunned by its length, Thalberg and MGM chief executive Louis B. Mayer demanded a shorter product. A four-hour version was edited by Stroheim, but Mayer, who still considered it too long, confiscated the film and had his assistants cut it down to 140 minutes. Despite huge discontinuities, critics throughout the world heralded Stroheim as a master, a genius, and nearly every director who saw *Greed* would cite it as inspirational.

However, the "difficult" label persisted, and eventually it would destroy one of Hollywood's brightest careers. With Stroheim under tight supervision, MGM chanced a light operetta, *The Merry Widow* (1925), then another, *The Wedding March* (1928); both were profitable and well received. But overall, Stroheim felt that the studio system would no longer support his inventive spirit. He became insubordinate and Thalberg finally fired him. Stroheim was MGM's star property, and perhaps the greatest working director of the time, when he was dismissed. The famous feud between the irrepressible director and the penny-wise producer, comparable to the unstoppable force running straight into the immovable object, would serve as a lesson to directors everywhere.

He retreated from directing, traveled throughout Europe, wrote screenplays, and earned a modest income by acting, most notably in Jean Renoir's *Grand Illusion* (1937), returning to his familiar garb as a Prussian military officer. Stroheim briefly appeared on screen in a role of poignant self-mockery in Billy Wilder's *Sunset Boulevard* (1950), then quietly retired. He died in 1957.

What is left of Stroheim are the fits, the excesses, the rumors. Remembered by many of his contemporaries as one of cinema's greatest directors, Stroheim's influence waned after his retirement, largely because many of his films were shelved and became lost or destroyed due to deterioration of the film stock. (Efforts to salvage the remaining negatives are underway, and several videotape releases of his films have been announced.) Still, few people have seen any of his work in the last fifty years. Nevertheless, his ranking reflects his seminal contribution: bringing realism to movies. Erich von Stroheim was a director willing to document his sweeping vision at all costs, and he made the first significant steps toward showing Hollywood realism in cinematic art.

60

Born: June 16, 1872, Lodz, Poland
Died: August 30, 1938, Beverly Hills, CA

Even Lon Chaney bowed to Max Factor's makeup expertise.

—FRED BASTEN

The first makeup designed expressly for motion pictures was created by Max Factor in 1910, when he came to Hollywood to service the needs of more than 150 small independent studio lots that sprinkled the Southern California coastline. Sensing the wealth of opportunity, Factor decided to concentrate his efforts solely on creating the cosmetic products for the fledgling film industry. He quickly became the biggest name in movie glamour, and his innovative products reached far beyond Hollywood.

The first Factor innovation was the use of wigs. When called upon by Cecil B. DeMille to help outfit cowboys and Indians for *The Squaw Man* (1914), Factor interested the director in a new approach. Hollywood had been using wigs made of straw, tobacco, and Spanish moss in the silent days of moviemaking, but with the increasing use of close-up shots, the unnatural patches of hair were painfully obvious. For a more realistic look, Factor suggested wigs made with genuine human hair. When DeMille balked at the cost, Factor offered to rent the wigs to ease the picture's budget. Wig rentals proved to be a huge boon for Factor's business. He became the major supplier of wigs to almost all studios in Hollywood for half a century. The famous rugs that Max designed over the years were worn by John Wayne, Frank Sinatra, Fred Astaire, and Jimmy Stewart. To round out his full-service approach, Factor had most of his clients' wigs delivered directly to set locations.

Next, Factor focused on makeup essentials. In those early days, many stars were reluctant to wear full makeup. For example, cowboy star Tom Mix considered makeup unmanly, and he simply refused to wear any—until Factor had the rugged Mix filmed next to a male model wearing makeup. When Mix saw the results on screen, he relented. Other actors, like Lon Chaney, had favorite kinds of makeup from their years of experience on the stage, but most quickly bowed to the superior quality of Factor's greasepaint, which was graduated in tones that were more suitable for film lighting. Soon, his products were the exclusive choice of Charlie Chaplin, Buster Keaton, Mary Pickford, Gloria Swanson, and others.

When Hollywood cameramen began using panchromatic film, in 1928, they standardized their lighting, and Factor noticed an unnatural effect in the actors' faces. He experimented with a new range of colors, which resulted in products called panchromatic makeup, an achievement that won him a special Oscar that same year. He was also alert to the effects of Technicolor film, which caused images to appear yellow, red, or blue, and soon found a solution. For *Vogues of 1938*, starring Joan Bennett and dozens of attractive models, he developed a special base that yielded a matte finish, which did not reflect light from nearby colors into the camera. For both of these special considerations, Factor developed a solid block of makeup—a "cake"—that could be applied with a moist sponge; he housed the innovative product in a small tin canister and called it Pan-Cake makeup. It soon became extremely popular. In fact, on the set of *The Goldwyn Follies* (1938) a property clerk noticed that all of the tins filled with Pan-Cake makeup were disappearing. Apparently the dancers fancied the new product and were running off with it. The studio estimated the theft at hundreds of dollars a day. Amused and flattered, Factor released the makeup to the public that same year. The popular application created a revolution in women's cosmetics; Pan-Cake makeup became the fastest-selling product in the history of the cosmetics industry and is still used today.

He also invented many of the essential tools used by makeup professionals and consumers alike: the lip brush, powder brushes for smooth distribution of makeup, even a series of booklets for actors on the basic principles of character makeup. He popularized the concept of color harmony—matching lipstick to the color of a woman's hair, or color-coordinating the actor's face with the costume or setting.

Factor's prominence within the Hollywood community increased with each new starlet. When Greta Garbo arrived from Europe, Louis B. Mayer had her taken straight from the airport to Max Factor's studio for a consultation. Some actresses completely entrusted themselves to him in their search for a trademark look: the striking, dark, chiseled features of Joan Crawford, the vampy platinum blondeness of Jean Harlow, and the brassy red hair of Lucille Ball were all the work of Max Factor. In exchange for his services, Max would have starlets sign a token one-dollar contract with him that allowed him to use their image and endorsement on any or all of his products. Then he would advertise the exclusivity of his "contracts" with such stars as Bette Davis, Janet Gaynor, Rita Hayworth, and Ginger Rogers and feature their faces in campaigns aimed at American housewives. In fact, Factor set up sales counters inside many of the Los Angeles theater lobbies to catch women who might have just watched a movie starring a particularly glamorous Max Factor client.

In 1937, he traveled to Europe to open a series of salons. Returning after a similar trip in 1938, he died at the age of sixty-six. Max Factor came to California to start his own salon and found himself starting a global corporation. He adapted to the needs of his clients and learned the craft of filmmaking intimately; his pioneering products are the standard for movie makeup to this day. Over twenty-nine years, his dedication to serving Hollywood resulted in a revolution in cosmetics and provided a steady supply of state-of-the-art products for the film industry. His influence on Hollywood continued even after his death, when his son took over the family business and solved new makeup problems on television with Lucille Ball's famous show. Today, the Max Factor name symbolizes a standard of quality in consumer cosmetics worldwide.

61

THE LUMIÈRE BROTHERS

AUGUSTE LUMIÈRE
Born: October 19, 1862, Besançon, France
Died: April 10, 1954, Lyon, France

LOUIS LUMIÈRE
Born: October 5,1864, Besançon, France
Died: June 6, 1948, Bandol, France

*I never saw a more startled audience than that which saw the
Lumière Cinématographe exhibited for the first time.*

—J. AUSTIN FYNES

In 1894, Louis Lumière had just completed a factory for the production of photographic plates. He had over three hundred workers making more than fifteen million plates in his first year of business. The last thing on his mind was a new venture. But his father, a renowned painter and statesman, returned from a showing of Thomas Edison's Kinetoscope in Paris and charged his sons Louis and Auguste with the task of combining animated pictures with a projection device. The brothers found a way by 1895.

Edison's work was fascinating, but the Lumières knew the secret of making movies a success was in projection, and Edison's invention had only a small peephole that could be viewed by just one person at a time. If they could devise an instrument to cast images on a large canvas, they could beat their competition to market and get a firm foothold in the new industry. They started by examining Edison's process. Everything filmed by Edison's company had to fit into his studio and perform in front of a heavy, stationary

194

camera. Then, the recorded images had to be transferred to the peephole viewing device.

The Lumières believed the Edison group had been foolish to separate the camera and projector. Certain that the two could be integrated, they set to work. As the lead tinkerer, Louis developed a device for driving strips of film from the foot pedal mechanism of a sewing machine. In lieu of perforated film strips, which were difficult to come by in France, he used paper strips and punched holes in them by hand. But the paper was still too opaque to see through, so strong arc lamps were employed to study the animated images that developed on the paper.

The brothers applied for their first patent on February 13, 1895. No name was given for the device, simply a description: "an apparatus for obtaining and showing chronophotographic prints." Their father urged them to dub the contraption a "Domitor," but they settled for another name, the Ciné-matographe, a hand-cranked camera that required less film than Edison's and reduced the projection speed from forty-eight to sixteen frames per second. More important, the Cinématographe was housed in a single unit with a film projector for viewing by an entire group.

Best of all, it was lightweight, so the Lumières could venture outside to capture the real world. This was perhaps the most significant contribution the brothers made to cinema. By developing a single-unit device that was portable, they were able to document the outside world in moving pictures. They began by taking shots of their family members and employees at work and play, but soon the Lumières were filming anything and everything. With Louis doing most of the cranking, the brothers photographed about sixty subjects the first year, eventually building a catalog of more than 750 films in less than five years. Most were only one minute long and were simple recordings of everyday life. Although they tended to be unimaginative, featuring names like *The Arrival of a Train* or *Feeding the Baby,* they were outdoor scenes that showed movement and depth.

They were also, many of them, firsts. The first film ever projected was *Workers Leaving the Lumière Factory* (1895). The first screen comedy was *Watering the Gardener* (1896). The first newsreel and the first documentary belonged to the Lumière brothers. To raise funding for the mass production of the Cinématographe, the Lumières displayed these film firsts to industrialists on March 22, 1895, and prepared a public screening in Paris on December 28, 1895. The effects upon the unsuspecting audiences were baffling. Curious photographers and inventors rushed to the back of the room when they saw the image of an oncoming train entering the station.

By 1897, the Lumières were training camera operators for additional exhibition films and retooling their factory for the production and sale of film equipment to every corner of the world. Soon they followed Edison in renting their films to theater owners, offering a library that eventually grew to more than twelve hundred titles.

During the earliest years of the film industry, these short films played a critical role in giving the public an opportunity to see the marvel of motion pictures. Although the Lumières gave more presentations than any other organization, their films never matched the quality or creativity of others. As distribution became competitive, the Lumières were squeezed thin and ceased production in 1900.

Placing pioneers like the Lumière brothers in the bottom half of this ranking may seem ungenerous and overly severe, considering that their early work in the development of motion pictures resulted in a lightweight portable camera and the exhibition of films to large audiences. However, it's important to note that the Lumières were not the first to consider a projection system. They simply won the race by being the swiftest, refining many of the innovations that were invented by others, ignoring many of the patents on other inventors' processes, and beating the competition to market. Although their overall design of the Cinématographe is a forefather of the modern camera and projector, the equipment used in filmmaking today owes only a slight debt to their early mechanisms. These few considerations aside, the Lumières deserve a high place in film history. They were the first to take filmmaking out on the streets; they disseminated the essential tools and provided the inspiration that made filmmakers out of Alice Guy Blaché, George Méliès, and Edwin S. Porter. And their competitive spirit accelerated the race to make superior film equipment available in the earliest days of the industry.

62

WOODY ALLEN

Born: December 1, 1935, Brooklyn, NY

*I've always tried to dissuade people and tell them my films
are not all autobiographical.*

—WOODY ALLEN

Woody Allen made movies smarter. He also made them funnier, but his gift for appealing to the intellect of moviegoers has had a lasting effect on the way scripts are written today. He wasn't just an intellectual's filmmaker, he was a filmmaker for anyone who liked the clever, the inventive, or the unexpected delivery of dialogue. His scripts introduced humor that referenced popular culture and borrowed elements of absurdity and fantasy from such far-ranging influences as Groucho and Fellini. He respected the collective literacy of the audience and raised the standard for both comedies and dramas.

In the earliest days of television, Woody Allen was a gag writer for the immensely popular *Your Show of Shows* with Sid Caesar. Among his fellow writers were the cream of the comedy crop: Neil Simon, Mel Brooks, and *M*A*S*H* creator Larry Gelbart. After selling monologue jokes to a receptive Ed Sullivan in 1961, Allen felt his material might do well in Greenwich Village nightclubs, where stand-up comics were developing acts for humorous record albums. He spent his weeknights perfecting his timing and delivery in such New York comedy clubs as the Hungry I and the Purple Onion. Striking a chord with intellectuals, he created a style of humor that exorcised his fascination with death, sex, and violence, the same subjects that were on the minds of his audience.

The success of his routines led to several Broadway plays, small film acting assignments, and screenwriting stints before the first two films he directed, *Take the Money and Run* and *Bananas* (1971) demonstrated that Allen had a sense for what audiences would find funny. Both films, in which he wrote and starred, had fast-paced and inventive gags reminiscent of Allen's movie heroes, who include Charlie Chaplin and the Marx Brothers. These films introduced jokes that referenced social and political figures and current events.

Using cultural images in much the same way Jean-Luc Godard did in *Breathless* (1959), Allen had established the postmodern comedy. He seemed to be winking at moviegoers, sharing in their awareness of all that had come before in film history. Like Godard, Allen would make a film tribute to Humphrey Bogart, using the public's familiarity with his role as Rick in *Casablanca*. The classic film played a pivotal part in the adaptation of Allen's Broadway hit *Play It Again, Sam* (1972). Allen's next film, *Sleeper* (1973), is another homage, this time to Buster Keaton's deadpan reaction to the unpredictability of mechanical objects. He would go on to show his reverence for directors Ingmar Bergman in *Interiors* (1978), *Another Woman* (1988), and *September* (1987) and Federico Fellini in *Stardust Memories* (1980) and *Shadows and Fog* (1992). Many of these films are open testaments of his devotion to these literary and artistic influences.

By the time Allen had finished *Love and Death* (1975), his screwball offerings had lost much of their novelty, and many of the sight gags seemed more like television sketch comedy. But the introspective and bittersweet *Annie Hall* (1977) established a new brand of comedy, mixing sophisticated humor and experimental narrative structures. *Annie Hall* was a fresh and vital film. During scenes of dialogue with other characters, Allen would suddenly turn to the camera and address the audience, much as he did in stand-up performances. During an on-screen dispute about a literary classic, Allen would drag the real-life author into the scene and have him settle the argument. The film used flashbacks, animated sequences, discontinuous chronology, subtitles, and interior monologues to reinforce the soul-searching theme. The nebbish "Woody" persona, created over a number of films, now had a more relaxed and reflective quality, mirroring the spirit of the 1970s "me" generation. A quintessential satire on the psychoanalytical intellectual, *Annie Hall* proved to be an overwhelming success and won four Oscars.

Other filmmakers, including Paul Mazursky, Elaine May, and Richard Benjamin, followed in Allen's footsteps, making smarter and more self-aware comedies. A flood of stand-up comedians entered the film industry on the heels of Allen's success. Steve Martin, Harold Ramis, Richard Pryor, Amy Heckerling, and Albert Brooks all climbed the ranks from comic to screenwriter to director.

Annie Hall began a new era for Allen. Teaming with long-term collaborators, talented ensemble casts, and studios willing to give him limitless freedom, Allen has added unique creative touches to a long list of distinguished films, including *Manhattan* (1979), *Hannah and Her Sisters* (1986), and *Crimes and Misdemeanors* (1989). His finest films feel autobiographical and balance Allen's traditional Yiddish humor with a universal depth and insight. Somewhere in between his best and his worst are the entertaining films *Zelig* (1983), *Broadway Danny Rose* (1984), and *The Purple Rose of Cairo* (1985).

Movies made today, even the most mundane action thrillers and cop dramas, owe Woody Allen at least a small debt, for their humor now has to be smart. His irreverent intellectual comedies since *Annie Hall* have almost single-handedly killed off the slapstick comedy, and physical comedians like Chevy Chase, Robin Williams, and Jim Carrey now succeed only by blending their madcap antics with the smart retort.

63

CLARK
GABLE

Born: February 1, 1901, Cadiz, OH
Died: November 16, 1960, Hollywood, CA

*Gable was Gable in film after film. That was the foundation
on which stardom was built then.*

—MARSHA HUNT

Clark Gable first achieved fame on Broadway before a string of bit parts in silent films landed him *The Merry Widow* (1925). A speaking part in one of the first sound westerns, *The Painted Desert* (1931), made Louis B. Mayer take notice of the handsome actor, and Gable soon signed a lucrative MGM contract. He would remain their hottest property for more than thirty-five years. His blue-collar charm and mustachioed smile combined to create a dashing rogue whose rough exterior could not tarnish his inherent good nature. Crowned the "king of Hollywood," he molded the public's ideal of the leading man in more than sixty films.

MGM put him through romantic paces with Greta Garbo in *Susan Lenox: Her Fall and Rise* (1931), Joan Crawford in *The Possessed* (1931), and Jean Harlow in *Red Dust* (1932). Because several other actors in Hollywood were experiencing great success with gangster films, Mayer decided Gable should pick up a tommy gun. These roles irked Gable, who felt they would stereotype him and ultimately ruin his career. He complained to Mayer, viciously attacking the studio head for playing puppetmaster with his career. Mayer retaliated by lending Gable out to Columbia for light comedies. The famous tiff put Gable in the hands of director Frank Capra, whose *It Happened One*

Night (1934) swept all of the main Oscar categories, winning five, and put Gable firmly on top.

Clark Gable was an unlikely fellow to become a movie star. His legendary ears were initially considered too big, his speech was at first fast-paced and clipped, and producer Darryl Zanuck once stated that "he looks like an ape." But next to a variety of glamorous leading ladies, he remained confident and in charge. He was witty and handled physical comedy as well as he handled romance. He was what every woman wanted and every man wanted to be.

Back at MGM, Gable switched easily to bare-chested adventure in *Mutiny on the Bounty* (1935), another Oscar-winner that crystallized his image of male virility. Vehicles were created to capture the genuine camaraderie he shared with fellow actors; he was paired with Spencer Tracy for *San Francisco* (1936) and *Boom Town* (1940). Because of his overwhelming appeal, there was worldwide speculation that Gable would be cast as Rhett Butler in *Gone With the Wind* (1939); it had been reported in the gossip magazines that Gable was the ideal among readers of the Margaret Mitchell novel. As extensive tests were held for a proper Scarlett, producer David O. Selznick tried to woo Gable for the role of the southern gentleman. Gable wasn't interested, so Selznick floated Gary Cooper's name to the trades, testing the waters. But public demand was unyielding—the fans wanted Gable—and reluctantly he gave in. *Gone With the Wind* would give him the role of a lifetime and supplied him with the most memorable line of dialogue in Hollywood's golden era when he told Scarlett, "Frankly, my dear, I don't give a damn." The force of his personality helped the film become an instant classic and one of the box office champions of all time.

Steady profits rolled in from his films throughout the 1930s, but Gable's stardom lost all meaning to him when his new bride, actress Carole Lombard, became an early casualty of World War II. Just before boarding the plane that crashed, killing all aboard, she had encouraged Gable to enlist in the war effort. After her funeral, he immediately left the movies for combat service. It was another indication of the strong moral character Gable displayed both on and off the screen. When he was later asked to play a role in a war drama, he refused because of a subplot involving an adulteress. "I won't play a man who sleeps with a woman whose serviceman husband is overseas," stated Gable.

After his return to Hollywood, he played macho roles in *Mogambo* (1953) and *Run Silent, Run Deep* (1958). In the early fifties, he attempted an independent production venture, but his failing health made the task impossible. After three decades as Hollywood's male lead, Gable romanced Marilyn Monroe in John Huston's *The Misfits* (1961) before succumbing to a heart condition two weeks after filming was completed.

64

DAVID O. SELZNICK

Born: May 10, 1902, Pittsburgh, PA
Died: June 22, 1965, Hollywood, CA

Selznick's genius was in his commercial sense, his showmanship,
as well as his basic good taste.

—PETER BOGDANOVICH

In 1926, a young scriptreader named David O. Selznick joined fledgling MGM and rocketed through jobs in the story department until earning a promotion to supervisor of production. He quickly became known as a producer who could get efficient results out of a meager staff and bring a picture in under budget and on schedule. However, Selnick was also a stubborn perfectionist who would wield his authority with reckless disregard for the temperament of his stars or the authority of his superiors. While working at MGM, Selznick continuously engaged in disagreements with production genius Irving Thalberg; he got himself fired just one year after his appointment to the position.

However, Paramount Pictures, attracted by his reputation for efficiency, quickly made him the head of their production staff, in 1927. Selznick worked on several projects with no hint of the prima donna tendencies that MGM saw in him. But the Depression forced Paramount to juggle priorities; they wished to institute a temporary hiatus in all salaries, and when they informed Selznick of the payroll problems, he bolted to RKO. There, he instituted a production scheme modeled on the autonomous units that production pioneer Thomas Ince had espoused in his days at the Triangle studios. As head of seven assistant producers, Selznick concerned himself with every detail of RKO productions, particularly the Katharine Hepburn films *A Bill of Divorcement* (1932) and *Little Women* (1933).

Upon hearing of Selznick's repeated successes, MGM boss Louis B. Mayer sought to rehire him when Irving Thalberg took a leave of absence. Selznick agreed to a package that would give him creative control, and soon he was back at MGM making *Dinner at Eight* (1933), *David Copperfield* (1935), and other prestigious literary and stage adaptations of the 1930s.

Bent on establishing himself as a rogue independent, Selznick left MGM again in 1936 and launched International Pictures, where his first movie was the award-winning *A Star Is Born* (1937). Most of the films made under Selznick's new company would be distributed under the MGM flag, but with one difference: they would include Selznick's name over the title. He then set out to make his name a mark of superior excellence.

The scope of Selznick's bravado was illustrated in his most memorable triumph, *Gone With the Wind* (1939). Enlisting six directors, including William Cameron Menzies, King Vidor, and Victor Fleming, and calling on several screenwriters, including Ben Hecht, he released the picture to millions of eager fans. *Gone With the Wind* won ten Oscars and a place as one of the greatest box office successes in film history.

The tremendous profits were multiplied by other Selznick successes that same year, notably Alfred Hitchcock's *Rebecca*. Selznick's other talents included finding foreign film properties and acquiring their rights for a Hollywood version. Here, he was incredibly successful, and a remake of *Intermezzo* (1939) illustrated it. With the film, he revealed two European talents in Charles Boyer and Ingrid Bergman.

Ironically, a massive tax debt in 1940 forced stockholders of International Pictures to put the entire holdings on the block. Selznick immediately formed David Selznick Productions, but did not produce any movies until the mid-1940s. In many of his productions he had to assume a reduced role such as acting as a talent scout for Hitchcock's *Spellbound* (1945) and Carol Reed's *The Thin Man* (1949). Compared to his earlier years, his output was rather sparse. He did, however, produce *Duel in the Sun* (1946) and *Portrait of Jennie* (1948), mainly as vehicles for actress Jennifer Jones who later became his wife, but he rarely took an active part in his company's projects.

David O. Selznick accomplished what he had set out to do; his name became a symbol of exceptional quality in entertainment. Audiences began to recognize his seal of approval. Actors and directors were eager to be involved in his projects. MGM was glad to have his bright light shine upon their crown; Selznick was responsible for many of their biggest names, and the pristine MGM image is largely due to him. He would be remembered as the energetic loner, working outside the studio system to make polished films. Selznick's hard-won reputation would inspire the Zanucks and Goldwyns to follow his example and treat their names as a mark of excellence.

65

GREGG TOLAND

Born: May 29, 1904, Charleston, IL
Died: September 28, 1948, Hollywood, CA

Toland demonstrated how the cinematographer can and should suit his style to the feel of the script.

—KENNETH MACGOWAN

Gregg Toland has been called the greatest cameraman ever to work in films. At fifteen, he was hired as an office boy for William Fox, working his way through various jobs until he was assisting camera operators on large productions. When he wasn't busy on a movie set, he was tinkering with the tools of his craft, learning about photographic lenses and camera mechanics. By the time he was twenty-seven years old, he had become the youngest cameraman ever assigned to a first unit in Hollywood. Three years later, Toland's experiments had made him so popular that Samuel Goldwyn was forced to share his prized innovator with other studios or risk losing him.

Although he developed many of his skills in the silent era, the talkies made Toland a Hollywood hero. In the days of silent film, cameras were clumsy and noisy, which was tolerated at the time because the final product didn't require a soundtrack. But when sound films came into vogue, the loud camera ticks prevented acceptable recordings of the actors' voices. Sound equipment had to be kept far away from camera equipment, and this made some productions unbearably complicated and time-consuming. Toland devised ways of improving equipment to rectify this problem. In 1928, he invented a soundproof blimp-like housing that covered a camera and ensured that its mechanized noise would not reach recording devices. This development was significant for sound pictures because it allowed directors to close in on intimate moments between actors and capture their whispers without capturing the whir of winding film. The soundproof camera instantly became a standard throughout the industry.

Recognition brought Toland great opportunities. He went to work on some of the most beautiful films of the thirties. He was assigned as the lead cameraman on *Dead End* (1937), and his Oscar-winning work on *Wuthering Heights* (1939) and contributions to *Intermezzo* (1939) made him a sought-after name in Hollywood. Working with director John Ford on *The Grapes of Wrath* (1940), Toland would make technical experiments that would lay the foundation for another Ford film, *The Long Voyage Home* (1940).

A startling example of Expressionistic black-and-white contrast photography, *The Long Voyage Home* introduced razor-sharp images to the screen. Toland obtained this powerful clarity by using coated lenses, which he had custom-made for the film, and high-powered arc lamps. In effect, the lens could keep objects in the foreground and background of a shot in focus at the same time. The achievement was dubbed "deep focus," and the innovation would become the most famous in Toland's career. Unfortunately, explaining the benefits of deep-focus photography to Ford proved impossible. The stubborn director followed his own path in moviemaking and wasn't interested in exploring Toland's new compositions. Toland would have to wait for another chance to demonstrate the benefits of deep focus.

When Toland heard that the young Orson Welles was coming to Hollywood, he volunteered his services to RKO and introduced himself to the newcomer. Welles was exceptionally open-minded about Toland's exciting ideas, and soon they were put to the test on *Citizen Kane* (1940), the film that showcased the benefits of Toland's deep-focus lenses. The clear photography gave audiences a chance to examine Orson Welles's masterpiece to exhaustion, maintaining a rich and realistic look that exaggerated the sense of space in many scenes. Welles cleverly adapted his sets to highlight the benefits of deep focus, and he choreographed certain scenes to use the new lenses to create some powerful effect. In one sequence of the film, the title character, Charles Foster Kane, discusses his financial affairs with two men in a foreground set, then wanders far into the background to stand in front of several towering windows. The scene accomplishes two interesting visual tricks through deep focus: it allows the actors to carry on a dialogue in different planes without requiring editing, and it creates an optical illusion of small office windows that are revealed to be enormous as Kane retreats into the background.

Although Toland's deep-focus photography was slow to catch on with most Hollywood features, his own work on *The Little Foxes* (1941) and *The Best Years of Our Lives* (1946) employed it to award-winning success.

Toland continued to innovate through the years. He converted the light-weight and flexible Mitchell BNC camera, a model that found favor among television studios, for use on film sets. This camera was the outstanding choice for mise-en-scène, a style of shooting in which constant movement of actors through a set often requires the camera operator to adapt quickly. With greater camera control, Toland was able to satisfy a director's instructions for unprecedented perspective shots or fluid movement. This eliminated the reliance on editing to intercut between scenes and sparked a new trend in film structure; directors planned long continuous shots around the new mobility. Toland also developed a new antinoise device built into the housing of the camera, negating his own blimp invention and creating yet another industry standard.

Camera operators often wind up becoming directors, using the position as a stepping-stone to greater things, as many of the people on this list have already proven. But among those who chose the craft of photography as their lifelong pursuit, few have equaled Gregg Toland. Only the legendary achievements of Billy Bitzer and the widespread application of Linwood Dunn's optical printer have earned higher rankings here. Although most of Toland's techniques were applied to their fullest in television, he is best remembered for his far-reaching impact on some of the greatest films in Hollywood's golden age, and cameramen in both mediums still hold Toland in the highest esteem for his many innovations.

66

LILLIAN GISH

Born: October 14, 1896, Springfield, OH
Died: February 27, 1993, New York, NY

Gish is so hypnotic that the audience finds itself straining to catch the merest movement of an eyelash.

—KEVIN BROWNLOW

It was Mary Pickford who introduced Lillian Gish to director D. W. Griffith. As the quintessential waif, Gish fit the bill for the sentimental Victorian melodramas that became Griffith's speciality. Together, they clashed on the interpretations of some of silent film's greatest accomplishments, including *The Birth of a Nation* (1915) and *Orphans of the Storm* (1922). She openly shared her opinions with the famous director, who in turn shared his respect for her drive to add artistry to the new medium. His dramatic instinct for throwing a helpless victim into a cruel and tension-filled climax was heightened by Gish's transcendent innocence.

Credited with pioneering fundamental screen acting techniques, Lillian Gish was a true original. Her fragile, innocent face was a marvel of subtle nuances. Her expressive eyes and restrained gestures were the perfect match for Griffith's trademark close-ups. Other actors who had spent years refining their craft on the stage and in vaudeville shows continued with their broad, melodramatic movements on the film set; every action was accompanied with flailing arms that forced other actors to move out of their way and reposition themselves in the camera's eye. Emphasized by the flickers of film projectors, these jittering, overblown theatrics simply drew laughter from audiences. In contrast, the vulnerable and virginal Gish mesmerized moviegoers by exerting control over both her emotions and her body. She remained stationary and would simply stoop or cower slowly when another actor became agitated. With soft steps, she would glide slowly out of a scene, halting just momentarily before a final exit. Audiences had time to study and assess the finer points of her performances.

Even more amazing, Lillian Gish had no contemporaries or mentors in the field of screen acting. She imitated no one. All of the craft that she brought to her roles was instinctual. Many of her habits in movement and timing have become the time-tested preferences for capturing performances on film and are still in common use today. She was hailed as the first serious movie actress, and her early shorts became training films for scores of actors making the transition from the theater. Gish gracefully accepted the moniker "first lady of the silent screen."

Her most celebrated roles were popular largely because of her persistence in making them realistic. In *Broken Blossoms* (1919), she huddles in a closet while her abusive husband hunts throughout the house, looking to beat her. Griffith wanted to film just a few seconds of her terrified face, but Gish asked that the camera be left to roll on, as she added levels of fright to her beautiful countenance. The scene would prove to be the film's most powerful. In another film, *Way Down East* (1920), a perilous trip downriver on an ice floe was called for, and Gish insisted on performing in a real blizzard without a stunt double. The ice broke away from the crew, and Gish was left untethered. The scene captured the immediacy of the panic and became another hallmark in silent films.

After graduating from the Griffith stock company in 1923, she excelled at MGM studios in literary adaptations, including *La Bohème* (1926), *The Scarlet Letter* (1926), and *The Wind* (1928), as well as her first sound film, *One Romantic Night* (1930).

She decided to work with several minor studios and tried her hand at producing her own films in the late 1920s, exercising total control over scripts, supporting roles, crew members, and producers. She had her choice of directors; among the top helmsmen she selected were King Vidor and Victor Seastrom. She displayed a keen eye for talent and hired the witty Dorothy Parker to write the titles for the successful *Remodeling Her Husband* (1920), the first film Gish tried her hand at directing.

In the late twenties, Gish's popularity began to fade as talkies took the attention of audiences. She returned to Broadway in 1930, and continued to act on the stage for the next half century. Gish was resistant to sound pictures because she believed that silent features possessed a greater ability to touch people's emotions. Despite these feelings, some of her finest work was done in the sound era. Her majestic presence appeared again in the David O.

Selznick production of *Duel in the Sun* (1946). Her performance earned her an Academy Award nomination and, combined with a role in the Oscar-winning *Portrait of Jennie* (1949), signaled that Lillian Gish had a secure place in sound pictures. In fact, her angelic image earned her a powerful role in the cult classic *The Night of the Hunter* (1955), in which she embodied the soul of goodness; her scenes of reading scripture to ward off the coming evil are some of the most memorable moments in sound films.

A special Oscar was awarded to Gish in 1970 for her "superlative artistry," and she accepted honors from the Kennedy Center in 1982. Her last film appearance was at the age of ninety alongside Bette Davis in *The Whales of August* (1987). A poignant performance, it was a nostalgic curtain call completing the most respected body of work in the history of motion pictures. While accepting a lifetime achievement tribute from the American Film Institute in 1984, she recalled a favorite quote from John Barrymore that summed up the power of moving images: "That camera is more dissecting than anything that's ever been invented. You stay in front of it long enough and it tells what you had for breakfast."

67

WILLIAM CAMERON MENZIES

Born: July 29, 1896, New Haven, CT
Died: March 5, 1957, Beverly Hills, CA

*Menzies is one of the few talents ever to work in films whose influence
is literally impossible to overestimate. He was almost certainly the
greatest and most innovative visual designer ever to work on
movies, and there have been many greats in that field.*
—BILL WARREN

The pictures trapped inside the head of William Cameron Menzies needed a
large canvas to be fully realized, and as an art director in Hollywood, he got
his chance. His first assignment was *The Thief of Bagdad* (1924), with
Douglas Fairbanks. Menzies shocked the world with his use of colossal buildings in forced perspective and expansive lines of fences, walls, and railings to
dramatize the legendary chase sequences and create maximum tension. The
grandiose debut established Menzies as the king of set design, a reign that
lasted for three decades.

No doubt Menzies's *Bagdad* earned him commissions on, among others, *The
Son of the Sheik* (1926), *Two Arabian Knights* (1927), and Fairbanks's *Taming
of the Shrew* (1929) with Mary Pickford. He was the dominant influence on art
direction in the thirties and early forties, quite an achievement considering it
was a golden era for production designers; such talents as Anton Grot, Richard
Day, Perry Ferguson, Cedric Gibbons, and Van Nest Polglase were his contemporaries. Menzies would continue with more influential work on *The Dove*
(1928), which culled him the first Oscar ever awarded for art direction.

The few credits Menzies received as a director were completely forget-table, with a single exception—*Things to Come* (1936). This science fiction film had a far-reaching impact. Menzies's directorial techniques in the groundbreaking fantasy spectacle lacked any sign of a personal style, but the highly imaginative sets, particularly those depicting widespread destruction, bear the mark of his production design.

In *Things to Come,* the screenplay by H. G. Wells called for three distinct variations of the film's main setting, the city of Everytown. The first was a bustling metropolitan center, and the second shows the streets of the same city after it is leveled by the effects of a world war. The visual representations of postapocalyptic chaos became the most pervasive view of desolation in film. These images were not yet cliché, yet they have since been repeated in hundreds of futuristic films; the sets of strewn rubble, raging fires, twisted metal, and overturned machinery are recalled in *The Omega Man* (1971), *Damnation Alley* (1977), *Mad Max* (1979), and *Twelve Monkeys* (1995), among others.

Working with designer Vincent Korda, Menzies needed one final look for *Things to Come:* the reconstruction of Everytown into an advanced civiliza-tion in the year 2036. He resisted all common speculation and trusted his instincts about the way the world would look one hundred years into the future. The result was a utopian city of sleek skyscrapers connected to each other by mid-air walkways, levitating cars, and citizens draped in simple robes strolling in peaceful and methodical silence. *Things to Come* was an unadorned, antiseptic view that has become the most complete vision of a tomorrowland ever filmed, featuring a style of architecture that has become pervasive in science fiction films. Its influence can be seen in other films, notably Stanley Kubrick's *2001: A Space Odyssey* (1968).

Things to Come relied more on art direction than on crafty storytelling, so Menzies was the right man for the job. It cost $1.4 million to make and opened February 21, 1936, to enthralled fans in London. Other space films like *Invaders From Mars* (1953) owed much to Menzies's futuristic design, but with its complete view of the future, *Things to Come* created a picture of Earth as it might be, and all such films to date borrow extensively from its vision.

More artist than director, Menzies was regarded in his heyday as one of the most influential men in Hollywood circles, and producers would come calling on projects of critical importance, as David O. Selznick did with *Gone With the Wind* (1939). It the first time an art director had been listed in the credits as a "production designer." Menzies painted detailed and elaborate pictures of each scene, complete with correctly garbed actors. Coordinating the entire design team, including set construction and costume design, Men-zies worked closely with Natalie Kalmus to ensure spectacular use of Technicolor and hired famed set artist Lyle Wheeler to detail props and decor with historical accuracy. The famous "burning of Atlanta" scene was Menzies's conception. (He can actually be seen playing an extra; there is a band playing as the train returns with wounded Confederates, and Menzies appears on screen in uniform.)

Something of a swan song for Menzies, *Gone With the Wind* won him a second Oscar in 1939 for Outstanding Achievement in the Use of Color for the Enhancement of Dramatic Mood in the Production. Although only his standard services were required for Alfred Hitchcock's *Foreign Correspondent* (1940) and Anthony Mann's *Reign of Terror* (1949), Menzies's career is still unrivaled for the sheer magnitude of its artistry.

68

LUCILLE BALL

Born: August 6, 1911, Celeron, NY
Died: April 26, 1989, Los Angeles, CA

I didn't take well to movies and they didn't take well to me.
—LUCILLE BALL

As a product of several New York drama schools, Lucille Ball became extremely frustrated when her stage career turned out to be a series of misses, so in late 1929, Lucy decided to take a shot at Hollywood. She ended up as a walk-on Goldwyn girl in a Busby Berkeley chorus line for *Roman Scandals* (1933), won substantial praise for her work in another film, *Stage Door* (1937), and shortly thereafter signed with MGM to appear in more films. Unfortunately, her assignments were always as a bit player in B productions. In preparation for *The Big Street* (1942), Lucy went to see Max Factor for a makeover and left with a new look. Her hair took on a striking red hue that she would keep for the rest of her life.

In 1947, she teamed with husband Desi Arnaz for a live vaudeville-style tour and did some radio work for CBS that met with audience approval. The situation comedy of a wacky housewife and her husband was adapted easily to the growing medium of television, and Lucy and Desi Arnaz started *I Love Lucy* in 1951.

"Wasn't that girl just a bit player at RKO a few weeks ago?" movie stars would chuckle among themselves. Surely Lucy would destroy her chances of ever making it big in films, they speculated. After all, it was well known around Hollywood studios that the executives in charge frowned upon an actor who considered television parts. Television was the lowly, artless medium, and its stay-at-home appeal was hurting picture profits. To work in television was to play for the other team. You were a traitor. You were an outcast. You would never work in movies again.

Lucy's years of mingling with the dancers, singers, crew members, and makeup artists gave her plenty of connections, which she used to lure Hollywood talent to the lowly medium. Nearly all of her original TV technicians were from the film industry: cameramen, lightning and sound specialists, even Max Factor's son, had signed on to keep Lucy radiant.

The most prominent acquisition was director Karl Fruend. Desi Arnaz felt the show would need an experienced hand to preserve the look of the series over time. Karl Fruend was an Oscar-winning cameraman who had filmed *Metropolis* (1926) with Fritz Lang and the acclaimed *The Last Laugh* (1924) with F. W. Murnau. Fruend was extremely fond of Lucy, but he hated the idea of television; he considered it beneath him. Lucy pleaded with him and assured him he would have the best working conditions and the proper support. He could hand-select his staff. In addition, Lucy offered him a handsome and regular paycheck. Fruend took the deal, stunning his colleagues, and suddenly Hollywood was paying attention.

Arnaz and Fruend's first decision was how to record the episodes. They chose film instead of video, and their prophetic wisdom would lead to significant profits from reruns. (It was later discovered that the archives of many of the early classic TV programs that used videotape had been erased or ruined, destroying all chances of syndication profit.) Next, Fruend opted for a revolutionary three-camera technique for filming live television shows. The pioneering method was picked up by director Alfred Hitchcock, who adapted the process and used it extensively.

I Love Lucy had rippling effects in Hollywood. The instant popularity of the TV series made Lucy an overnight sensation. In just six months, more than ten million people were watching her series, and it retained the number one position until 1957. Her fame startled the film industry.

Eventually, Lucy's success was also instrumental in mending the relationship between the film and television industries. Her show was the first to give studios an opportunity to pitch their upcoming movies through cameo TV appearances. Stars who knew Lucy from the studios—some of them among the biggest stars in Hollywood—might have vowed never to work in television, but broke down and made their first appearances with the outrageous redhead, usually at union scale. William Holden, John Wayne, Bob Hope, Rock Hudson, Richard Widmark, and Orson Welles all stopped in at the Ricardo residence and made television history.

Lucy's return to theatrical features was heralded as the prodigal coming home. Her subsequent film work in *The Long, Long Trailer* (1954) and

Yours, Mine, and Ours (1968) demonstrated television's ability to create bankable stars for future full-length features. By the time Delbert Mann's presentation of *Marty*, originally shown live on the Philco Playhouse, had transcended the small screen to win four Oscars, including Best Picture of 1955, the lines were blurred. Many Hollywood directors and screenwriters were convinced that work on television could only help their careers. In fact, television would soon produce the next generation of stars on both sides of the movie camera.

In 1962, after lengthy divorce proceedings, Lucy assumed control of RKO, the same studio where she had struggled to become a movie star. She was the first female studio head in Hollywood since Mary Pickford had a stake in United Artists; she headed production of more than fifty TV series, including *Mission Impossible* and *Star Trek,* and in 1967 she sold the studio for a $10 million profit. Lucille Ball had become the first film actress to make the transition from movies to television and back again to movies successfully. Her trailblazing success forever connected the two industries.

69

SAMUEL ROTHAFEL

Born: July 9, 1882, Stillwater, MN
Died: January 13, 1936, New York, NY

Samuel Rothafel was the first great showman and supreme impresario of motion picture exhibition.

—EMILY GWATHMEY

Samuel Lionel Rothapfel began his career in motion pictures by projecting movies to drunk miners in the back room of a Pennsylvania saloon in 1905. A one-man operator, he painted his own advertising posters, rented chairs from an undertaker, exchanged his own films, and ran the projector for six shows a night. After raising enough money to travel to New York, Rothapfel struck out on his own in grand style. When he arrived, Rothapfel approached the owners of a number of New York establishments, including the Paramount, Strand, Knickerbocker, Rialto, Rivoli, and Capitol theaters. He offered them a partnership proposition: he would manage them all and introduce motion pictures to their theatrical offerings.

He decided to shorten his name to Rothafel, which was displayed over his many theaters. Soon he would be known simply as "Roxy," and his venues would begin showing films to aristocratic audiences that shied away from the bawdy entertainment of vaudeville houses. Rothafel saw an opportunity to present a luxurious environment for displaying movies to a better class of customer. His theaters would become superior to all others, and Rothafel would refer to them as "pleasure palaces."

His flagship was the exemplary Roxy Theater in New York City. When it opened in 1927, it was advertised as the largest theater built since the fall of Rome. It had private apartments, a hospital staffed with nurses, a radio broadcasting booth, a kitchen, and a waiting room that could comfortably hold more than two thousand people. Boasting one of the first wide-screen theaters, the Roxy had a canvas forty-two feet tall. The specially commissioned Kimball organ had three consoles facing all areas of the theater, and New York's finest organists were hired to play every night. Most important, it had six box offices and ticket sales of $100,000 a week.

The palatial quality of Rothafel's theaters was extraordinary. Many of his finest picture houses were decorated with an opulent "rococo" flair, an excessively elaborate architectural style highly fashionable at the time. To make visitors comfortable, he installed thick carpets, cushioned seats, balconies, and enormous restrooms. To add a regal appearance, Rothafel installed crystal chandeliers, oriental rugs, marble floors, and gilt-edged paintings. To make his environment more elegant and accommodating, he hired uniformed attendants and built relaxation rooms decorated in Venetian, Elizabethan, and colonial motifs.

Also contributing to the opulence were the huge organs that played accompaniment to silent films, adding comedic sound effects and heightening the dramatic mood. Rothafel imported international soloists to sing before screenings and kept a staff of master organists that included Carl Stalling, Lew White, Deszo Von D'Antalffy, and Dr. C. A. J. Parmentier on the payroll. Many of the musicians would move on to Hollywood in the sound era as composers; others would join Rothafel on the radio.

In 1923, the National Broadcasting Company approached Rothafel about broadcasting a live program from the Capitol Theater in New York, which had fifty-three hundred seats and room for eighty musicians in the orchestra pit. As the host of a variety show, *Roxy and His Gang*, Rothafel presented his popular performers and organ music to audiences around the city. The broadcast ran weekly until 1931, and it encouraged thousands of moviegoers to come see a real radio show before their movie started.

During the 1930s, Rothafel's genius for theater design was sought by other entrepreneurs. He was consulted by the Rockefellers, who wanted a dazzling launch for a concept venue called Radio City Music Hall. Rothafel accepted the project with characteristic enthusiasm. He sailed to Europe to study the great architecture of European playhouses. On the return trip, on the deck of an ocean liner, Roxy's original concept for the Music Hall came to him. He envisioned the stage and surrounding coves to be designed as sunbeams shining above an ocean of theater patrons. The final decoration was a spectacular model of the modern theater, with glass, aluminum, and chrome styled in art deco geometric patterns. Unlike any other theater in the world, the Radio City Music Hall featured a host of mechanical wonders—including eight elevators, pulleys, and cranes underneath the stage—as well as the usual comforts that had become the trademark of the theater king.

With an unmatched devotion to the moviegoing experience, Sam Rothafel became known as the "high priest of the cathedral of motion pictures." His legacy lives on today in the multiplex theaters, with their video arcades and espresso bars. He was truly one of film's most interesting characters never to set foot in Hollywood.

70

AKIRA KUROSAWA

Born: March 23, 1910, Omori, Japan

His complex subject matter and superb pictorial sense were equal
to those of any Western filmmakers.

—RICHARD STROMGREN

In 1936, young Akira Kurosawa worked as an assistant director and screen-writer in an Eastern cinema studio by day, but studied Western painting, literature, and political philosophy at night. A subtle blend of these passions found their way into his noteworthy scripts, particularly *Judo Saga* (1943), and he began to formulate a distinct, personal style as a scenario writer under the tutelage of Japan's premiere director, Yamamoto Kajiro. However, the film that made a name for the young artist was *Drunken Angel* (1948), on which Kurosawa was both scenarist and director. The film also marked the beginning of a collaboration with the actor who would be forever associated with him, Toshiro Mifune. After years of serving as an apprentice, Kurosawa finally emerged as one of the most promising new directors in postwar Japan.

Then came *Rashomon,* the Grand Prix finalist at the Venice Film Festival in 1950. *Rashomon* stunned audiences with its innovative exposition and drew international raves for its artful composition. Not even the unorthodox structure of *Citizen Kane* (1941) used cinema to probe for truth as Kurosawa had. The film details the same event from four different points of view. Filled with dynamic acting and surprising plot twists, *Rashomon's* clever narrative was accompanied by rich, black-and white visuals; Kurosawa used harsh streams of light that penetrate the branches of a forest as a metaphor for the truth-seeking theme of the film. His skillful movement of the camera and reliance on long shots also complemented the complex and circular story. But the buzz over *Rashomon* centered on the deconstructed plot; this fresh approach to storytelling had great influence over future screenplays. In fact, the heralded script of Quentin Tarantino's *Pulp Fiction* (1994) owes much to the jumbled chronology in *Rashomon.*

In Kurosawa's next film, *The Seven Samurai* (1954), the director paid tribute to the Hollywood western and introduced the wandering *chambara* or swordsman tradition with which he would be most closely associated. The Japanese sixteenth-century civil war repeatedly gave Kurosawa a setting for themes of heroism, and his series of samurai films represented his most influential and commercially successful efforts. *The Seven Samurai* is a clever scenario in which poor villagers employ the aid of mercenaries to rid their town of the depradations of a war lord. The film expertly walks the fine line between morality tale and tense action thriller. It sparked several Hollywood remakes of notable influence, most obviously *The Magnificant Seven* (1960). Several filmmakers would also borrow the elegant scripts of Kurosawa's other samurai films, including *Yojimbo* (1961) and *Kagemusha* (1980). From *Yojimbo,* Sergio Leone would create the perfect vehicle for his spaghetti westerns with Clint Eastwood in *A Fistful of Dollars* (1964). More recently, Walter Hill's *Last Man Standing* (1996) used a Depression-era setting to re-create *Yojimbo's* story with Bruce Willis in the lead. Despite his own adaptations of gangster films and period epics, Kurosawa's public best loved the violent fight scenes of these samurai classics.

The two most appreciated aspects of Kurosawa's films are his themes and his imagery. He is considered one of the finest screenwriters in film history, blending dialogue with equal parts of understated absurdity and powerful poignancy. Central to his scripts are questions of morality, and he often places his characters in inventive situations that force them to face ethical dilemmas. His detailed visual style is reminiscent of traditional Japanese art, but his photography maintains a modern look that favors high contrast and vivid color to emphasize the exploration of truth in many of his films.

Famous literary works were carefully mined by Kurosawa. He successfully adapted the plays of William Shakespeare to the screen in *Throne of Blood* (1957) and *Ran* (1985), tackling the tormented spirits of Macbeth and King Lear, respectively. Both films were hailed as among the finest film versions of the Bard's plays. He has also written his own scripts based on Dostoevsky's *The Idiot* and Edgar Allan Poe's *The Masque of the Red Death.* Many of Kurosawa's literary adaptations were never filmed but were later collected and published in books.

Ikiru (1952) is generally cited as Kurosawa's best film, ironically it was made during a period of depression in the Japanese film industry. His most accessible films, in which economy of style and minimal dialogue allowed for international appeal, were well received in the West. Looking to migrate to Hollywood in 1968, Kurosawa agreed to shoot the war spectacle *Tora! Tora! Tora!* for 20th Century–Fox. Halfway through the Pearl Harbor attack scene, he was replaced with another director and gave up ideas of traveling abroad.

Unquestionably, Kurosawa is the best-known Eastern filmmaker. He assimilated his knowledge of ancient Japanese traditions into a modern Western art form, influencing many writers and directors along the way. His bold visual style and humanist stories had tremendous impact on the execution of films by George Lucas, Satyajit Ray, Steven Spielberg, Andrei Tarkovsky, and Tony Richardson. And his success and influence on American cinema garnered attention for Kenji Mizoguchi, Yasujiro Ozu, and other Asian directors. In his heyday, Kurosawa's work was so highly regarded that veteran Hollywood director Billy Wilder expressed his frustration by saying, "I'm just going to sign up with a Japanese team and sit on the bench and wait for Kurosawa to break his leg."

71

MARILYN MONROE

Born: June 1, 1926, Los Angeles, CA
Died: August 5, 1962, Los Angeles, CA

For the entire world she became a symbol of the eternal feminine.

—LEE STRASBERG

While working as a parachute inspector in the Radio Plane factory in Burbank, California, a starry-eyed Norma Jean Baker began supplementing her income by modeling in bathing suits for pinups and glamour photos for just fifty dollars a session. Those photos became instantly popular, and the photographer sold over a million copies for a $750,000 profit. By spring of 1945, after bleaching her hair, she had posed for pictures that graced the covers of more than thirty national magazines.

Howard Hughes saw the famous photographs and gave her a screen test for RKO, but he took too long making a decision, and talent scout Ben Lyon convinced Darryl F. Zanuck to beat Hughes to her signing. She started with Fox at $125 a week. In a meeting with Lyon on July 23, 1946, it was suggested that she change her name to Marilyn Miller, but Norma offered Monroe, her grandparents' last name.

After appearing in non-speaking parts, she gave the first glimpses of her true talent in *All About Eve* (1950). But it was with the 1953 features *Gentlemen Prefer Blondes* and *How to Marry a Millionaire* that Monroe broke through and became world famous. Her strut in a red dress in *Niagara* emblazoned her in the minds of moviegoers. Then nude calendar photos she had posed for years earlier appeared in the debut issue of *Playboy* magazine, and Monroe was the talk of the town. Soon she was the top star of the year. Marriage to baseball hero Joe Dimaggio boosted her standing as America's favorite trophy.

She lacked the disarming power and self-confidence of the screen sirens who preceded her—Marlene Dietrich, Greta Garbo, Jean Harlow, and Mae West. And yet this very lack of self-confidence was the key to her success among adolescent males of the 1950s. Her sense of innocence and natural sexuality made her seem vulnerable and nonthreatening. She was not a femme fatale who used her powers to manipulate; rather she appeared baffled by her allure, and this made her doubly attractive. Her status as a sex symbol is the gauge that all starlets are measured against, and rarely does an actress approach her radiant sexuality.

When Monroe grew tired of the dumb blonde stereotype, she took steps to take control of her own destiny. Joining the famed Actors Studio in New York, she met playwright Arthur Miller, whom she married in 1956. She formed Marilyn Monroe Productions in 1956, and produced a film version of the Broadway play *Bus Stop* (1957) in which she starred. She also starred in *The Prince and the Showgirl* with Laurence Olivier that same year.

Her comedic sense won over audiences in Billy Wilder's *Some Like It Hot* (1959). Monroe proved that she possessed a serious talent, but following *The Misfits* (1960), her marriage to Miller ended and, depressed, she was hospitalized for psychiatric care and treatment of physical problems.

Habitual tardiness on the set of *Something's Got to Give* (1962) got her fired. The movie was never completed, and one month later, on August 5, 1962, Marilyn Monroe was found dead in her Brentwood, California, home from an overdose of sleeping pills. Her premature death would elevate her status from superstar to goddess, and she would vault to the top of the list of stars, like James Dean, who had also died too young.

Since her suicide, Marilyn Monroe has remained in the public eye, an icon of popular culture. Her likeness has become the most widely reproduced in Hollywood history, recently surpassing the enormous popularity of Charlie Chaplin's, and can be found on every conceivable collectible item. The U.S. Postal Service minted a commemorative thirty-two-cent Marilyn Monroe stamp in 1995; Mattel issued a *Seven Year Itch* Barbie doll; and ironically, her fifty-year-old photos are still among the bestselling celebrity calendars annually. Skyrocketing from pinup girl to essence of screen sexuality, she gave hope to millions of young people who dreamed of becoming a superstar.

72

VITTORIO DE SICA

Born: July 7, 1901, Sora, Italy
Died: November 13, 1974, Paris, France

A filmmaker who was clearly more experienced and, indeed, more interested and skillfull in penetrating the depths of individual psychological reactions than Rossellini.

—BOSLEY CROWTHER

Roberto Rossellini's classic *Open City* (1946) is frequently considered the first film in the Italian neorealistic movement, a postwar period of experimental film that was characterized by the resourcefulness of its directors, who shot on the streets, used ordinary people as actors, and focused on the dramatic situations commonly found in daily life. Rossellini's work *is* complex and gritty, but many purists cite the work of Vittorio De Sica as the truest representation of the genre. Certainly, De Sica's films became the popular favorites, changing the face of films entirely and casting the director as a central figure in Italian films.

The handsome Vittorio De Sica began as an actor, first appearing in the sound film *Vecchia Signora* (1931). He used his good looks to surprising success as a matinee idol in Italy, and his countenance graced more than 150 Italian films, as well as plenty of teenage gossip magazines. After graduating from light comedies during World War II, De Sica, like Rossellini, made realistic films that reflected the social tragedies of postwar Italy. His poignant movies were emotional plays about downtrodden people struggling to keep their faith in the goodness of man.

The first of such films, *The Children Are Watching Us* (1942), shaped Italian film production by rejecting most of Hollywood's conventions. These films were made in collaboration with scriptwriter Cesare Zavattini, a major proponent of realism in film. Zavattini's scenarios eschewed trite or clever story devices, focused on working-class settings, and were emotionally charged. To carry these values through, De Sica hired untrained actors and shot on the streets. The film was welcomed enthusiastically by audiences in impoverished Rome.

De Sica's next film, *Shoeshine* (1946), established him as the "artist of the poor." The deceptively simple story is about young street urchins hustling stolen blankets in an effort to buy a horse. They wind up in a reformatory where they experience corruption and dehumanization. The plain narrative style of the story powerfully illuminated the social injustices in European societies after the war. *Umberto D.* (1952) was an ambitious comment on the problems of old age, but audiences found it too bleak and it was a financial disaster at the box office. However, De Sica's attempts to combine a documentary feel with sophisticated elements of humor were generally considered important. These techniques became the focus of the French New Wave directors, who studied what they called "cinema verité," the cinema of truth. De Sica's work had a major impact on their films, notably in the stark feel of Jean-Luc Godard's *Breathless* (1959).

The height of this truth-telling neorealism movement was De Sica's *The Bicycle Thief* (1949), arguably the most popular Italian film ever made. It is a touchstone of its kind, telling the story of a poor man whose relationship with his son is tested following the theft of a bicycle. Filmed without studio techniques, it had a fresh, improvisational quality. To heighten emotion, De Sica compressed scenes to their core feelings. All of the action takes place on the back streets of Rome, away from the beautiful fountains and piazzas the city is famous for; instead, these are the dirty and crowded buildings where laundry hangs from windows, people toss their garbage in the gutter, and those without jobs hang around in doorways staring at passing strangers. The film achieves an air of authenticity by cutting actual documentary footage into some segments, a technique found today in the films of Spike Lee and Oliver Stone. The film is prominently ranked on almost every critics' annual poll of all-time greats and was extremely influential, especially among directors; the Indian director Satyajit Ray, who saw the film as a young boy visiting Rome, credits it with compelling him to become a filmmaker, and Woody Allen called it an example of near-perfect film direction. De Sica received international acclaim and awards, including an Oscar for Best Foreign Film.

De Sica continued acting to finance some of his own projects; he directed Sophia Loren and Marcello Mastroianni in *Yesterday, Today and Tomorrow* (1964). Vittorio De Sica made twenty-five films in his career and received four Academy Awards, including an Oscar for *The Garden of the Finzi-Continis* (1971), which is not regarded as a neorealist work. His methods made others aware of the beauty that can be plainly captured through the lens.

73

NATALIE KALMUS

Born: January 20, 1892, Boston, MA
Died: November 15, 1965, Boston, MA

*In her reign, Kalmus supervised and guided the intricate color process
on some of the great classics.*

—ALLY ACKER

Inventor Herbert T. Kalmus could never have guessed that his wife's contribution to film history would surpass his own. After all, it was Herbert who created a color method for film. An MIT graduate in 1915, he saluted his alma mater, "Tech," by patenting Technicolor, then waited for Hollywood to make him rich. But Hollywood took its time, and moviegoers sat through many dull experiments with color. Early innovators tried staining or hand-tinting film stock. This resulted in strange night scenes of complete blue, or kissing scenes covered in red. Color was inconsistent, its gradual development lacked the overnight impact of sound, and talkies had proved they could succeed in black and white, so most movie studios had given color the pink slip.

Still, Natalie Kalmus wouldn't let interest in color wane. She campaigned tirelessly for Technicolor, pitching studio heads and traveling abroad to educate foreign filmmakers. With all of her efforts, however, feature film studios remained reluctant to purchase the technology. Finally, Natalie came upon a better idea—after years of looking for buyers, she would start looking for renters. Essentially, Natalie Kalmus turned the process of Technicolor into a full-blown service.

Kalmus's "package deal" was a complete crayon box for studios. Traditionally, color was used sparingly in films to save cost: the 1925 *Ben-Hur* used color only in biblical scenes. But Kalmus offered the equipment, cameramen, and makeup, costume, set, and prop designers, all for a flat rate. She leased to producers an entire team of Technicolor experts, and her laboratory was solely responsible for the final output.

An extreme perfectionist, Kalmus learned the business of making movies in the studio system and tailored her organization to fit the needs. She was part technician, part artist, part entrepreneur, and she studied the technical aspects of the process thoroughly. She became a master of color, understanding its place in dramatic composition and its power to affect emotions. Because Technicolor required intense light, she learned to counter the effects of reflected glare on certain colors by hand-picking fabrics, paints, and makeup to achieve distinct contrast between neighboring hues. When her color needs couldn't be met on the set, she had her staff develop special dyes to correct the problem in the lab. In many cases, she was involved with a film for as long as the director, being present from planning stage until the final prints were made.

Despite a year of delivering a distinct color signature on films like *The Adventures of Robin Hood* (1938) and *The Wizard of Oz* (1939), Kalmus was having trouble justifying the high costs of Technicolor. As 1939 approached, she feared color was on the block again. *Gone With the Wind* (1939) changed all that. Its brilliant use of color placed the film far ahead of the other outstanding films of that productive year. Studio executives then put Technicolor at the top of their wish list for the really big productions. Kalmus's contribution to *Gone With the Wind* all but secured the future of color films.

Kalmus struck a seven-year sweetheart agreement with Walt Disney granting him exclusive use of Technicolor in animated films, making the process popular in animation departments. She also made trips abroad several times a year to help other film industries develop a Technicolor process. In 1948, she packed an entire crew and flew to England to train British crews extensively on appropriate use of color in costumes, makeup, and set design. Her suggestions were right on the mark for Michael Powell's *The Red Shoes* (1948) and the ballet melodrama became the exemplary Technicolor film.

Although Kalmus had several capable lieutenants, she tackled the toughest assignments herself. Director John Ford wasn't much for consultants, but he carefully listened to Kalmus when he used Technicolor on *She Wore a Yellow Ribbon* (1949). She explained to Ford that many directors overused the process and didn't take advantage of her ability to custom-manufacture special hues. Ford gave her great latitude, and *Yellow Ribbon* was truly a joint effort between the two, defining the look of the color western.

Kalmus enjoyed a monopoly for close to twenty-five years. Virtually every color film made between 1925 and 1950 (representing 12 percent of all Hollywood features over that time) was produced using Technicolor, and Natalie insisted that her name be credited as color consultant on every one. Throughout the forties, she made $65,000 annually. When the Kalmus patent expired, in 1949, the Eastman Kodak Company was ready to dethrone Queen Natalie and introduced a rival process. By 1952, the studios no longer needed Technicolor's specialized equipment and expensive consultants. The vogue for wide-screen and 3-D movies, which couldn't be produced with Technicolor cameras, hastened the demise. Even studios who used the process to make their original master prints could no longer afford the expense of Technicolor, so when it came time to make duplicate prints, many Technicolor classics were sent out in a cheaper two-color process.

Natalie Kalmus saved color films from an early death, and her legacy remains—color films prevailed. By 1954, more than 50 percent of American features were made in color, and the figure reached 94 percent by 1970. Today, black-and-white films cost more to make than color films. Her Technicolor company is still in business, using a different, more economical procedure to get color results. Preservationists like director Martin Scorsese are championing the return of the process, which they find superior in quality and best for longevity.

74

GENE SISKEL
Born: January 26, 1946, Chicago, IL

ROGER EBERT
Born: June 18, 1942, Urbana, IL

*They are the most recognized, the most watched, and the most
influential critics in the world.*

—DONALD LIEBENSON

Born on Chicago's north side, Gene Siskel graduated from Yale and joined
the *Chicago Tribune* in 1969, when journalism was in its heyday and the
"American New Wave" was taking over cinema. Films were suddenly very
hot, and papers were leaning toward first-person opinions. After the success
of Judith Crist at the *New York Herald-Tribune,* it suddenly became fashionable to have dedicated film critics rather than gossip columnists covering
the arts. Siskel became the *Tribune's* film critic with a twice-a-week column,
which has lasted more than nineteen years. In 1975, WBBM-TV introduced
his opinions to television audiences.

Later that year, a local TV producer capitalized on a crosstown rivalry
between Siskel and a newspaperman from the *Chicago Sun-Times* as the basis
for a new kind of television show. Roger Ebert, who had recently become the
first film critic to win the Pulitzer Prize for Distinguished Criticism, would share
his opinions on newly released movies with Siskel during the half-hour program.

A product of Urbana, Illinois, Ebert began a newspaper career at age
fifteen as a sportswriter and worked his way through school. He was a Ph.D.

candidate in English at the University of Chicago before dropping out to become a film critic in 1967, when he began reviewing films for the *Chicago Sun-Times*. Before joining the television show, he had produced a 1973 TV special, *The World of Ingmar Bergman,* and had also followed in the footsteps of James Agee and other critic-screenwriters by scripting the cult film *Beyond the Valley of the Dolls* (1970).

Together, these experienced journalists picked apart movies and each other at the same time. The show struggled at first, but through appearances on public television, it built a following among those yearning for a critical film vocabulary. A slew of copycat programs followed in the early 1980s. Although many of them emulated the format exactly, viewers remained loyal to the original, responding to its authentic feel. In Siskel and Ebert, they saw two genuine, well-informed newspapermen energetically defending personal opinions in front of millions of onlookers.

The "thumbs up, thumbs down" trademark that embodied the sum of their comments didn't appear until 1986, eleven years into their partnership, but the famous signal, conceived by Ebert, quickly became the gauge that millions looked for in advertisements. The power of their thumbs still frightens today; those simple gestures can make or break a movie's opening-week receipts. Many studios lock S&E out of advance screenings and refuse to provide the show's producers with movie clips or trailers, giving up national exposure to avoid receiving a disfavorable digit.

Their influence has also saved some films from premature death. Documentary filmmaker Errol Morris benefited from the attention they gave his offbeat *Gates of Heaven* (1978) when most of the mainstream media did not even review his film. Director Louis Malle's intellectual *My Dinner With Andre* (1981), from a script by Wallace Shawn, was having trouble holding theater bookings until Siskel and Ebert gave it "two enthusiastic thumbs up"; it added additional showings and eventually had nine hundred playdates nationwide. Billy Bob Thornton got a career boost when the critical pair pointed to his excellent script for *One False Move* and his stellar work in *Sling Blade,* a film headed straight for video that went on to earn Thornton an Oscar.

The weekly broadcast has also provided the critics with a platform for championing the merits of such technologies as laserdisc and digital videodisc (DVD). They have been instrumental in educating the public about the ongoing efforts to preserve classic films, and they have used their show to draw support for the fight against film colorization, often hailing black-and-white films in special editions of the program.

The continuing expansion of their influence is astounding; Siskel provides film criticism on the *CBS This Morning* program, and Ebert posts his electronic reviews for millions of subscribers to CompuServe's online service.

Both men have their columns nationally syndicated in more than three hundred combined newspapers. The various film books of Roger Ebert alone have sold more than seven hundred thousand copies.

Now into its twentieth season and the winner of five Emmy Awards, Siskel and Ebert's program is aired on 180 U.S. stations, and the straightforward commentary of the bickering midwesterners is reportedly broadcast to a staggering 95 percent of all television sets in the nation.

75

WILLIS O'BRIEN

Born: March 2, 1886, Oakland, CA
Died: November 8, 1962, Los Angeles, CA

*O'Brien was a bloody genius, you know. He was the best trick man
in the business. Nobody in his class.*

—MERIAN C. COOPER

Willis O'Brien was a San Francisco cartoonist when the sculpting bug bit
him in 1913. A year later, he began making small replicas of prehistoric creatures in his garage at night, molding rubber to a wooden figurine with move-
able joints, then filming them moving against miniature sets. Working alone,
O'Brien invented almost all of the commonly used practices of a process
known as stop-motion animation—techniques that have remained relatively
unchanged for eighty years.

After completing a number of shorts for Edison's Biograph company,
including his first film, *The Ghost of Slumber Mountain* (1918), O'Brien first
used his innovative techniques in his animated sequences of several mon-
strous beasts in *The Lost World* (1925), a feature-length film starring Wallace
Beery. The story involves an Amazon expedition's encounter with a world of
strange prehistoric beasts that battle with each other for survival. In the film's
climax, several of the dinosaurs escape captivity and terrorize the citizens of
London. The two-hour film was all but destroyed in 1929, when an ambitious producer ventured to make a remake and burned all the existing prints
to prevent unfavorable comparisons. Some 16mm copies surfaced later;
trimmed in half so its running time coincided with the schedules and atten-

tion spans of young audiences, the film was shown in elementary schools. Those who have seen it are entranced by its thrilling re-creations of dinosaurs that come to life, and the concept has been duplicated endlessly ever since. Animator Bob Clampett cites *The Lost World,* particularly a scene in which a long-necked dinosaur swims under the ocean, as the inspiration for his sea serpent puppet in the popular 1950s Beany and Cecil TV show. Steven Spielberg recalls its startling jungle scenes as the inspiration for *Jurassic Park* (1993) and its sequel, which took the name of O'Brien's seminal film.

By the 1930s, Hollywood had a bad case of jungle fever, setting dozens of features like *Tarzan the Ape Man* (1932) in the Dark Continent. Sparked by a trip to Africa, producer Merian Cooper sought to blend O'Brien's striking effects with a good story. The final script became the most famous and influential special effects film ever made, one that coined the term "monster movie." *King Kong* (1933) led Depression-era audiences to a mysterious place where ancient creatures fight savagely for survival and villagers live in fear of the beast called Kong—a name created to emulate the short, rough sound of the title of Cooper's documentary *Chang* (1927). Originally *Kong: The Eighth Wonder,* the title was shortened to *King Kong* after scriptwriter Ruth Rose wrote the line "He was a king in the world he knew."

To this day, *King Kong* is regarded as the masterwork in stop-motion technique. O'Brien's ability to combine live action seamlessly with animation created the illusion that New York City really was under attack. Meticulously scaling several models of the giant gorilla, O'Brien often labored on his own for months to create just seconds of screen magic.

Also important to O'Brien's work was the mixing of live-action mechanical models with stop-motion animated footage. One particularly exhilarating shot in *The Lost World* features the large, intricate head of a brontosaurus poking into a window, an effect O'Brien created using a large armature attached to a crane. Close to the finale of *Kong,* the ape chases Fay Wray to a hotel in a scene that illustrates O'Brien's attention to detail and sophisticated mix of live action and stop-motion animation. O'Brien, using two sets, one full-scale and one miniature, cuts between real car crashes, a miniature hotel marquee hurling through the air, fleeing pedestrians, and, ultimately, a real marquee smashing into pieces; as the ape rips the sign from the building, faint clouds of dust add to the realism. This subtle mix of small models with large mechanical beasts is standard today; witness *Jurassic Park.*

Inspired by O'Brien's animation in *King Kong,* a small army of young storytellers appeared, kids with home-made figurines and 16mm cameras. Legendary special effects man Phil Tippett, who gave life to the menacing AT-AT walkers in the ice fight of *The Empire Strikes Back*, and created life-like dinosaurs for *Jurassic Park* and its sequel, cites O'Brien as a mentor. Spielberg, George Lucas, Will Vinton, and George Pal all received their first glimpse of their futures by watching O'Brien creatures at work. O'Brien gave his most famous disciple, the young animator Ray Harryhausen, his first shot at moviemaking with *Mighty Joe Young* (1949), another story about a giant ape, which scooped up the Academy Award for O'Brien. Harryhausen would later score big on his own with *The 7th Voyage of Sinbad* (1958) and carry the torch of stop-motion technique into a new generation of films, among them *RoboCop* (1987).

The movie monsters of *Jaws* (1975) and *Alien* (1979) owe their eyeteeth to O'Brien. His *King Kong* continues to tower above the classic fantasy films of all time. It has been shown on television more than any other film. Memorabilia is still in high demand—an original poster sold for $112,500 in 1994. To this day, Kong remains the Eighth Wonder of the World, and O'Brien stands alone as the pioneer of a unique film craft.

76

SHIRLEY TEMPLE

Born: April 23, 1928, Santa Monica, CA

I look forward to Shirley someday winning as great a popularity as an actress as she has as a child star.

—JOSEPH SCHENK

While enrolled in dance class at the age of three, Shirley Temple was plucked from a pack of tiny beauties and tested for a new series of kid pictures from the Hal Roach studios called Baby Burlesks. Designed to capitalize on the success of Roach's Little Rascals, the idea behind the Burlesks series was to have little girls mimic the flirtatious vamps so popular in adult features of the period. Among the talented toddlers, Shirley gave some of the most sophisticated impersonations of modern-day stars.

The charm of the tiny performer emerged over the next few years in a series of supporting roles until *Stand Up and Cheer* (1934) established her undeniable maturity at age five. She could sing and dance with the best of them, but it was her stunning ability to talk to adults on a deeply emotional level that warmed the hearts of audiences and made her an international phenomenon.

She was hailed as the face of prosperity and helped to lift the spirits of a nation following the stock market crash of 1929. Other Depression-era stars like Fred Astaire provided escapism for audiences, but Shirley awakened the hopes for the coming generation. Children loved her movies, adults were astounded by her genuine determination and relentless optimism, and 20th Century–Fox was counting its blessings with record hits like *Little Miss*

Marker (1934) and *Baby Take a Bow* (1934). The height came with *Bright Eyes* (1934), which produced her popular song "Good Ship Lollipop."

A special Oscar "in grateful recognition of her outstanding contribution to screen entertainment" was awarded to Shirley in 1934, her first year of feature acting. Toys exploited her charming smile; drinks were named after her; and big names like Gary Cooper signed to costar with her. At her best, Shirley's performances were not simply the standard for child acting but rivaled those of many of the period's full-grown stars. Each subsequent film was increasingly profitable, and by 1935 she was a star with a huge following that flocked to *The Little Colonel* (1935), *Wee Willie Winkie* (1937), and *The Little Princess* (1939). At the box office, she outperformed all other actors in 1938.

The original choice for Dorothy in *The Wizard of Oz* (1939), Shirley lost out to Judy Garland. Seeking a new image, she selected roles in films that focused on the problems of teenagers in *I'll Be Seeing You* (1944), *Since You Went Away* (1944), then tried to ease into ingenue parts in *The Bachelor and the Bobby-Soxer* (1947) and *Fort Apache* (1948). But her efforts were in vain. As is the fate of many child actors, like Jackie Coogan, her popularity waned as she entered her teens. The audiences that adored her as a child simply didn't follow her into a new career. Sensing her appeal had forever vanished, she "retired" in a celebrated event held by her studio in 1949.

Already an American institution, she entered Republican Party politics in the late sixties in San Francisco. A bid for a California seat in Congress failed in 1967, but President Gerald R. Ford appointed her U.S. ambassador to Ghana. In her own lifetime, she has seen her films broadcast weekly on television and her image immortalized in works of art.

Temple's instant rise and subsequent fall made child actors and their families aware of the questionable longevity of a film career, prompting them to take proper care in investing their profits from early success and to position themselves to ease the transition into adult roles. Among those to benefit from her example were Elizabeth Taylor, Roddy McDowell, and Ron Howard, among many others.

77

YAKIMA CANUTT

Born: November 29, 1895, Colfax, WA
Died: May 24, 1986, Hollywood, CA

Yakima Canutt, the first and perhaps the best of the great stuntmen,
transformed a suicidal gamble into a modern profession.

—CHARLTON HESTON

Stuntmen who journeyed to Hollywood in the 1920s most likely found work in the breakneck comedies of Mack Sennett or the cowboy vehicles of Tom Mix. Mix was a perfectionist who swore that audiences could tell a real cowboy from a fake, so he recruited heavily from rodeos and ranches. In 1917, Mix met a trick rider named Eddie Canutt, who was often billed as "the Man from Yakima."

Yakima Canutt, or "Yak," followed Mix to Hollywood, where over the next fifteen years he worked steadily as a cowboy actor and stuntman. Specializing in horse falls and wagon wrecks, Canutt built a solid reputation as a man who would come on in the final scene of a western and leap from the hero's horse to tackle a villain on the run. He was frequently used as a second-unit director on action westerns, also serving as stunt double for every actor in the production, even the women. During this active period, Canutt claimed he had broken every bone in his body.

In 1920, he met an unknown actor named John Wayne. From Yak Canutt, Wayne learned the nuances of a real cowboy, how to handle a horse and take a punch. In fact, the Duke was on the scene when Yak made one of his great contributions to movies—the art of the screen punch. To add to the realism of movie fights, he positioned the camera to film an actor over the shoulder of the actor throwing the punch, so his fist could pass several inches in front of the target's face while giving the illusion of a direct hit. The choreography of the punch in fight scenes is, of course, a staple of all action films.

Yakima Canutt would go on to be a stunt double for Wayne in a variety of roles, but taking punches for John Wayne wasn't the extent of his portfolio. He would jump into a saddle from a second-story window or lead a horse straight off a cliff. His talent for executing a series of hair-raising stunts, precisely planned, made him the popular production specialist in Hollywood, and the credit "Action by Yakima Canutt" appeared on many of his films.

Seeking to minimize his injuries, he devised mechanisms that went unnoticed by the camera but triggered actions that made stunts safer and more predictable. He cleverly rigged his stirrups to break open and release his foot at the proper time and his cable rigs became the standard means of training horses to fall as if a bullet had stopped them short. Many of these tricks were adapted from rodeo; their unconventional methods were initially controversial, but Canutt invited Humane Society inspectors to judge his work and documented safety rules for other productions using animals.

After hundreds of silent horse operas, the physical demands caught up with the aging performer. Yak made a clever transition from stunt double to coordinator and reserved his body for special occasions only. One was *Gone With the Wind* (1939). He stood in for Clark Gable, navigating a horse-drawn wagon around the falling buildings of Atlanta as it burned; in another memorable scene, he took a bullet in the face from Scarlett O'Hara, then tumbled backward down a flight of steps. He was forty-four years old at the time.

Another special case was John Ford's *Stagecoach* (1939). Canutt was hired to supervise the stunts, but when the time came for the dangerous work, he stepped in as both cowboy and Indian—even portraying a woman. The climactic scene, involving a runaway stage, required Yak to leap to a coach railing to the team of horses before drawing the stage to a halt. Well into his sixties, the cowboy star worked on the epic chariot race in Cecil B. DeMille's *Ben-Hur* (1959) and contributed to *Spartacus* (1960) and *El Cid* (1961). His work in later years included stunts with motorcycles and automobiles, and his choreography of a spectacular car chase in *The Flim-Flam Man* (1967) is widely regarded as the all-time best example of high-speed thrills.

Yakima Canutt made hundreds of films in his prolific career, and some of his finest are still available on video, including *Wild Horse Canyon* (1925), *The Devil Horse* (1926), and *The Iron Rider* (1927). He was awarded the only special Oscar presented for stunt work, in 1966, for making it not only more artistic but also safer. He lived to the age of ninety, remained active in films until 1976, and helped establish his son in the same profession.

Every day, hundreds of stunt performers are acutely aware of his influence. He made his biggest impact on the profession through the vast number of safety guidelines he conceived and documented. By generously passing on a legacy of knowledge and skill, he elevated the stunt profession to become a vital part of the artistry of film.

78

SAM PECKINPAH

Born: February 21, 1925, Fresno, CA
Died: December 28, 1984, Inglewood, CA

Violence, with Peckinpah, sometimes becomes a psychic ballet.

—ROGER EBERT

Sam Peckinpah spent his formative years as an assistant to Don Siegel, the director who would later make the Dirty Harry films starring Clint Eastwood. Both Eastwood and Peckinpah would become forever connected to screen violence in the western, but while Eastwood simply refined the style of the genre, Peckinpah explored its soul.

Peckinpah was first placed in the saddle writing and directing episodes of western series, including *Gunsmoke* and *The Rifleman,* in the early days of television. A 1957 rough outline of a script for *One-Eyed Jacks* (1961) led to a bizarre portrayal of Billy the Kid by method actor Marlon Brando, and a directing exercise titled *The Losers,* on TV's *Dick Powell Theater* in 1963, employed startling slow-motion gun battles, a celebrated effect that Peckinpah would use to excess in later films.

His introduction to Hollywood moviemaking was rocky; he battled with studio executives over the production of his first feature, *Major Dundee* (1965) and was virtually blacklisted for being too difficult. However, his brutal and disturbing *Straw Dogs* (1971) raised the controversial Peckinpah into the echelon of Arthur Penn, Francis Ford Coppola, and other directors who were putting a personal stamp on films inside long-established genres. These artists were referred to as the purveyors of the American New Wave, the result of French film influences on Hollywood.

Next, a trilogy of stylistic, elegiac horse dramas addressed the mythological masculinity of cowboys, a theme that would flow through the rest of Peckinpah's work, starting with the release of *The Wild Bunch* (1969). *Wild Bunch* did have important impact; first, it stripped away all of the heroic values that John Ford had created in his years of making outstanding westerns with John Wayne. Unlike the majestic pillars of the Monument Valley settings in Ford's films, Peckinpah's locations were bleak and unvarnished, and the violence was gratuitous and realistic. Also, the actions of cowboy stars in Peckinpah stories were predicated on the thematic message, not a personal code. The unspoken rules of the macho cowboy no longer applied. There was no moral clarity in the films. The extended and unjustified violent outbursts of gunslingers became a metaphor for misguided attempts to resolve situations that had no distinct right and wrong sides.

By the time Peckinpah's next films, *Junior Bonner* (1972) and *Pat Garrett and Billy the Kid* (1973), had finished their runs, some critics had convicted him of killing off the western. On the other hand, he has been credited with turning the genre from moral simplicity to moral complexity. His elegiac tones and lyrical execution make it almost impossible to watch typical action westerns with the childlike excitement they once invoked. Ironically, it would be twenty-five years before Clint Eastwood's *Unforgiven* (1992) would restore order to the western, tipping its hat to both the beauty of Ford's calm and the conscience of Peckinpah's chaos.

Peckinpah's greatest influence on film was through his handling of violence. The masterful slow-motion scenes in *Wild Bunch* reverberated throughout the films of the 1970s. The technique became synonymous with its director. It was imitated in shootouts in cop dramas and gangster films, and spoofed in comedies. Recently, the work of Robert Rodriguez in *El Mariachi* (1992) and *Desperado* (1995) has mocked the slow-motion style by bringing it to a crawl.

Though the term "cathartic" had been applied to the violent nature of his earlier work, Peckinpah was later blamed for simply glorifying violence in *The Getaway* (1972) and *Bring Me the Head of Alfredo Garcia* (1974), and the ensuing increase in tasteless and irresponsibly violent films is often attributed directly to him.

Still, Peckinpah sparked a debate about violence in films that surfaces perenially—it seems every year brings a real life crime that its perpetrators claim was inspired by a movie. Few directors have affected the way in which action scenes are choreographed and recorded. In an effort to emulate the stylized sequences that Peckinpah repeatedly produced, a slew of talented filmmakers, from Martin Scorsese to Quentin Tarantino, have added even more bullet holes and blood to their climactic shootouts. Few, however, ever achieve the elegiac quality that Peckinpah infused, even during his most chaotic screen moments.

79

JACKIE COOGAN

Born: October 26, 1914, Los Angeles, CA
Died: March 1, 1984, Santa Monica, CA

The boy was one of the miracles of the movies.
—KEVIN BROWNLOW

The ambition of a stage mother both created and destroyed the film career of Jackie Coogan. His parents had placed the talented youth in vaudeville stage shows at an early age. One day while passing a restaurant, the Coogans noticed screen star Charlie Chaplin exiting a side door and approached with little Jackie in tow. They introduced the child to Chaplin and invited the famous comedian to an afternoon performance. When he saw the precocious six-year-old hamming it up on stage later that day, Chaplin was captivated.

A child with a sparkling countenance, Jackie first appeared in a film when he was eighteen months old, sitting patiently through *Skinner's Baby* (1916). When Chaplin gave him a brief screen role in *A Day's Pleasure* (1919), featured alongside the Little Tramp character, he was impressed by how Coogan handled his suggestions and immersed himself in a scene. Chaplin believed the youth had a future and decided to feature Jackie in his next film.

Chaplin's *The Kid* premiered in New York City in January 1920 to packed houses and made Coogan a household name. It was a highly anticipated event and soon became the all-time box office leader, surpassing D. W. Griffith's *The Birth of a Nation*. In the film, Coogan's sad-eyed waif upstaged Chaplin with a tremendous range of emotions that seemed beyond a child of his age. He was hailed as a new sensation. Coogan's parents complained that despite the huge receipts from the film, they made nothing. Chaplin, who despised the forthright Mrs. Coogan, offered to secure a position for Jackie's father at the First National studio at an inflated salary.

Meanwhile, Jackie Coogan went to work on other First National productions, including the popular *Peck's Bad Boy* (1921). Like all Chaplin protégés, Coogan was seen internationally, so his following was immense. He performed in a number of young adult roles based on literary classics—*Oliver Twist* (1922), *Little Robinson Crusoe* (1924), *Tom Sawyer* (1930), and *Huckleberry Finn* (1931).

It's hard to exaggerate the success of Jackie Coogan. His fame made him the first major Hollywood child star, a crown he would carry for twenty-three films over a lucrative ten-year period. In 1923, his parents decided to switch studios from First National to MGM, where they agreed to a historic contract that provided a signing bonus of $500,000, an additional $22,000 a week as salary, and a 60 percent stake in the profits from all his films, the first being the appropriately titled *Long Live the King* (1923). Little Jackie was suddenly one of the highest-paid stars in Hollywood. He became a millionaire before Shirley Temple was even born.

His entire life became front page news, and a well-publicized haircut was filmed for posterity in *Johnny Get Your Hair Cut* (1927). With puberty came declining popularity, and by the mid-thirties he was washed up. He tried many comeback attempts but never completely succeeded. In 1935, an auto accident claimed his father's life and killed three others; Jackie was in the car at the time, but survived. The tragedy indirectly resulted in a landmark legal decision that forever protected the rights of child actors.

Coogan's widowed mother married Arthur Bernstein, a friend of the family and formerly Coogan's business manager. Jackie suspected that the newlyweds were frivolously spending his fortune, so in 1938, at the age of twenty-four, he asked his parents for a portion of the $4 million he had amassed as a star. His new stepfather refused. Coogan sued to collect, but a loophole in the law enabled the couple to whittle away his childhood earnings before the courts settled the dispute. By the time the trial started, the sum had dipped to just $700,000. Coogan was awarded half and, after paying his legal fees, collected less than $250,000.

However, as a result of the case the California legislature passed the Child Actors Bill, designed to protect the assets of child stars; it is commonly referred to as the Coogan Act. Thanks to Coogan, young movie actors' income is managed by the court and financial specialists.

He married the leggy Betty Grable in 1937, but had to struggle to support her, and they were divorced just three years later, in part because of the intense emotional strain from the trial. Coogan was effectively blackballed in the film business by his stepfather, a popular and powerful producer. After army service in World War II, Coogan kicked around film lots but found greater success in television as the perpetual optimist Uncle Fester on *The Addams Family*.

In the mid-1970s, Coogan was instrumental in the re-release of *Oliver Twist*, a film that had been lost for fifty years. A negative print with no intertitles had been recovered in Yugoslavia. The film, starring horror icon Lon Chaney as Fagin and Coogan as Oliver, was edited together with the assistance of Coogan's recollections and released to the home video market. It contains moments of stunning poignancy thanks to a child star whose tribulations resulted in the legal precedent that protects all young actors to this day.

80

FEDERICO FELLINI

Born: January 20, 1920, Rimini, Italy
Died: October 31, 1993, Rome, Italy

I prefer cinema of lies, lies are much more interesting than truth.
—FEDERICO FELLINI

Federico Fellini had written scripts for Roberto Rossellini before coming into his own as a director of impressive films in the 1950s, when the form in vogue was neorealism, a rough-hewn documentary approach to giving films a more realistic feel. By the 1960s, Fellini's work began to change and reflect a flamboyance that would mark him as a unique visionary. He was among the few film storytellers to document his entire life through his body of work. His films adopted metaphorical images, like Ingmar Bergman's, but Fellini infused his movies with surreal sequences that did for cinema what Picasso had done for painting.

A onetime crime reporter and caricaturist, Fellini began his film career with original stories for Rossellini's *Ways of Love* (1948). From scripting sympathetic characters, he advanced to directing startling performances with the powerful debut of *La Strada* (1954). Poetic and moving, it revealed Fellini's ability to mix the grotesque with the sublime. Instantly, his name gained international attention.

Widespread acceptance of Italian films was achieved through *La Dolce Vita* (1960), which matched the depth of its story with striking and unforgettable images, particularly scenes of Anita Ekberg, the film's sex interest, playfully kicking up water in Rome's landmark Trevi Fountain. The reflective, intelligent drama about soul searching left an impression on young filmmakers, Woody Allen and Paul Mazursky prominent among them. It received overwhelming critical support and was a box office success despite condemnation from both the Catholic Church and the Italian government, which felt the film mocked religion and exploited the ills of society.

By the time the furor over *La Dolce Vita* died down, Fellini was lionized throughout the world. Unprepared for this sudden attention, he became paralyzed by the global fixation on him, began to feel suffocated by his creativity, and struggled to summon the will to make another film. After months of reclusion, he resurfaced with a film that brilliantly made light of his own personal panic: *8½* (1963), an acerbic satire on celebrity status. With his demons behind him, Fellini forged ahead to *Juliet of the Spirits* (1965), his first color film. Like their predecessors, both films garnered unflagging raves from reviewers and fans, and Fellini was well on his way to legendary status as a filmmaker with a singular style.

By *Fellini—Satyricon* (1970), depicting the bawdy adventures of pre-Christian bisexuals, the look of Fellini's films had changed. His newfound signature featured absurdist humor and crisp, vivid images from extreme and unusual viewpoints. During this period, Fellini pushed the limits of his craft and set the tone for the bizarre fantasies with which he would be closely identified. His most fantastical scenes, featuring intense color, striking makeup and costumes, radical camera angles, and a host of eccentric and outlandish characters, would soon show up in the dream sequences and nightmarish flashbacks of thousands of films by others. Such scenes prompted the coining of "Fellini-esque," describing a collage of dream sequences which reflect real-life fears and paranoia.

As his work became less focused, Fellini indulged his own eccentricities to excess. There were some financial failures and critical disappointments before *Amarcord* (1974) reaped his fourth Oscar as Best Foreign Language Film. Unfortunately, his visions now required bigger budgets, and his sporadic box office returns scared investors away. By the 1980s, the damage was done: no one was willing to finance his surreal fantasies. He completed his last film, *Voice of the Moon*, in 1990 with his own money.

Fellini was awarded a special Oscar for lifetime achievement in 1993. As do the autobiographical films of Ingmar Bergman and Woody Allen, Fellini's stories assumed a distinctive style that was marked by bold exploration of the human psyche. The day after his fiftieth wedding anniversary, he suffered a stroke and went into a coma at age seventy-three, never to recover. The legendary Japanese director Akira Kurosawa expressed the sentiments of film lovers around the world by telling a friend, "Fellini's death has upset me; the idea that we will never again see a new Fellini film is unbearable."

81

LENI RIEFENSTAHL

Born: August 22, 1902, Berlin, Germany

Film is the greatest medium for propaganda ever invented.
—JOSEPH GOEBBELS

Among the most tragic and bewildering stories in film history is the career of Leni Riefenstahl. A director whose captivating films set artistic standards in the medium, she was eventually banished from her country and from her trade, living the rest of her life under a merciless cloud of controversy. Her misfortune was partly a historical one: her rise to glory as a director of international acclaim coincided with the rise of Nazi Germany's bid for world domination.

Leni Riefenstahl was a young ballerina who began dancing in the ethereal mountaineering pictures of director Arnold Fanck in the golden age of German cinematic production. A screen actress of incredibly magnetic allure, with a following as enthusiastic as Dietrich's, Riefenstahl became obsessed with directing. She passed on several offers to act in Hollywood; instead, she grabbed a camera and headed outdoors to begin filming.

With Fanck's encouragement, she formed a production company in 1931 and directed herself in *The Blue Light* (1932), a magical alpine fable. Like Fanck, she had an innate sense of natural lighting and instinctively knew how to photograph the Alps to capture nature's pageantry, but there was visual drama in her indoor setups, too. After much experimentation and guidance from Fanck, she also showed a unique talent for editing. It looked as if Riefenstahl would become one of the world's premiere feature filmmakers.

Her international reputation, however, would come from her first effort at documentary filmmaking, commissioned as a record of the 1934 Nürnberg Nazi rally. If *Triumph of the Will* (1934) was indeed pure propaganda, then pure propaganda never looked so good. Riefenstahl rehearsed extensively to prepare for Hitler's now-famous speech, digging trenches for low-angle shots, building towers for long crowd shots. Then, she edited the images against a soundtrack of marching goosesteppers. The result was a film of rare emotional and visual magnetism. In its propaganda aspect, the film showcased Nazi power to a naive German public, emphasizing unity, superiority, and the charisma of its leader, Adolf Hitler.

Hitler's regime rewarded Riefenstahl with additional funding and equipment for *Olympiad* (1938), a study in the beauty of the Aryan physique filmed during the 1936 Olympic games. Once again, Riefenstahl demonstrated an uncanny command of emotional reactions to imagery. She shot a beautiful nude sequence to open the film, looking back at the origins of the modern Olympics in the ancient games. Her Greece was filled with blond-haired, blue-eyed athletes. Still, the compositions were all interesting, and the film launched widely influential techniques in sports photography that are universally used today in television sports broadcasting. Experimenting extensively, she strapped the camera to everything—moving automobiles, ascending balloons, elevator lifts. Extreme close-ups, low angles, and montage were used gratuitously. She applied the rich sound and lighting techniques used in fictional movies when shooting real life events, extruding documentary footage of high visual impact. No later film about sports has been able to resist the use of Riefenstahl's seminal camera angles and heroic framing. Many directors have credited Riefenstahl's impact on their films; George Lucas has said that the final ceremony in *Star Wars* is taken shot for shot from the presentation of medals in *Olympiad*.

Riefenstahl's effectiveness backfired in the aftermath of World War II. Her apparent collaboration with the Nazi cause made her persona non grata in postwar Germany, and she was threatened with physical harm. She fled to France, where the government briefly imprisoned her. She lived and worked in Africa for nearly two decades before returning to her homeland. Despite every effort to distance herself from the Third Reich, Riefenstahl was castigated by her fans, shunned by the film industry, and deprived of all opportunity to continue practicing her craft.

For the remainder of her ninety-two years, speculation of her knowledge about Hitler's primary aim has loomed over her. In 1982, she participated in a lengthy documentary that attempted to separate the driven artist from the Nazi conspirator, but did little to restore her image. According to Riefenstahl, when she was a young director she was approached by Minister of Propaganda Joseph Goebbels, who never clearly stated his intentions.

Despite her vehement denials to the contrary, historians point to memos between Hitler and Riefenstahl, as well as testimony from survivors, suggesting she clearly understood the assignments. One writer said of Riefenstahl's role in moving mass audiences, "Only a naïf or rank opportunist could have so disingenuously separated the medium from its message."

Political motivations aside, she was a filmmaker of immeasurable potential. Had she not become synonymous with Hitler's mesmerizing image, she could well have become an unstoppable creative force. Other than Orson Welles, she is probably the most untapped filmmaking talent to date, and her work is studied more than any other documentary director's. She is exemplary among women in the trade, and her genius has been cited by directors the world over. Her influence can be seen weekly in the sports broadcasts that borrow heavily from her point-of-view angles, slow-motion sequences, aerial shots, and underwater photography. Her mystical images of nature continually show up in fantasy films and dream sequences.

Her ranking on this list suffers only because of her limited output and the relatively small number of movie lovers who have been exposed to her documentaries. Leni Riefenstahl influenced filmmakers in one other important way: after *Triumph*, documentary filmmakers could no longer be passive observers. Their medium would inherit a whole new scrutiny, as audiences tried to determine the slant of their supposedly objective viewpoint. At the core of her infamy is the question of a director's social responsibility.

82

STEVEN SPIELBERG

Born: December 18, 1947, Cincinnati, OH

Spielberg and George Lucas—they aren't wunderkinder anymore.
They have to produce.

—JUDITH CRIST

Today, the motion picture business is a high-stakes game that requires deep resources to stay competitive. As the average budget for an action movie rises above $100 million, there is little room for films that cannot draw audiences by the millions. Currently considered Hollywood's premiere power broker, self-taught filmmaker Steven Spielberg is perhaps the person most responsible for this condition. His successes have consistently outperformed those of his peers, and collectively his films have been seen by more people than any other director's in the history of Hollywood. This phenomenal track record has pushed Spielberg to uncharted heights in Hollywood and established him as the prototype of the twenty-first-century filmmaker. His films have virtually become entertainment industries in themselves, creating opportunities to franchise film stories and characters into consumer merchandise, multimedia computer games, and television shows. To sustain this long line of profits, every film must be a blockbuster—and nobody creates blockbusters like Steven Spielberg.

Spielberg's short film *Amblin'* (1969) led to an assignment directing Joan Crawford in the pilot episode of Rod Serling's *Night Gallery* series in 1970. For a brief period, he continued directing installments on other series, including *Columbo* and *Marcus Welby, M.D.* His keen sense for dramatic structure earned him a feature-length made-for-TV movie, *Duel* (1971), which became a critical surprise. The film was released theatrically and became a solid commercial success.

After *The Sugarland Express* (1974), he leveraged the rich hertitage of Hollywood's most exciting and profitable genres: fantasy, horror, and science fiction. He realized that films like *Dr. Jekyll and Mr. Hyde, Metropolis, Nosferatu,* and *The Cabinet of Dr. Caligari* had outgrossed many of the films of esteemed directors like Jean Renoir, Charlie Chaplin, and D. W. Griffith. So Spielberg decided to make a monster movie.

Jaws (1975) launched Hollywood's alarming climb to the blockbuster era by becoming the highest-grossing movie of all time, breaking the record set by Francis Ford Coppola's *The Godfather* (1972). *Jaws* was a unique thriller that spawned several sequels and send-ups. It began the summer tradition of competing action films, all vying for the spending money of baby boomers by using action-oriented scripts and special effects. By the time Spielberg's follow-up hit, *Close Encounters of the Third Kind* (1977), was released, he had put himself into a elite stratosphere of huge financial players, where filmmakers could hardly risk a failure.

Inevitably, there would be colossal flops, like the disappointing *1941* (1979), *Empire of the Sun* (1987), *Always* (1989), and the $60 million *Hook* (1991). But along with the flops, there was a steady stream of monumental successes. In *Raiders of the Lost Ark* (1981), which introduced the adventurer Indiana Jones, Spielberg attempted to re-create the feeling that cliffhanger serials had given him as a kid. Two other Indiana Jones movies would follow, both directed by Spielberg, and the character's youth would be chronicled in a George Lucas television series.

By *Raiders*, he had established himself as a director with a rare insight into the type of entertainment that struck a familiar and friendly chord with mainstream audiences. His films were eagerly anticipated, and his name on a film, even if only as producer, assured audiences of quality escapist fare. He topped the box office again with *E.T. The Extra-Terrestrial* (1982), which was immediately hailed as the definitive Spielberg classic, becoming the largest money-maker to date; it was the impetus for dozens of films that put children and aliens together.

Tired of the perception that he was a "soft" director, Spielberg became interested in stories that had more challenges than simply earning enormous receipts. He set out to earn respect for his technical skill with some more thought-provoking projects. His first attempt, the exceptional adaptation of Alice Walker's controversial novel *The Color Purple* (1985), was well received by audiences, but Spielberg's direction was ignored by the Academy. Finally, he received the critical acknowledgment he sought with *Schindler's List* (1993), a sprawling exposé of the Holocaust; it garnered seven Oscars including Best Picture, Best Director, and Best Adapted Screenplay. Subsequently, each film would make more than $100 million, proving that his artful endeavors did not have to come at the expense of ticket sales.

As a savvy executive producer, Spielberg backed *Poltergeist* (1982), *Gremlins* (1984), *The Goonies* (1985), *Back to the Future* (1985), and *Who Framed Roger Rabbit?* (1988), among hundreds of others. Through his production company, Amblin Entertainment, Spielberg diversified into TV projects, including *Amazing Stories*, the daily animated series *Tiny Toon Adventures*, a throwback to the Leon Schlesinger productions of Warner Bros. cartoons, and the undersea adventure *SeaQuest DSV*. Soon, Spielberg's empire became a well-oiled entertainment machine.

Spielberg's business acumen was evident in his $70 million special effects adventure *Jurassic Park* (1993). The most aggressively marketed film in history, its $1 billion worldwide revenues (including merchandising) shattered all previous movie records. His second computer-generated dinosaur film, *The Lost World* (1997), made $100 million in just five days, the shortest time ever.

Steven Spielberg's name at the helm of an entertainment project has come to symbolize a standard of quality that is surpassed only by the Disney studios and the MGM of the forties. With a new production company he cofounded, DreamWorks SKG, he is poised to continue his winning ways. He is able to hand-pick more ambitious projects such as *Amistad* (1997), that allow him to showcase his directorial skills, while keeping a tight grip on more profitable productions that DreamWorks develops by leveraging his considerable clout. His expanded offerings of feature films, TV productions, multimedia projects and merchandise may soon have major studios scrambling to catch up.

83

SAM WARNER

Born: July 23, 1888, Baltimore, MD
Died: October 5, 1927, Los Angeles, CA

*Adding sound to movies would be like putting lipstick
on the Venus de Milo.*

—MARY PICKFORD

The first talking movie was a short test film prepared in 1889 by W. K. Laurie Dickson for demonstrating to Thomas Edison the idea of synchronized sound. Essentially, the sound system featured crude voices recorded on a disk, sort of a gramophone hooked up to a Kinetoscope. The "story" featured assistant Fred Ott saying hello to the inventor. Unfortunately, sound capabilities were extremely costly to distribute in Kinetoscope systems nationally and so they were sold with silent moving images only. The Edison Labs continued with sound film experiments throughout the early days of film, but Edison eventually abandoned sound movies after a fire in his lab destroyed much of the research in 1914. Furthermore, the growing number of movie theaters were being built without sound system of any kind. The future of sound movies seemed grim, but the determination of Sam Warner would shepherd the first genuine talking picture to the screen and quickly secure the future of talkies.

Sam Warner and his three brothers owned a bicycle shop in their hometown of Youngstown, Ohio. Like many others at the turn of the century, they saw motion pictures and became obsessed. In 1903, on the advice of brother Sam, they bought a projector, rented a copy of Edwin S. Porter's *The Great Train Robbery*, traveled to the surrounding mill towns, and moved smoothly into a lucrative business showing moving pictures on tours throughout the Ohio River Valley. Progressing into distribution, the Warners purchased their first theater, located in a two-story building on South Mill Street in New Castle, Pennsylvania.

Sam Warner soon took leadership as the guiding force of the Warners' future. He transformed the company into a film production studio in 1913 and moved the outfit to California in 1917; six years later, Hollywood welcomed the official Warner Brothers Pictures, Inc. Under Sam's care, Warners was known for its tightly budgeted, technically advanced films, including landmark efforts using Natalie Kalmus's Technicolor process.

But Warner pictures struggled in an increasingly competitive marketplace. What Sam felt they needed to leap ahead of the pack was movies with sound. By the mid-1920s, there had already been a number of experiments to produce a workable sound system. The best of the bunch belonged to William Fox's Movietone system, but theater owners were scratching their heads over it because there were problems with amplification and proper synchronization. Many theaters decided against incurring the expense. After all, they were making good profits with silent features; a sound film had yet to prove worthy of the headaches.

One by one, movie studios ditched their plans for the production of sound films, and it looked as though silent movies would prevail forever. Director D. W. Griffith claimed, "When the century has passed, all thought of our so-called talking pictures will have been abandoned." Bucking the trend, Sam Warner persuaded his brothers to invest in a patented device called the Vitaphone. It was an imperfect system, recording music and voices on a coated disc, but it reproduced sound faithfully and synchronized well with on-screen images. To persuade exhibitors of the benefits of the Vitaphone, Sam sent his brothers around the country with a sampling of sound shorts, including the twelve-minute *Don Juan* (1926) starring John Barrymore. The first film with complete synchronization of a musical soundtrack, it also featured some sound effects. However, theater owners were still reluctant; they saw the shorts as novelty films, and what they wanted was a feature-length hit.

The Warners could hardly afford a failure; they were near bankruptcy already. On the other hand, that meant they didn't have anything to lose, either. Sam knew William Fox was still working on the Movietone sound system, and if Fox installed new equipment in exchange for exclusive contracts with key distributors, it would mean certain death for Warner films. So Sam ran out and purchased the rights to *The Jazz Singer,* a Broadway play based on Sampson Raphaelson's 1922 short story "The Day of Atonement," and tried to lure George Jessel into playing the lead. Jessel, however, demanded too much money, so Sam went to entertainer Al Jolson and told him Jessel wanted the part. Jolson jumped at it.

Though confident the sparkling Jolson would carry the first talkie, Sam would never see the premiere. Just twenty-four hours before *The Jazz Singer* (1927) launched a new era in motion pictures, Sam Warner died of a cerebral hemorrhage. His brothers, all rushing from the film premiere to be at his side, also missed one of the most historic moments of the twentieth century.

Warner Bros. *Jazz Singer* was a sensation. Jolson sang several songs and ad-libbed many of the short dialogue sequences. By the time he muttered the immortal line "You ain't heard nothing yet!" audiences were cheering loudly. Lines outside theaters were consistently long for months. The incredible curiosity over *the Jazz Singer,* owing much to the fact that it was the screen debut of one of the year's most talked-about entertainers, convinced theater owners of the merits of sound. The enormous receipts saved the studio from financial ruin and made it invincible. Warner Bros. became the leader in full-length all-talking color films, producing a hundred pictures a year by 1930 and controlling eight hundred theaters worldwide.

Sam Warner's unflagging commitment to *The Jazz Singer* guaranteed the future of sound, but it didn't secure the adoption of the Vitaphone. By 1930, the awkward system of sound-on-disc had been almost entirely supplanted by a host of sound-on-film processes. Nevertheless, Sam Warner's big gamble had paid off. At the first Academy Awards presentation, on May 16, 1929, a special Oscar was presented to Warner Bros. for producing the pioneering talking picture that revolutionized the industry.

84

JEAN-LUC GODARD

Born: December 3, 1930, Paris, France

He's the definitive influence, if not really the first film artist,
of the last decade.

—ORSON WELLES IN 1971

In 1956, several of the French film critics who had made the popular *Cahiers du cinéma* journal so widely read decided to grab their 16-mm cameras and practice what they preached. By 1959, such independently produced films had brought international prominence to three major figures of the New Wave phenomenon. François Truffaut's *The 400 Blows* and Alain Resnais's *Hiroshima, Mon Amour* displayed a sense of exploration and commercial appeal. But the critical acclaim was focused on Jean-Luc Godard, whose Humphrey Bogart homage, *Breathless* (1959), was perhaps the most original film made since Orson Welles debuted with *Citizen Kane.* The film put Godard in the forefront among New Wave directors and created a new set of aesthetics in filmmaking.

Shot without a script, *Breathless* had a loose home-movie quality and bucked all conventions of continuity, camera angles, sound, and narrative. References to American pop culture gave the film an authentic and realistic quality. In one scene, the film's star does an impersonation of Bogart; among its memorable successors is the moment in *Raging Bull* when Robert De Niro, as Jake La Motta, rehearses a Marlon Brando monologue from *On the Waterfront* (1954). Godard's daringly original film marked a reaction against the Hollywood film, and he instantly rose to fame for articulating the postmodern aesthetic of the French New Wave.

Ultimately, the landmark features of *Breathless* would free filmmakers of a narrative language more than six decades old. Godard's success with sparse sets and hand-held cameras signaled to aspiring directors that good movies could be easy to produce and affordable. His use of inconsistent point-of-view angles, shock editing, and jump cuts demystified the craft of editing. The absence of well-constructed plotlines placed greater emphasis on character. In the next four years, hundreds of low-budget films were made by dreamers with no prior experience, and such established artists as Sam Peckinpah, John Cassavetes, Robert Benton, and Arthur Penn borrowed these techniques for their own projects.

A large part of Godard's attraction for filmmakers is his role as an essayist. Many of his films are homages, juggling filmic references from detective, suspense, musical, and comedy genres. Looking to stimulate discussion to promote a greater understanding of the language of film, Godard make movies largely about the making of movies. His startling films showed a confidence in their minimalist approach toward dialogue, scenery, and camera movement. By stripping the process of filmmaking down to its basic elements, Godard hoped to understand what lies at the center of the medium. Often his scenes would continue long after actors had delivered their lines, and even after they had wandered off camera. Godard wanted to elict thought by allowing audiences time to explore the depth of possible meanings in these stark scenes. These unorthodox methods caused some filmmakers to revere Godard as a genius, while others believed his experimental techniques were excessive attempts to regain the sense of groundbreaking work that had brought him such fame with *Breathless*.

Godard remained influential during the 1960s, appearing on the *Cahiers du cinéma*'s list of top filmmakers in every year for a ten-year span. He continued to question traditional filmmaking techniques, preferring the absence of technique altogether, and in subsequent films he continued his intellectual quest for a new narrative structure.

Of all the New Wave artists, Godard remained the most stylized and abstract, continually experimenting with virtually every cinematic convention. Although critics praised these efforts, audiences began to lose their interest. Many moviegoers found his work too intellectually challenging, and others could no longer see the value in his work. Still, there were flashes of his early brilliance in *My Life to Live* (1963), *A Married Woman* (1964), and *Masculine-Feminine* (1966). By *Weekend* (1967), however, most traces of the Godard of *Breathless* were gone, and the New Wave was essentially over.

At the height of his popularity, he was constantly sought after to direct American productions. Screenwriter Robert Benton asked if Godard would direct a script of his that would become *Bonnie and Clyde* (1967). Godard turned down the project; subsequently it was made with a New Wave feel by

Arthur Penn, starring Warren Beatty. During the 1970s, Godard remained prolific but focused on political stories, often made for television. In the early 1980s, he was involved in efforts to secure a large budget for a Hollywood production of a biographical film about Las Vegas founding father Bugsy Siegel. The film was originally set to star Diane Keaton, with Godard directing, but once again Warren Beatty became involved; he produced and starred in *Bugsy* (1991) himself, and Barry Levinson directed.

Godard is a director whose image as a revolutionary new artist often overwhelms his actual influence on the films we see today. Because his later films were heavily introspective and self-indulgent, his international appeal suffered and his following was reduced mainly to curious film students and die-hard fans. For this reason, he is listed well below other directors who have not shared similar adoration. Still, Godard ranks high among the greatest visionaries of the cinematic art form. Although his subsequent films never achieved the stature or influence of *Breathless,* he continues to dominate the best efforts to explore the essence of film.

85

ROBERT DE NIRO

Born: August 17, 1943, New York, NY

I had to decide early on whether I was to be an actor or a personality.
—ROBERT DE NIRO

Robert De Niro is perhaps the finest character actor of his generation, a modern-day Fredric March, handsome enough to play the leading man and plain enough to disappear into roles with just the slightest disguise. He brought authenticity to the screen in the sweeping movement toward realism in films of the 1970s, primarily in roles that examined the darker recesses of the human psyche. Hundreds of movie actors have made obvious attempts to match his intensity, but few are able to exude the subtle complexities that have characterized his performances.

De Niro dropped out of high school in 1960 to pursue a career on Broadway. Joining the Actors Studio, he studied method acting under Marlon Brando's legendary instructors, Stella Adler and Lee Strasberg. Brian De Palma gave De Niro one of his first chances to showcase his talents in *The Wedding Party* (1969) and recommended him for the part of Ma Barker's drug addicted son in Roger Corman's *Bloody Mama* (1970).

An award from the New York Film Critics drew attention to his moving performance as a dying baseball player in *Bang the Drum Slowly* (1973), and when they saw him in *Mean Streets* (1973), audiences knew they were watching someone special. Following Francis Ford Coppola's *The Godfather Part II* (1974), De Niro was called "the New Brando," having gracefully re-created many of the subtle behaviors that Marlon Brando had originated for Don

Vito Corleone. The performance gave De Niro the first Oscar ever awarded twice to the same film character (Brando won it in 1972). Remarkably, at age thirty, De Niro had developed into a counter-culture hero; his name was placed in the titles of hit records and foreign films.

De Niro's gifts were best employed in films that emphasized character over plot, beginning with *Taxi Driver* (1976). As cinema's most memorable psychotic, the haunted and tragic Travis Bickle entered the mainstream cultural fabric as a symbol of our desperate search for fulfillment in an increasingly detached society. In what became the trademark of his technique, De Niro studied for his role: he passed the test for a cab driver's license and cruised New York streets in twelve-hour shifts for several weeks, researched the symptoms of mental illness, and investigated the rituals and superstitions of Vietnam Special Forces veterans.

In a range of compelling performances, De Niro applied more psychological and physical transformations. For *Raging Bull* (1980), he gained sixty pounds to play the faded boxer Jake LaMotta in scenes that represented only minutes of the entire film, and during a sparring session with Joe Pesci, he got lost in the moment and accidentally broke the costar's rib. For the role of Max Cady in *Cape Fear* (1991), De Niro paid an oral surgeon $25,000 to have his teeth temporarily altered to appear ill-tended; he also stained his skin for months with vegetable dye to simulate the look of real tattoos.

These credible transformations characterized the gritty "street" feel in the films of Martin Scorsese, the director with whom De Niro has collaborated more often than with any other. In fact, the success of Scorsese's films is mostly due to De Niro's willingness to immerse himself completely in each role and to go to extreme lengths to understand his characters. Furthermore, securing De Niro as a star in a film was often crucial to the financing of Scorsese's films. In all, they have made eight films together, with a scheduling delay preventing a ninth—De Niro was originally to play Jesus in Scorsese's *Last Temptation of Christ* (1988). It is almost inconceivable to suggest another actor who would have lent the same level of veracity to this body of work, and no other actor has made such an indelible mark on the career of a director since John Wayne last appeared in a John Ford western.

De Niro's depiction of a returning Vietnam War veteran in *The Deer Hunter* (1978) sparked a controversy that cost him the Oscar he deserved in 1978. After Universal Pictures had already spent nearly $250,000 on their Best Actor campaign, there was a backlash from veterans' groups objecting to the suggestion that vets were uncommunicative loners on the brink of committing violent acts. Jon Voight, who played a more appealing vet in *Coming Home* (1978), won the statue. Ironically, *Deer Hunter* garnered awards for director Michael Cimino and the supporting performance of Christopher Walken. In fact, many insiders felt that De Niro's allegiance to New York filmmaking upset Hollywood loyalists in the Academy and was more responsible than the veterans' groups for his loss.

His tour de force in *Raging Bull* did bring him the Best Actor Oscar, and strong performances in *True Confessions* (1981), *Once Upon a Time in America* (1984), and *The Mission* (1986) placed him among the most respected actors of his generation. Cashing in on his ability to produce respectable grosses, De Niro took less challenging roles throughout the eighties and nineties to finance his own New York–based film production company, but his reputation has suffered little over the years.

With his gift of rendering reprehensible antagonists human and complex, De Niro has remained one of the most watchable men in movie history. Critics continue to regard him as a creator of powerful screen characters, and fans are drawn to his films in the hopes of getting a glimpse of the private personality behind the characters. Like Brando before him, Robert De Niro's naturalistic style often feels immediate and improvisational, and his effect on younger actors is reflected in the smoldering intensity and explosiveness of Sean Penn, Johnny Depp, Mickey Rourke, Gary Oldman, Eric Roberts, Michael Madsen, and scores of others.

86

FRED ASTAIRE

Born: May 10, 1899, Omaha, NE
Died: June 22, 1987, Los Angeles, CA

To be in a picture with Fred Astaire was every dancing girl's dream.
—ANN MILLER

Fred Astaire's spirited, inventive dancing was characterized by crisp, coordinated steps. He rehearsed extensively and demanded his partner share his dedication. During the Depression and World War II, Astaire distracted millions of troubled minds by dancing up the walls, over the furniture, on roller skates, and in costumes that ranged from the dapper tuxedo of a gentleman to the disheveled rags of a hobo. He is remembered as the quintessential hoofer, a talented man of modest looks who turned his sense of timing and humble charm into a ticket to stardom. More important, his happy-go-lucky demeanor assured Depression-era crowds that prosperity truly was just around the corner.

Fred was dancing at age four and touring the vaudeville circuit at age seven; his first successful partnership was with his sister Adele. In 1917, the Astaire siblings tapped into international fame with such Broadway hits as *Funny Face* (1927) and *The Band Wagon* (1931). Adele tired of dancing in 1932, and Fred had to find a new partner.

After a famously unflattering Hollywood test, Fred first stepped onto the screen in an obscure number with Joan Crawford in *Dancing Lady* (1933). Later that year, he appeared with Ginger Rogers in *Flying Down to Rio,* their first of their ten films, which included *The Gay Divorcee* (1934), *Top Hat*

(1935), and *Swing Time* (1936). Their routines started international dance crazes, notably the revival of interest in the carioca and fandango, but they were more closely associated with an intimate style of dance that provided an upbeat distraction from the sour spirits of the stock crash. Astaire personally outlined the routines and trained Rogers to keep in step with him. Up on the screen, in perfect harmony, Rogers and Astaire seemed effortless and elegant, caught in a timeless celebration that embodied hope and harmony.

Although exuberance was the key to Astaire's success, he was also driven to experiment with the wide-open possibilities of dancing in films. He choreographed sequences in which the camera turned over to follow him up the walls of a room and across a ceiling; he incorporated firecrackers into tap routines. More fundamentally, he revolutionized the structure of the genre.

Before Astaire, movie musicals were simply revues, a smattering of individual songs and spectacular dance numbers. The films of Busby Berkeley, with their elaborate stage sets and casts of thousands, were the touchstone. MGM's musicals existed primarily to showcase Broadway sensations or present-day hit recordings. Astaire saw other possibilities. He integrated songs and intimate "celebratory" dances that reinforced the plot points or themes of the script. He made his films more story than song and brought sophistication to the musical, substantially revising a long-standing tradition in the movies. Stars of the old-school films, like Al Jolson and Eddie Cantor, saw their popularity wane; musical directors who could not adapt to the integration, like Berkeley himself, found their projects financially undesirable to studios.

In 1946, Astaire temporarily retired; long rehearsals and personal travails had taken their toll, and he required an extended break. After his return, hits such as *Easter Parade* (1948), *Daddy Long Legs* (1955), and *Silk Stockings* (1957) marked Astaire's passage through the brilliant Technicolor era. His partners changed as often as his costumes: Eleanor Powell, Lucille Bremer, Judy Garland, Cyd Charisse, Audrey Hepburn, Leslie Caron, Ann Miller, Vera-Ellen, Barrie Chase, and his personal favorite of them all, Rita Hayworth. He served as an inspiration for the next wave of screen dancers; talents as diverse as Mikhail Baryshnikov, Patrick Swayze, and Gregory Hines credit his example. Inanimate objects often served as willing dance partners: tables, chairs, revolving doors, golf clubs, hat racks. These imaginative routines challenge the creativity of his contemporaries; the legendary Gene Kelly spoke of Astaire as "one of the greatest dancers who ever lived."

In 1949, Astaire was honored with a special Academy Award for his contributions to the musical film. He stopped dancing in 1971 but continued to act in films into the early eighties. The Astaire musical, with its unmatched grace and sophistication, still left plenty of room for the imagination of modern choreographers like Bob Fosse, but Fred Astaire's technical excellence is still regarded as the greatest in the history of film.

87

FRANCIS FORD COPPOLA

Born: April 7, 1939, Detroit, MI

I knew he had a future in film.

—ROGER CORMAN

The son of composer Carmine Coppola, Francis was raised in a New York suburb among a community of Italian-Americans. After earning a master's degree from the UCLA film school, he worked on several soft-core porn films for Roger Corman; then, in 1968, he was offered his first directorial stint, the disappointing *Finian's Rainbow*. But Coppola bounced back. At just thirty-one years old, he won his first Oscar, for the screenplay of *Patton* (1970), and was approached by Paramount for a film adaptation of a story about a family of immigrants.

Paramount had been approached in 1970 by author Mario Puzo, who was peddling a twenty-page screen treatment entitled *Mafia*. He wanted $12,500 for a script and the rights to have a novelization published independently. Paramount agreed, and while Coppola struggled to cast the leading roles for nearly eight months, Puzo hammered out a book. By the time the director was ready to begin shooting, Mario Puzo had a bestseller called *The Godfather*, which had already sold seven million copies.

The Godfather (1972), starring Marlon Brando, became an instant cinema classic, won the Best Picture Oscar, and was the highest-grossing film in movie history. Better still, it was solely responsible for the revival of the gangster movie, a formerly beloved genre that had been lifeless for twenty-five years. Coppola had been asked by leaders of Italian-American organizations to refrain from using the terms "Mafia" and "Cosa Nostra," so Puzo skillfully substituted the word "family," and refocused the picture to be an intimate portrait of generations shaped by a criminal legacy. Hundreds of films that used Mafia subplots would feel compelled to strictly follow the "code of honor" conventions established in *The Godfather.*

Coppola's fame and fortune skyrocketed. He wrote the screenplay for *The Great Gatsby* (1974), then wrote and directed *The Conversation* (1974), which garnered the Palme d'Or at Cannes. It seemed Coppola was at the top of his game. So why, many people asked, would he stoop to taking on a sequel?

The Godfather Part II (1974), a bold telling of parallel stories spanning more than eighty years, sent shock waves through the industry. Filmmakers were amazed that a sequel could be so powerful. Traditionally, sequels were frowned upon by directors, who felt they were traveling old territory for commercial gain exclusively. But *Godfather II* was such an elegant companion piece to the original that the two films looked as if they had been shot together, then edited apart. Legendary director Billy Wilder called the sequel "certainly among the five best American pictures ever made." Producer Philip D'Antoni said he felt a deep sense of regret that he had declined the follow-up to *The French Connection* after seeing Coppola's master handling of the elaborately constructed story, which he cowrote with Puzo. *Godfather II* became the most successful sequel ever, taking in $28.9 million in domestic receipts. It scooped up six Oscars, including one for Robert De Niro. It became the first sequel to win Best Picture, and the first time two actors were awarded Best Actor Oscars for the same character (Brando and De Niro both won honors for portraying Vito Corleone). Shamefully overlooked by the Academy was the artful photography of Gordon Willis, which arguably influenced more cinematographers than any film since *Citizen Kane.*

The *Godfather* films eventually earned more than $800 million combined, and echoed the previous attempts of D. W. Griffith and Edwin Porter to simultaneously build dramatic tension and advance a story by intercutting separate storylines. The slew of Mafia films that followed were pathetic imitations, including *The Godfather Part III,* Coppola's own disappointing reunion.

Next, Coppola turned Joseph Conrad's *Heart of Darkness* into *Apocalypse Now* (1979), a brilliant $30 million war movie that struck an emotional chord at Cannes, where it won the Palme d'Or; it also won two Oscars, for sound and cinematography. *Apocalypse* did for Vietnam battle epics what *Godfather* had done for the gangster genre. The Vietnam War had been presented as a patriotic mission in *The Green Berets* (1968), then movie audiences discovered the psychological horrors of war in *Coming Home* (1978), *The Deer Hunter* (1978), and other films that dealt with returning soldiers. But

Apocalypse, which used a slow and steady stream of disturbing, chaotic images and mesmerizing dialogue to establish the idea of an ever-present enemy, broke a Hollywood taboo by depicting the true nature of combat. The film's vivid graphic battle scenes set the ground rules for all Vietnam War films that followed, including *Casualties of War* (1989) and *Platoon* (1986).

The decade of box office disasters that followed unfortunately established Coppola as a modern-day Erich von Stroheim. *One From the Heart* (1982) was a $26 million preoccupation, and forty different drafts of *The Cotton Club* (1984) couldn't put any jazz into the $48 million sinker. Steady directorial efforts on *Peggy Sue Got Married* (1986), *Gardens of Stone* (1987), and *Tucker: The Man and His Dream* (1988) did nothing to save Coppola's American Zoetrope production company from $30 million in debts and a 1990 bankruptcy. Perhaps the sole artistic high point during this period was his direction of *The Outsiders* (1983) and *Rumble Fish* (1983).

In weighing the considerable contributions of Coppola, one must consider the opportunities he provided an impressive group of young actors. Among those whose careers got started under Coppola's guidance are Matt Dillon, Diane Ladd, Mickey Rourke, Roseanna Arquette, Nicolas Cage, Patrick Swayze, Laurence Fishburne, Rob Lowe, Emilio Estevez, and Tom Cruise. Just as Corman had done for him, Coppola set new talent loose on Hollywood.

Born: November 19, 1938, Cincinnati, OH

I'm going to colorize Casablanca *just to piss everybody off.*

—TED TURNER

In 1970, young Ted Turner used profits from his father's billboard-advertising company to purchase a financially troubled UHF television station in Atlanta, Georgia. Within three years, WTBS was one of the few truly profitable independent stations in the United States, and by 1975, it was the first to broadcast "superstation" programming by satellite to a national audience. After Turner launched the CNN twenty-four-hour news format and Turner Network Television in 1988, he became a media mogul, reaping huge advertising revenues and influencing the viewing habits of millions of people around the world.

His appetite for swallowing companies continued in the mid-1980s. Along with the MGM/UA Entertainment Company he purchased for half a billion dollars in 1986 came the entire Metro-Goldwyn-Mayer archival collection of four thousand films—a stellar library of rare prints, as well as many unseen and many established classics. Seeking to make these films more appealing to television fans, and therefore more profitable, Turner invested heavily in a process that electronically colorizes old films through the use of computers. The era of colorization ushered in the most fevered debates about creative ownership and film preservation since the French legal wranglings over film authorship in the 1930s. Poised to control a significant portion of the world's most endearing classics, Turner alone may determine the future of cinema's past.

The heart of the argument was whether the viewing experience was, and should be, in black and white or whether the limitations of yesterday's technology was simply forcing audiences to watch stories without color. Consumer testing had revealed that many people did not watch movies made in black and white. Turner wished to provide these films with tints and dyes that would approximate the actual colors that would have been visible on the set. He argued that many of these films would have been made in color if issues of technology and prohibitive costs had not prevented it. Turner also went to great lengths to convince his detractors that expert technicians would be consulting photos, storyboard sketches, set paintings, and production notes, and other archival materials in order to determine the proper colors for backgrounds and costumes before tinting the films.

Film historians, critics, professional filmmakers, and fans all protested the process of colorization. They believed that black-and-white films were part of the collective culture and that altering them would be revisionist. They explained that color film stock had indeed been available to some MGM directors who simply preferred the range of moods and emotional overtones achieved best through black-and-white photography; for example, the expressionistic lighting of film noir classics would be rendered ineffectual in color. Furthermore, they argued that it would be inappropriate to "restore" colors by referring to old photos of set pieces, costumes, and props that audiences were never intended to see in color.

But Turner proceeded anyway. On September 9, 1986, the first colorized film, the James Cagney musical *Yankee Doodle Dandy* (1942), was shown on WTBS. Violent protests came from every corner of the film community. Retired directors, including Billy Wilder and Orson Welles, took offense at the idea of altering their works. Contemporary directors, notably Woody Allen, argued that many films were deliberately made in black and white, like *In Cold Blood* (1967), and therefore would not be presented in the spirit of their creators if colorized. Welles's dying wish was to have his lawyers "keep Ted Turner and his goddamned Crayolas away from my movie." In a gesture of goodwill, Turner, who owns the rights to *Citizen Kane,* entered into a legal agreement that protects *Kane* from anything that might alter its original black-and-white imagery.

Turner abandoned his colorization project in 1993 when it became clear that it was an expensive personal indulgence that failed to earn favor with viewers. By that time, nearly 230 movies had been tinted.

One result of the colorization debate was a renewed interest in film preservation. A black-and-white print cannot be colorized unless it is of sufficient quality to handle chemical treatment. Perhaps partly as a way to soften his public image as a destroyer of film, Turner made the decision to fund large restoration projects. Many of Lon Chaney's films, unseen for decades, have recently been preserved in beautiful 35mm prints. Turner Classic Movies, which now holds Warner Bros. and RKO pictures in its growing collection, has theatrical re-release plans for various classics, including *Gone With the Wind* (1939), Robert Wise's *The Haunting* (1963), and John Boorman's thriller *Point Blank* (1967).

A footnote to the debate was a 1996 French court ruling that Turner had violated the rights of director John Huston by televising a colorized version of *The Asphalt Jungle* (1950), a film that Huston had expressly wished to remain unaltered. It was the first decision that stated that "colorization of a black-and-white movie violated the moral rights of its authors." At the conclusion of a legal battle that lasted nearly ten years, Turner was ordered to pay the executor of John Huston's estate, actress Anjelica Huston, damages that totaled roughly $84,000. Today, Turner's stations enjoy worldwide audiences of more than eighty million, and a recent sale of Turner Broadcasting to Time Warner is expected to earn him close to $3 billion in the next five years.

89

CLINT EASTWOOD

Born: May 31, 1930, San Francisco, CA

From laconic TV star to laconic genre star to laconic superstar.
—MICHAEL BARSON

The Old Western was taking a beating in the 1960s. American New Wave directors like Sam Peckinpah and Arthur Penn attempted to revisit the genre and demystify the allure that stalwarts John Ford and John Wayne had spent years solidifying. Overseas, a new actor was interpreting the gunslinger as the nameless hero of Sergio Leone's "spaghetti" westerns. Clint Eastwood would rise through a career of cowboy roles to carry Wayne's torch to a new generation of film lovers. His performances in more than fifty films have left a permanent mark on action roles, and today's macho screen idols are indebted to him for much of their style and delivery.

Eastwood shared billing with a talking mule in *Francis in the Navy* (1955), and his first significant role came in Leone's *A Fistful of Dollars* (1964). Originally titled *The Magnificent Stranger,* and based on Akira Kurosawa's *Yojimbo* (1961), it was the debut of the fearless loner that Eastwood would portray in other Leone westerns shot throughout Spain, Germany, and Italy. *For a Few Dollars More* (1965) and *The Good, the Bad, and the Ugly* (1966) were solid hits in Europe and eventually reached cult status in America. Eastwood, fresh off the trail as Rowdy Yates in television's popular series *Rawhide,* seemed a perfect choice for the postmodern films, playing a moralistic cowboy out of place in a snakepit of nasty caricatures.

Back in the States, Eastwood made *Two Mules for Sister Sara* (1970) and

The Beguiled (1971), establishing himself as the heir to the cowboy throne vacated by the ailing John Wayne. Ironically, these films were directed by Don Siegel, who helped Wayne make a graceful exit in *The Shootist* (1976).

The nihilistic overtones of the Eastwood persona took shape under Siegel's hand in *Dirty Harry* (1971) and its four sequels. The title role was offered to John Wayne, Paul Newman, and Frank Sinatra before Siegel settled on Eastwood. The films about the driven detective Harry Callahan were a backlash against sixties liberalism; feminists and pacifists attached misogynistic and right-wing connotations to the film's ultra-conservative values.

At the height of the feminist movement, Eastwood became the model of masculinity. His laid-back manner and independent spirit were expressed by an economical acting style. His characters spoke only when necessary and revealed their feelings reluctantly. Anything else that needed to be communicated was usually handled in the script with Hollywood's oldest and most frequently used prop—a gun. The liberal bias of the times did not stop Eastwood, and he stayed on the top of box office and celebrity polls for the next twenty-five years.

Eastwood became a respected director himself with *Play Misty for Me* (1971) and almost single-handedly kept the western alive throughout the decade, starring in, as well as directing, *Joe Kidd* (1972), *High Plains Drifter* (1973), and *The Outlaw Josey Wales* (1976). He became the biggest name in westerns since John Wayne, but their acting styles were markedly different. Where Wayne was direct and aggressive, Eastwood was reluctant and lazy. Where Wayne was charismatic and kind, Eastwood was terse and cold. To combat the widespread perception that his range was limited, Eastwood accepted a number of roles in broad comedies and dramas.

Eastwood tried to revitalize the western with *Pale Rider* (1985), but without success. However, *Unforgiven* (1992) became a critical triumph as well as a solid $100 million commercial hit. From a script Eastwood had secured in the 1970s and left undeveloped for over fifteen years, *Unforgiven* was a morality tale set in the West that seemed to defy a postmodern label. It had a new western look, not as antiseptic as John Ford's films and not as gritty as Leone's. It was not particularly romantic, nor was it a sly wink at the past. Essentially it was an elegiac film that restored the power of the genre. It was selected as best film of the year by the National Society of Film Critics and won the Directors Guild Award in 1992. It also collected four Oscars, including Best Picture and one for Eastwood as as Best Director.

Today's screenwriters and action stars work diligently to copy his immortal one-liners, steely delivery, and box office success. Sylvester Stallone, Arnold Schwarzenegger, Bruce Willis, Steven Seagal, Jean Claude Van Damme, and Chuck Norris all rely heavily on the Eastwood influence, muttering glib one-liners under their breath and restricting themselves to minimalist facial expressions—squints, lip curls, gritting teeth. (Leone once said of Eastwood, "He had only two expressions—with a hat and without a hat.")

In four different decades, Clint Eastwood has consistently performed among the elite ranks of superstars. He had an unprecedented twenty-year run in the annual Quigley poll of theater owners' top ten box office draws, and on the overall list of the top draws since 1933 he is preceded only by the Duke. He is the rare action star who has escaped stereotypical roles by financing his own highly artistic endeavors with paychecks earned from his macho roles. And like the Duke, Eastwood is still a leading action hero well into his sixties; *In the Line of Fire* (1993) and *Absolute Power* (1997) were both $100 million blockbusters.

DALTON TRUMBO

Born: December 9, 1905, Montrose, CO
Died: September 10, 1976, Los Angeles, CA

Trumbo took a great big invisible bow.
—ORSON WELLES

When McCarthyism ruled the 1950s, the House Un-American Activities Committee (HUAC) feared that communism was threatening the United States. Focusing their attention on Hollywood, the committee launched an aggressive campaign against the studios—against screenwriters in particular, the men and women who penned the words that HUAC suspected were chipping away at the patriotism of moviegoers. Of all individuals in the film industry forced to testify during the red scare, 60 percent were screenwriters. And the highest-paid screenwriter at the time was Dalton Trumbo.

Trumbo was a novelist who came to commercial and critical success easily with his scripts for *Kitty Foyle* (1940) and *Thirty Seconds Over Tokyo* (1944). His name had come to the attention of McCarthy successor John S. Wood while compiling a list of Hollywood Communists. Wood had extremely thin evidence that leftist messages existed in films, and when asked to produce specific passages of dialogue, he often cited lines that had been scripted by Trumbo.

Trumbo was easy prey for Cold War hysterics; he had actually been a member of the Communist Party and had voiced his left-wing sentiments freely. A high-profile and prolific screenwriter with an excellent track record of profitable films, he had recently signed a contract with MGM for more than $3,000 a week. Most of all, his dialogue was characteristically preachy and tended to espouse liberal ideals.

Wood included Trumbo among a group of nineteen "unfriendlies" in a 1947 subpoena. Eventually, only eleven were called to testify; one of them subsequently bolted the country for Germany. The remaining group became infamous as the Hollywood Ten—Edward Dmytryk, John Howard Lawson, Lester Cole, Albert Maltz, Alvah Bessie, Samuel Ornintz, Herbert Biberman, Adrian Scott, Ring Lardner Jr., and Trumbo.

Fearing the entire picture business itself would be blacklisted, many studio heads rushed to cooperate with HUAC by instituting means of "testing" the political affiliations of their contracted employees. The Hollywood Ten urged their fellow filmmakers to stand firm. They themselves refused to be divided and employed legal representation as a group. Their brave message unified the creative community, and luminaries in other fields, most notably Albert Einstein and E. B. White, lent support publicly and joined in fund-raising efforts. When called before the committee, the Hollywood Ten exercised their Fifth Amendment rights by refusing to act as informers against others or answer any questions about their political beliefs. All ten men were convicted of contempt.

Their appeals went all the way to the Supreme Court, which refused to review their cases, deferring to appellate justice Bennett C. Clark's assertion that "the motion picture industry plays a critically important role in the molding of public opinion and motion pictures are, or are capable of being, a potent medium of propaganda dissemination which may influence the minds of millions of American people." Denied their appeals, the Ten were sentenced in 1949 to prison terms of one year each. Trumbo wrote about his involvement with HUAC and his incarceration in a book called *The Time of the Toad* (1950).

Throughout the fifties, the blacklist took full effect in Hollywood, altering the career paths of hundreds of actors, directors, production specialists, and screenwriters. Many of them were falsely accused. Most found ways to continue working in the industry. While still behind bars, Trumbo began the first of more than thirty screenplays he would sell using several "fronts." He enlisted his friend Ian McLellan Hunter to pose as the writer of *Roman Holiday* (1953) and secretly collected $40,000 from Paramount for it.

Trumbo also peddled some of his finest scripts during this time under pseudonyms, the most famous being Robert Rich. When Trumbo gave the bogus name as screenwriter on *The Brave One* (1956), he didn't anticipate that the film would be awarded an Oscar for Best Screenwriting. "Robert Rich" was called to collect the Academy Award, and no one came forward to accept the honor. Gossip and innuendo quickly spread about the origins of the script. Industry insiders knew Trumbo deserved the statuette, but the entire incident was shielded from the public. The following year, the Academy's board voted to make any admitted Communists or those unwilling to testify to HUAC ineligible for an Oscar. It was Hollywood's way of signaling to Congress that it still had the problem under control.

However, in the wake of the Robert Rich award, a series of events hastened the end of that dark decade of political persecution. Blacklisted screenwriter Nedrick Young came forward just before the 1959 Academy Awards ceremony to declare that he was the "Nathan Douglas" who had written the nominated script for *The Defiant Ones* (1958). In 1960, director Otto Preminger boldly admitted that Trumbo was behind the typewriter on his film *Exodus*; later that year, actor-producer Kirk Douglas risked repercussions and courageously placed Dalton Trumbo's real name on the credits of Stanley Kubrick's *Spartacus*. The attention drawn to these powerful films and the man behind their inspirational scenes effectively erased the blacklist. Publicly humiliated and sensing the Oscar ceremony would become a farce, the Academy rescinded its previous decision but did nothing to rectify their previous mistakes; Robert Rich is still listed as the winner in the Academy's official records.

Sparked by a new sense of freedom, Trumbo lent his unique gifts to the scripts of *Lonely Are the Brave* (1962), *The Sandpiper* (1965), *Hawaii* (1966), and *Papillon* (1973). His directorial debut came in 1971 when he scripted and filmed a version of his own 1939 antiwar novel *Johnny Got His Gun*. Lung cancer abruptly ended his career as a director; he was confined to his home for the next five years.

In 1975, the Academy corrected the credit for *The Brave One* and gave the famed screenwriter a special Oscar for his contributions. The award was presented to a bedridden Trumbo, just one year before a heart attack would end his life. Sixteen years after his death, Trumbo was honored with another corrective Academy Award, this time for the Oscar-winning screenplay of *Roman Holiday*, a film he had written more than forty years earlier.

Dalton Trumbo courageously withstood a long period of political repression to emerge the most successful and resilient survivor of the Hollywood blacklists, and his triumphant comeback embodied the strength of Hollywood's liberal heritage.

91

DENNIS HOPPER

Born: May 17, 1936, Dodge City, KS

The whole Hollywood establishment had to stop and reassess, because at the exact time Easy Rider *came up, Hollywood had just sunk millions into several very big clunkers, and here comes this film making a fortune. It changed the industry.*
—PAUL SCHRADER

As a member of the cast of *Rebel Without a Cause* (1955) and a close friend of James Dean, Dennis Hopper belonged to a generation intent on revolting against the homogeneous middle-class lifestyle that America embraced in the 1950s. His direct and forceful personality marked him as a difficult star and isolated him from the major studios. Working outside the bureaucracy, Hopper developed a new perspective on films that would bridge the gap between old pros and young fans; eventually it would also put Hopper back in the graces of the studios.

From the beginning of his career, Hopper sought roles that would not stereotype him. His rebellious nature found companionship among other actors training at Lee Strasberg's Actors Studio. During work on Henry Hathaway's *From Hell to Texas* (1958), Hopper experienced difficulty in finishing a scene and insisted on more than a hundred takes of his improvisational techniques. Hathaway was furious; the studio was furious. Hopper was relegated to B-movie roles for the next ten years.

At the same time, studios were out of sync with young adults, a fast-growing slice of the moviegoing market. Hollywood's best attempts to attract them were films like *Doctor Dolittle* (1967), *Paint Your Wagon* (1969), and *Hello, Dolly!* (1969). Such films failed repeatedly, and Hollywood honchos began paying closer attention to the ideas of Dennis Hopper.

"The only thing you can make with a big budget is a big, dishonest, impersonal movie," Hopper told them. To reinforce his point, he conceived a film that would serve as a low-budget attack on societal norms. He approached producer Roger Corman about a psychedelic road movie that would deliberately embrace the hippie aesthetic. When Corman passed on the idea, Hopper financed the film himself, and the anti-Establishment *Easy Rider* (1969) became his first attempt at directing. Hailed as a new direction in film, it was cowritten by Terry Southern, who collaborated with Stanley Kubrick on *Dr. Strangelove* (1964). It cost $400,000 to make and won raves at the Cannes festival before opening to sellout audiences in the States. It became a monumental hit, making more than $16 million, and dramatically changed the tone of pictures in the following decades, demonstrating to Hollywood that the future audience with the discretionary spending power would be youths, who wanted films whose style and issues reflected their own.

The success of *Easy Rider* ushered in a wave of such new films. Baffled film executives witnessed the notorious sequences of Peter Fonda, Jack Nicholson, and Hopper consuming hallucinogenic drugs in a New Orleans cemetery and realized they had to hire a younger batch of directors to make the kinds of films teenagers would find interesting. They searched the film schools for talent; among their notable discoveries were Bob Rafelson, Steven Spielberg, Martin Scorsese, Peter Bogdonavich, Francis Ford Coppola, and George Lucas.

Ironically, Hopper was not one of the directors courted. He continued producing independently and directed two more films, showing only slight signs of his *Easy Rider* talent: *The American Dreamer* (1971) and the experimental, drug-induced *The Last Movie* (1971). The latter film had critics reporting Hopper's early death as a trend-setting artist.

Throughout the seventies, as a serious drug habit and vocal outbursts made him unattractive to most U.S. productions, Hopper become a creative globetrotter. For the next fifteen years, his film work was done in such films as Australia's *Mad Dog Morgan* (1976), West Germany's *The American Friend* (1977) and France's *The Sorcerer's Apprentices* (1977).

Hopper temporarily enjoyed a comeback when Francis Ford Coppola cast him (some say typecast him) as an edgy photojournalist in the Vietnam epic *Apocalypse Now* (1979). The film's antiwar message was a perfect fit with Hopper's history as the voice of the sixties. Several 1986 performances—in *Blue Velvet, Hoosiers,* and *River's Edge*—propelled another comeback. Hopper then found opportunities to direct again with *Colors* (1988) and *The Hot Spot* (1990).

Playing a series of flipped-out villains has turned Hopper into an eccentric character actor, and many film buffs are not aware of the magnitude of his influence. But his uneven career cannot change the fact that in one shining moment he had a hunch that, when acted upon, instituted a phenomenal shift in popular culture.

92

RICHARD HOLLINGSHEAD

Born: February 25, 1900, Camden, NJ
Died: May 13, 1975, Villanova, PA

During the 1950s, drive-ins truly did help keep the film industry afloat.
—KERRY SEGRAVE

Fascination with open-air theaters goes back to Ebbets Field, in Brooklyn, New York, where Marcus Loew, to boost spirits dampened by World War I, put on a free exhibition of *Wrath of the Gods* (1914) for an audience of more than twenty-one thousand. The lesson of the event was overwhelming: Americans loved the great outdoors as much as they loved the movies.

The first to exploit this dual passion was Richard M. Hollingshead Jr. In 1930, while employed as manager of his father's auto parts store, Hollingshead worked out several ways of mounting a Kodak projector to the hood of his car. He experimented in the front yard of his home, nailing a makeshift screen to a tree and placing speakers discreetly behind bushes to broadcast sound.

In his driveway, he tested the concept on his neighbors and noticed that cars parking behind his weren't able to see the entire screen. He solved this problem by elevating the front wheels with wooden blocks to adjust the angle for optimum viewing. These wheel ramps became the basis for U.S. Patent 1,909,537, the first ever awarded for open-air theaters, on May 16, 1933.

Later that year, Hollingshead gathered $30,000 from a few investors and scouted a Camden, New Jersey, site as the location for a revolutionary commercial venture. He broke ground on the first "drive-in" theater, and three weeks later, on Tuesday, June 6, 1933, he opened the gates to cars at twenty-five cents each. A three-speaker "directional sound" system was provided by the RCA Victor Company. Because light travels faster than sound, a slight delay was audible from the back row.

Refinements continued over the next several years, and by 1948 there were over a thousand drive-ins nationwide. Well suited to modest postwar lifestyles, the drive-in gave families a chance to pile into their car and go to a movie without any fuss. Because the average drive-in had a capacity of about five hundred cars, most were built outside metropolitan areas, making them perfect for leisure drives on weekend getaways.

Drive-in movies reached their height of popularity in the 1950s, when about forty-two hundred spread across the country, some boasting as many as two hundred fifty screens. The film industry was suffering as television began to take its toll on the theatergoing habit, but drive-ins flourished and kept studios alive, providing up to 25 percent of all box office revenues.

Popular teenage hangouts, drive-ins came under the scrutiny of fundamentalist Christians in the fifties. To counter their theaters' reputation as teenage love dens, drive-in owners introduced bingo games, laundromats, and beauty parlors—anything to support the family concept—but sex-crazed patrons remained the stereotype, and owners dropped the frills. Soon after, drive-in managers began booking B movies for an audience they felt was no longer paying attention to the screen.

Because they catered to fairly small communities, some theaters tried gimmicks to encourage audiences to travel a little farther than usual. The All-Weather Drive-In, on the outskirts of Copiague, New York, had both heated and air-conditioned indoor seating for twelve hundred, as well as twenty-five hundred parking spaces, plus a restaurant right on the premises. On the enormous twenty-eight-acre lot, patrons actually had to be shuttled from their car to the concession stand. In 1948, Ed Brown's Fly-In Theater in Asbury Park, New Jersey, had enough room for twenty-five airplanes. Pilots could land at the theater; when the movie was over, a Jeep would taxi the planes back to an adjacent airfield and off they went, back home.

By 1962, competition from television had reduced the number of drive-in theaters to a mere fifteen hundred. Today, fewer than nine hundred drive-ins exist, many of them doubling as huge flea markets during the day. This decline will eventually push Richard Hollingshead out of the ranks of cinema's top influencers and back into the realm of forgotten pioneer. Still, Hollingshead's idea became a unique movie phenomenon that lasted for many years, and his relentless pursuit made open-air movie theaters a permanent part of American culture.

93

MELVIN VAN PEEBLES

Born: August 21, 1932, Chicago, IL

Here they come, an endless row of black filmmakers, charging up the road.
—MELVIN VAN PEEBLES

Like the main character in his first film, *Watermelon Man* (1970), director Melvin Van Peebles woke up one day and realized he was black. After writing screenplays in beat-era San Francisco and bohemian France, Van Peebles ended up in Hollywood working on scripts with black themes. Disgusted with their lack of authenticity, Van Peebles saw an opportunity.

With a $50,000 loan from comedian Bill Cosby and a paycheck from his directorial debut, thirty-eight-year-old Van Peebles scraped together $500,000 and took just nineteen days to shoot a gritty, angry independent film that would become a cultural landmark. *Sweet Sweetback's Baadasssss Song* (1971), filmed in Watts, created something revolutionary—a new black cinema.

Rife with sexual themes, graphic violence, and vulgarity, *Sweetback* received an X rating from an all-white panel of the MPAA upon its release. Of the two theaters in the country that booked it, one deleted scenes from the movie. Enraged, Van Peebles sued and got the film restored to its original form in a highly publicized federal case. The publicity paid off. Black Americans flocked to see *Sweetback*. Black Panther Huey Newton hailed it as a "spiritual" masterpiece. *Sweetback* became the hottest film in the country, taking in just over $14 million, and Van Peebles was lionized as the soul of black popular culture.

Before the release of *Sweetback*, the depiction of blacks in motion pictures was largely influenced by white filmmakers, who, in small and subtle ways, often perpetuated stereotypes through sheer disregard or unwittingly reinforced prejudices. Over the decades since D. W. Griffith's overtly racist *Birth of a Nation* (1915), several black filmmakers had attempted to counter these negative images. The greatest effort in this area was the pioneering work of Oscar Micheaux, an African-American filmmaker active for three decades after World War I. The son of former slaves, Micheaux provided significant opportunities for black actors and craftsmen, and history has since recorded him among the most significant, albeit controversial, figures in reshaping the image of blacks in popular culture. Despite these efforts, black cinema remained a segregated part of the film industry and was relegated to underground status. The social and political legacy of the 1960s, however, combined with burgeoning economical and cultural power in the black community, made the timing right for *Sweetback*'s success.

To Hollywood, *Sweetback* had another message: blacks would pay to see black films. The exploitation had begun. Releasing *Shaft* in late 1971, MGM turned a cool $20 million profit. (Richard Roundtree, its star, made just $13,500.) *Sweetback* had introduced a new market segment to film studios, much as *Easy Rider* (1969) had unearthed the commercial potential of youth-oriented films.

Van Peebles's film shockingly illuminated a cultural gap between blacks and whites. Typical "blaxploitation" films contain bleak settings, militant protagonists, police brutality, and inexhaustible sexual appetites, usually backed by a soundtrack containing a healthy dose of electric funk. Van Peebles encouraged critics to view black films as foreign films, with a language and rituals unknown to white America. Many of the film's detractors, including prominent members of the civil rights movement, argued that these blaxploitation films trivialized the problems of drugs, misogyny, and violence that afflicted urban centers in the seventies, but Van Peebles defended the angry message of the film as reflecting the true sentiment of African Americans.

After *Sweetback*, Gordon Parks and Sidney Poitier suddenly found financing for films. Television shows echoed their successes; the music industry mimicked their soundtracks. The movement opened doors for black actors, producers, and directors. Within a year, the market was flooded with sixty blaxploitation movies, and many of them blatantly copied *Sweetback*'s dialogue, fashion, music, and themes. From action films like *Superfly* (1972), *Foxy Brown* (1974), *Dolemite* (1975), and *Death Force* (1978), a fresh batch of new stars emerged—Pam Grier, Jayne and Leon Isaac Kennedy, Rudy Ray Moore. An entire subgenre of black films contributed entries in horror, western, comedy, and musicals: *Black Caesar* (1973), *Blacula* (1972), *Blackenstein* (1973), *Black Belt Jones* (1974), and *Avenging Disco Godfather* (1976), to name a few. These films were often campy and uninspired, but they reinforced Van Peebles's contention that black audiences would support any enterprise that let them see themselves reflected in mainstream popular culture. Actor Ossie Davis would sum it up by saying, "Seems to me there's a lot of money in just being black these days."

Resurgent interest in the blaxploitation genre sparked recent spoofs and sequels, including *I'm Gonna Git You Sucka!* (1988) and *The Return of Superfly* (1990), and director Quentin Tarantino nostalgically borrowed the look, feel, and stars of the era in *Jackie Brown* (1997). More serious contributors, primarily Spike Lee, would later move black films far beyond stereotypical exploitation, but credit Melvin Van Peebles for dramatically changing the face of film for an entire generation.

94

JOHN CHAMBERS

Born: September 12, 1922, Chicago, IL

You can actually read emotion through those animal faces.
—CHARLTON HESTON

Before entering the film industry, John Chambers was an army dental technician, specializing in prosthetics for wounded soldiers. In 1953, he applied his knowledge in NBC's makeup rooms, where his most memorable creations were the pointy ears of Mr. Spock for television's *Star Trek* series.

In 1967, Chambers was approached by producer Arthur Jacobs, who was itching to make a sci-fi fantasy movie that would rival the excitement of *King Kong.* Jacobs had acquired a screenplay by *Twilight Zone* creator Rod Serling, based on a Pierre Boulle novel about a world inhabited by a race of intellectually advanced simians, and secured Charlton Heston as the lead. While pitching the idea to Darryl and Richard Zanuck at 20th Century–Fox, Jacobs sensed their reluctance to take a chance on a monkey movie. Fox wanted to see proof that *Planet of the Apes* was a plausible idea.

So Jacobs arranged for a sneak preview. He commissioned Chambers to make a prototype mask. In a brief test, Chambers put an ape face on veteran actor Edward G. Robinson, who ran lines with Heston in a five-minute filmed rehearsal. After screening the test, Fox decided to gamble $5 million that Chambers's makeup could be accepted on a realistic level.

With six months to prepare, and $1 million allotted for materials, Chambers went to work. More than a thousand extras would need to be turned into simians. Chambers left that job to his associate, Dan Striekpeke, who created masks that pulled snugly over the head.

Masks wouldn't do for the main actors; they were claustrophobic and rigid, restricting movement and making the actors look stiff and expressionless. Chambers needed a solution that would allow for the subtleties of fine acting, unhampered by the makeup. After all, Jacobs had recruited a stellar field of actors. (Robinson, who was exhausted by the long makeup sessions in the test, turned down a role, as would Orson Welles, who was offered General Ursus.) After experimenting with a variety of substances, he settled on a rubbery material called latex, which Lon Chaney had frequently incorporated into his monsters' faces. Latex had been used sporadically in makeup effects throughout the history of Hollywood, but generally it was regarded as too difficult to apply to the human face. Besides, most actors would need to look consistent over months of shooting; latex was too coarse and unruly for predictable results every time.

Chambers called all of the principal actors to his workshop and made several molds of each actor's face with plaster of Paris. Then, he created plaster busts and poured small amounts of latex over them to arrive at a thin skin. He punctured the skin with tiny pores, so his masks would breathe as actors perspired under them, and developed special makeup paint that allowed him to detail the latex skins without closing the pores in the foam rubber. Another Chambers innovation was custom-made, nonirritating adhesives that kept the latex firmly fastened to the skin. These developments were especially important, considering that many actors would be in their costumes for up to fourteen hours at a time. The latex skin was applied in sessions that lasted as long as eight hours. The finished creation was a talking ape that, when photographed in extreme close-up, showed audiences details and subtleties previously unseen.

The debut of *Planet of the Apes* (1968) was an unqualified success, reaping $15 million in domestic receipts. It generated four sequels and millions of dollars for Fox. Chambers received an Oscar and repeated his performance in *Beneath the Planet of the Apes* (1970), this time using latex to display the effects of radiation on a race of telepathic mutants. Other actors who donned the monkey makeup in the series included Claude Akins, John Huston, and Paul Williams. Historian Michael Druxman said of the film, "The real star is makeup artist John Chambers, whose contribution to [the movie]—more than any other single factor—was responsible for the motion picture's success."

Chambers may well deserve credit for saving the horror film genre. After a period of fantastic drive-in movies, film trends were shifting toward realism. Horror film directors, working with low budgets and cheap effects, had to keep their cameras at a distance and simply couldn't produce the thrills that captivate audiences. Chambers's latex revolution brought movie monsters closer to the camera than ever before. Suddenly, fantasy filmmakers were introducing us to terrifying new faces, and sometimes taking us right down into their throats. Chambers would go on to apply his innovations to other films, including Steven Spielberg's *Jaws* (1975), and the realism of his makeup accomplishments has extended to everything from *Mask* (1985) to *Mrs. Doubtfire* (1993).

95

MACK SENNETT

Born: January 17, 1880, Danville, Quebec, Canada
Died: November 5, 1960, Hollywood, CA

He that is without humor among you, let him cast the first pie.
—MABEL NORMAND

Mack Sennett's ambition to become an opera star never got further than the circuses and burlesque theaters he performed in at the turn of the century. Joining Biograph studios in 1909 as an actor and scriptwriter, he picked up directing and editing tips from D. W. Griffith. He left three years later to start a venture in Los Angeles that would become a beacon for clowns, barnstormers, roustabouts, prizefighters, mimes, acrobats, vaudevillians, and rodeo riders. His studio was known as a laboratory for the wildest experiments in pratfalls, stunts, and comedic sight gags, and he received a special Oscar in 1937 for lasting contributions to the slapstick comedy genre. Often overlooked is the sheer volume of films that Sennett churned out in an effort to satisfy the hungry, volatile film industry in its fragile infancy.

As the owner of the Keystone Company, Sennett recognized the demand for a constant, entertaining stream of short films to round out the movie bill at theaters across the country. To accomplish this, his assembly-line method produced nearly one film a day without benefit of scripts or preparation. He created a breakneck formula for making low-budget variations on the same two themes—sex and violence. Sennett's Bathing Beauties were only slightly less famous than his ingenious group of comedians gathered together as the Keystone Kops. Throughout the 1920s, no other troupe came to characterize silent comedy better.

Through happenstance, Sennett comedies developed a distinct style: devoid of logic, full of anarchy, completely over the top. Utilizing the latest camera tricks and high-speed techniques, Keystone highjinks centered around the chase; incompetent officers in baggy uniforms dashed off cliffs, swung around corners, and never slowed down. Often Sennett would rush to an automobile accident or building fire with equipment in tow and have his actors improvise on the spot. When the fledgling Charlie Chaplin arrived just one year into Keystone's success, Sennett explained the key to his profitable output by saying, "We have no scenarios. We get an idea, then we follow the natural sequence of events until it leads to a chase, which is the essence of our comedy."

The corner of 8th Street and Figueroa in Los Angeles became a favorite Kops intersection, where Sennett would spill liquid soap on the street to aid with the highjinks. Needless to say, safety wasn't the main concern; Sennett encouraged the gratuitous use of bricks, plaster of paris bottles, and of course an ample supply of cream pies (a delicious addition incorporated by Fatty Arbuckle). He employed engineers to build special wind machines, intricate plumbing works, electrical apparatus, trick cars, and whatever could be swung from piano wires. He also collected a menagerie of animals to throw into the comic mix: horses, great Danes, elephants, giraffes, lions, and dogs trained to smoke and drink.

The feverish demand for Sennett comedies cannot be understated. His Keystone shorts were shipped all over the world, so quickly that often no attempt was made to retrieve prints before the next shipment. Sometimes he would have his directors simultaneously film with four separate cameras, then simply send negative stock directly to international destinations rather than taking the time to duplicate prints.

A paranoid and argumentative leader, Sennett rode roughshod over everyone. He didn't care too much for writers, and his feelings for a particular actor or comedian would vary from week to week, but the success that prompted Sennett to anoint himself "the king of comedy" would also give rise to other royalty. Besides Chaplin, his talent searches yielded such incredible talent as Fatty Arbuckle, Harold Lloyd, Gloria Swanson, Ben Turpin, Chester Conklin, W. C. Fields, and Bing Crosby. To help him direct more than a thousand one- and two-reel comedy shorts, Sennett hired Frank Capra and George Stevens, among other talented directors.

In 1914, Sennett's company produced the first American feature-length comedy, *Tillie's Punctured Romance*. Such successes as *His Bitter Pill* (1916) and *The Shriek of Araby* (1923) followed before the introduction of double features and animated cartoons signaled the end of Keystone shorts. The stock market crash of 1929 cleaned out Sennett's bankroll, and he retired broke in 1935. Still, the real riches of the Sennett system remain in film vaults today. His studio produced nearly every comic invention ever recorded on film.

96

Born: November 7, 1942, New York, NY

His concern is what's true to his characters and what's right for their feelings.

—STEVEN SPIELBERG

Upon close examination of his career, Martin Scorsese appears to be two separate filmmakers. First and foremost, he is an obsessive student of cinema—hailing from a generation of college-educated filmmakers like Steven Spielberg, George Lucas, and Francis Ford Coppola—who borrows heavily from past masters to produce highly effective movies. On the other hand, most of Scorsese's work contains a sense of raw, unschooled direction that is truly rare among today's filmmakers. His unsurpassed knowledge of film history has allowed him to subtly and skillfully make well-established techniques seem completely original and has helped him enlist the talents of Hollywood's forgotten craftsmen. He has directed some of the cinema's finest films—*Taxi Driver* (1976), *Raging Bull* (1980), and *GoodFellas* (1990)—and his celebrated body of work is often credited with establishing a "modern cinema," a major shift in moviemaking trends of the last thirty years that has seen the proliferation of films that disregard conventional narrative structure and emphasize character over plot.

In his youth, Scorsese suffered from a series of ailments that kept him close to home in the Little Italy section of New York City. Believing himself to be destined for the clergy, he studied at a Catholic seminary for one year before his interest in filmmaking led him to New York University. In 1964, he received a bachelor's degree in film communication; then spurred on by praise of his *It's Not Just You, Murray* (1966) and other short films, he stayed at NYU to complete his master's degree while editing the rockumentary *Woodstock* (1970). Eventually, Scorsese would return to the university to teach filmmaking and film history classes, inspiring such budding student directors as Oliver Stone and Spike Lee.

Already present in Scorsese's early films were his trademark verité style and kinetic camera work, as well as his authentic view of small-time Italian-American hustlers. *Who's That Knocking at My Door?* (1967) showed what the talented new director could accomplish on a small budget. This attracted the attention of legendary B-movie producer Roger Corman, who asked Scorsese to leave New York for the backlots of Hollywood. Corman was interested in a sequel to his hit *Bloody Mama* (1970), and Scorsese was eager to test the waters in Tinseltown. The result was *Boxcar Bertha* (1972), a directing job critics labeled "yet another Bonnie and Clyde clone," but nevertheless a profitable venture for Corman.

Working under the tight constraints of a low-budget production gave Scorsese the savvy he needed to complete *Mean Streets* (1973). The film featured Robert De Niro and Harvey Keitel as young cousins becoming small-time hoodlums on the streets of New York. Although he shot most of the film in Los Angeles, Scorsese insisted that the exteriors of the city be captured in New York for authenticity, and his own autobiographical touches of street life in tenement neighborhoods gave the film added realism. *Mean Streets* became his breakthrough, was the hit of the crowds at the Chicago Film Festival, and got Hollywood's attention.

Suddenly, Scorsese was offered high-profile projects with the support of major studios. He had critical as well as box office success with the big-budget *Alice Doesn't Live Here Anymore* (1974), a film with feminist overtones that struck a chord with audiences in the wake of women's liberation and led to a popular television series, *Alice.* However, the characteristic touches that made Scorsese a promising talent were missing from most of his Hollywood films of the period, including the lukewarm *New York, New York* (1977). When he strays from the familiar settings and themes of his hometown, Scorsese films seem forced. His attempts at "mainstream" material, like *The Color of Money* (1986), the sequel to the 1961 classic *The Hustler,* and Scorsese's 1991 remake of the classic *Cape Fear* (1962), often perform well at the box office but lack the power of his more personal films.

The streets of New York played a central role in the highly influential *Taxi Driver* (1976), from a script by Paul Schrader, a story about a Vietnam vet's feelings of isolation and detachment from society. Robert De Niro plays psychotic Travis Bickle, a cabbie with a penchant for guns who fixates on a twelve-year old prostitute played by Jodie Foster. The infamous blood-letting that concludes the film has become an indelible moment of American cinema, and the film's intense character exposé is considered seminal in the modern cinema. The film entirely abandons traditional plot developments for a methodical, almost documentary, examination of Bickle's troubled existence. The role of Travis Bickle made De Niro an international star and Schrader a sought-after screenwriter. *Taxi Driver* received the Palme d'Or at the Cannes Film Festival and was nominated for three Oscars.

Taxi Driver featured a haunting score by legendary film composer Bernard Herrmann, who died just days after completing it. It would also mark a series of "rediscoveries" instituted by Scorsese. To avoid trouble with the MPAA board over the film's vivid bloodbath finale, Scorsese contacted special effects pioneer Linwood Dunn, who washed the negatives in sepia tones to tame the reddish hues to brown, which secured the film a favorable rating. Repeatedly throughout his career, Scorsese would use his vast knowledge of film's legends to summon famed title designer Saul Bass, New Wave cinematographer Nestor Almendros, and other artists of the past for his projects.

In 1980, Scorsese made what some believe to be his masterwork. *Raging Bull* told the real-life story of middleweight boxing champion Jake La Motta. The scenes filmed inside the ring, with their dreamlike imagery and gritty intensity, remain unsurpassed among boxing films, and De Niro's performance has become almost as famous as the picture itself. For the fight sequences, De Niro worked with one of America's foremost trainers; he was believed to be as fit as the top professional boxers. For the later scenes of an older La Motta, De Niro reportedly flew to Italy for three months of solid eating and gained over fifty pounds.

Raging Bull was instantly hailed as a classic, winning Scorsese the National Society of Film Critics Award for Best Director. However, despite being nominated for seven Academy Awards, including Best Director, the film picked up only two Oscars, one for De Niro's performance and one for Thelma Schoonmaker for editing.

The collaboration of Scorsese and De Niro continued in *The King of Comedy* (1983). Overall, they have made eight films together; although Scorsese tends to use actors repeatedly, like Harvey Keitel, Terri Garr, Barbara Hershey, Nick Nolte, Rosanna Arquette, and Joe Pesci, no other actor has been as closely identified with Scorsese's most successful films. Scheduling problems prevented De Niro from taking the role of Jesus in Scorsese's controversial *The Last Temptation of Christ* (1988). The Paul Schrader script, based on the novel by Nikos Kazantzakis, was a pet project that Scorsese had nurtured for nearly a decade before shooting began. His interpretation of the life of Christ, played by Willem Dafoe, explored Christ's final days and became an international scandal, as religious groups declared it blasphemous. Riots accompanied many screenings, and theater chains refused to book it. During the troubling production, Scorsese decided to supplement his income with experimental projects, including an episode of Steven Spielberg's TV series *Amazing Stories,* several commercials for fashion designer Giorgio Armani, and Michael Jackson's 1987 music video "Bad."

As his stature as a prominent filmmaker increased, Scorsese began producing films, including *The Grifters* (1990), *Mad Dog and Glory* (1993), and *Clockers* (1995). With his direction of *GoodFellas* (1990), Scorsese returned to familiar territory. Based on the book *Wiseguys* by Nicholas Pileggi, it is the story of gangster Henry Hill, a real-life informer who revealed the inner workings of the Mafia to Pileggi. The brutal tale, filled with excellent performances by Pesci, De Niro, and newcomer Ray Liotta, proved to be extremely popular, and Scorsese was nominated for a Best Director Oscar, as well as receiving awards from the National Society of Film Critics, New York Film Critics, and L.A. Film Critics for Best Director. He returned to mobsters with *Casino* (1995), an account of the final days of organized crime in Las Vegas.

A lasting achievement of Martin Scorsese, and one that has endeared him to film lovers, was the establishment of the Film Foundation in 1990. Dedicated to ensuring the survival of America's film heritage, the organization, headed by Scorsese and cofounded by George Lucas, Steven Spielberg, Woody Allen, Francis Ford Coppola, Stanley Kubrick, Robert Redford, and Sydney Pollack, supports a public crusade for the preservation of film that Scorsese has led since 1979. His campaign for more lasting films resulted in the creation of a new Eastman Kodak color film stock that will not fade as quickly as the current stocks. Scorsese also initiated the fight against Ted Turner and the colorization of black-and-white films, denouncing the process as a threat to America's cultural heritage. He continues to resist what he calls "the physical erosion of the integrity of our cinema through its deliberate material alteration by producers, distributors, and broadcasters in search of a fast buck." In 1992, Scorsese addressed a congressional subcommittee on behalf of the Directors Guild of America, to champion the Film Disclosure Act, a bill that passed and that requires all films to be labeled when they have been altered for television or video distribution.

Martin Scorsese has proved to be one of cinema's greatest artists and toughest champions. His box office success pales in comparison to some, but he is revered among aspiring filmmakers. Although he has never won an Academy Award, Scorsese is generally considered to be one of the best American directors working today. He received a Lifetime Achievement Award from the American Film Institute in 1997, an honor usually bestowed on directors posthumously, and he holds the unique position of being a director widely praised and appreciated well before his career is over.

97

KARL STRUSS

Born: November 30, 1886, New York, NY
Died: December 15, 1981, Los Angeles, CA

There are few better photographers; his work is more than excellent.
He is highly artistic and I cannot too highly recommend him.

—CECIL B. DEMILLE

Columbia graduate Karl Struss began a career in commercial photography in New York in 1916. Working extensively with autochrome film developed by the Lumière brothers, he was regarded as an early master of color photographs and soon began publishing articles in photographic journals and experimenting with new technologies. Motion photography became an increasing fascination that turned into a business opportunity in 1919, when he left the East Coast for Hollywood. In just a few years, Struss would become a celebrated cinematographer and provide film photography with its most influential lighting effects.

Immediately upon seeing a portfolio of Struss's work, producer Jesse Lasky hired him to shoot publicity stills. Drawn to the Rembrandt-like lighting in Struss's photos, Lasky sent his most beautiful starlets to Struss and asked him to work his magic on their promotional stills. Struss turned his camera on Gloria Swanson first, and eventually most of the silent era's greatest names were framed by him. His beautifully artful platinum prints drove up the demand for fan photos, and his characteristic lighting style was reproduced in the famous shots of photographer George Hurrel fifteen years later.

Lasky couldn't shake the idea that Struss might be better used behind a hand-cranked camera. He urged his favorite director, Cecil B. DeMille, to consider the quality of Struss's stills and determine whether the photographer would be useful on a movie set. DeMille took one look at the photos of Swanson and put Struss to work immediately on *For Better, for Worse* (1919). Over a three-year stint as a cameraman, Struss was often called on by DeMille to finish one or two scenes as a second-unit director, which he did on *Male and Female* (1919), *Forbidden Fruit* (1920), and *Poisoned Paradise* (1923).

When Struss went freelance in 1924, he quickly found work as a director with Thomas Ince, then worked on various films until DeMille tracked him down and invited him back for a European trip to assist on the location shots of *Ben-Hur* (1926). Upon his return to Hollywood, Struss would receive offers from almost every major studio.

For his next project, he accepted a position as second cameraman to Charles Rosher on *Sunrise* (1927), an ambitious drama by the established horror director F. W. Murnau. Struss was given great latitude on the set of *Sunrise* and used many of his own techniques to create lush, fluid imagery that seems to transform each scene smoothly into the next. Struss handled lighting on the scenes of the Big City sequences and was given responsibility for the crane-and-dolly shots of several water sequences. Making use of experimental film stock, some of the earliest panchromatic negatives available, Struss was able to capture dreamlike images of light reflected off water that contributed to the film's most memorable moments. Borrowing heavily from expressionistic lighting, Struss shot exteriors with much more light than German cinematographers had used when formulating their shots. After Struss noticed that much of his personal style had reached the screen, he demanded to be listed as a cinematographer in the film's credits and share equal prominence with Rosher. Murnau, who is often credited for the immense influence of *Sunrise,* claimed to have rarely looked through the camera lens, relying heavily on the expertise of his cameramen. He relented, and Struss got the credit he deserved.

The majesty of *Sunrise* is achieved through the suggestive power of Struss's photographic techniques. Its hallmark was the use of lighting to support the theme of the film. It has been called the most beautifully photographed silent film ever and was praised endlessly by the critics as the preeminent example of filmmaking for its time. The film was a tremendous influence on Orson Welles, and the French New Wave artists perched it high upon their critical pedestal. Film noir directors returned to it frequently for insights into creating mood.

Struss was quickly adopted by the industry. Asked by Louis B. Mayer to represent his trade union in the foundation of the Academy of Motion Picture Arts and Sciences, Struss was one of only fifteen cameramen invited to the first meeting to christen the organization. When the group tallied their ballots for the first annual Academy Award presentation, he would become the first Oscar winner for cinematography. There was no Best Picture category that year; but *Sunrise* received a special Oscar for "Unique and Artistic Picture." Later that year, the American Society of Cinematographers (ASC) inducted Struss into its prestigious club. He would become one of its cornerstone members, even serving as the subject of a documentary short called *The Cinematographer* in a 1949 series the ASC sponsored about their craft.

After *Sunrise,* Struss would market himself as an "artist photographer." He held out for projects that let him explore motion pictures as a means to express thought pictorially instead of by titles or dialogue. While waiting for choice projects, he maintained his expertise in modern photographic processes and continued to develop custom lenses.

In 1927, Struss moved to United Artists, where D. W. Griffith expressed an interest in having the young cinematographer aid him on four pictures, including *Battle of the Sexes* and *Drums of Love.* Struss jumped at the chance to work alongside and share screen credit with the legendary Billy Bitzer. The experience proved to have other benefits: UA's other stars, Mary Pickford and Charlie Chaplin, would use Struss for *Coquette* (1928), *The Great Dictator* (1939), and *Limelight* (1952). He was unavailable to oblige a young Orson Welles on *Citizen Kane* (1941) but was loaned to RKO to help Welles with *Journey Into Fear* (1942). These films highlighted the rich visual imagery that came to be a trademark of Struss's work.

His lighting techniques were so widely imitated, however, that he felt compelled to break away from the confinements of cinematography and took up an interest in special effects. During an eighteen-year stint at Paramount, Struss continued his experiments with trick lenses and unusual filters, leading to the eerie transformations in *Dr. Jekyll and Mr. Hyde* (1932) and *Island of Lost Souls* (1933).

When other cinematographers came up to Struss's level in the 1950s, he began a second wave of influence. Captivated by the attempts of studios to experiment with 3-D films, he signed on for such B-movie projects as *Rocketship X-M* (1953) and tried his hand at wide-screen effects for the CinemaScope craze. His multi-eye view in *The Fly* (1958) became one of science fiction's most indelible images, although many felt Struss was "slumming" by lending his experience to these low-budget shockers. However, Struss refused to be pigeonholed as a one-dimensional talent and continued to apply his inventive photographic ideas to a steady stream of film and television work up until 1970, when he retired.

Struss summarized his role in film history best when he wrote to a London exhibitor in 1921: "I believe I am the first of the American pictorialists to have entered the field of motion picture photography with the view of improving the presentation of films photographically."

98

BUSBY BERKELEY

Born: November 29, 1895, Los Angeles, CA
Died: March 14, 1976, Palm Springs, CA

Jesus, now Berkeley's going through the roof!

—JACK WARNER

The U.S. Army made a choreographer of Busby Berkeley. During World War I, he was assigned to train groups of twelve hundred men for parade drills, and he conducted aerial observations for a small army film unit. Upon his release, Berkeley took his newfound skills to Broadway, where his choreography of five shows in 1928 dazzled the eyes of Sam Goldwyn, who, two years later, brought Berkeley to Hollywood. In just one decade, Busby Berkeley would do much more than show dancers how to move—he would show directors how to move, too.

His first film experience was a musical sequence in Eddie Cantor's *Whoopee!* (1930), featuring a young Lucille Ball among a chorus of the Goldwyn Girls. Berkeley designed a grand-scale number using symmetrical formations filmed with some overhead shots. The result was an abstract visual style that would eventually become his favored technique. Employing huge chorus lines, special lighting, and mirrors, the Berkeley musicals for MGM and Warner Bros. created an escapism of happiness and prosperity throughout the Depression and into World War II. Even costumes and props got the Berkeley treatment—Ginger Rogers wears a suit of coins as she sings "We're in the Money" in the opening number of *Gold Diggers of 1933,* one of the many obvious metaphors that characterized Busby's work. Freudian symbolism appears in his campy Carmen Miranda vehicle *The Gang's All*

Here (1943), featuring a line of beautiful girls waving to the audience with overblown bananas in a surreal sequence; the film was a favorite among homesick sailors and GIs.

However, Berkeley's choreography is important less for its movement of the dancers than for its movement of the camera. To overcome the limitations of sound stages, he ripped out walls and drilled through ceilings and dug trenches for his film crews. When a desired effect could not be accomplished with traditional film equipment, he had his budget expanded to include costs for developing custom rigs. His innovations explored ideas that the stationary camera could not. He wanted to take the audience through waterfalls and windows. He wanted lines of dancers to fall away to reveal scenery that in turn would fall away to expose an even larger setting. His dreams were big, but his determination to see them actualized was even bigger.

Even his worst attempts resulted in eminently watchable movies of exhilarating movement, but his best efforts produced startling effects that bordered on surrealistic dream states. In the quintessential Berkeley films *Footlight Parade* (1933) and *42nd Street* (1933), cameras mounted on tracks are sent soaring past a multitude of dancing legs, flailing arms, and orchestra instruments. In all, he directed more than twenty musicals, including an underwater sequence with aquatic star Esther Williams.

The high production costs of his spectacles became a liability when a new breed of sophisticated musicals learned to integrate music and drama, an approach that countered the bravura dance numbers he made famous. Attempting the transition to other directorial assignments, Berkeley suffered a well-publicized nervous breakdown, then retired in the mid-1950s. But he lived long enough to see a revival of his films by an appreciative new generation. Part circus and part stage, his musical numbers became a staple of the moviegoer's diet, and other studios were forced to match his flamboyance. Few films, however, ever matched the wonder of a Busby Berkeley production.

99

JOHN HUBLEY

Born: May 21, 1914, Marinette, WI
Died: February 23, 1977, New York, NY

Our marriage vow was to make one noncommercial film a year.
—FAITH HUBLEY

For most young animators, working for Walt Disney was the dream of dreams. But for John Hubley, collaborating on *Snow White and the Seven Dwarfs* (1939), *Pinocchio* (1940), and *Bambi* (1942) was unfulfilling. Hubley came to Hollywood in 1935 on a floodtide of new talent that had been recruited to support the Disney studio's ambitious plans for animated features. He quickly tired of the anthropomorphic characters of Disney's stories. He despised the detailed drawings. He hated the gag-a-minute mentality and yearned to try the more contemporary approaches practiced by Saul Steinberg and other abstract illustrators. So he left Disney.

Hubley joined the newly formed First Motion Picture Unit (FMPU) in 1941 and moonlighted on a series at Columbia Pictures. He was not afraid to voice his personal opinions and expounded the possibilities of a new movement in animation. Earning the respect of his new colleagues, Hubley played a vital role in the newborn United Productions of America (UPA), a studio he cofounded when FMPU sold off its animation division. Under his leadership, UPA became the monogram for fiercely independent cartoons. While other studios rushed to keep up with Disney standards, UPA went the other way entirely.

As supervising director of UPA, Hubley was vocal about the direction the studio needed to take. He embraced a stark style that emphasized story development over character development. He encouraged his staff to experiment with modern drawing forms, odd angles, unusual textures, and color combinations. It was a clean slate; the rules were all gone. Out were the smooth movements of Disney. Out were the 3-D backgrounds of Fleischer. Light and shadow replaced color. Fuzzy, floating shapes stood in for baroque backdrops. A wavy line could symbolize a tree. Knees did not have to bend when a character walked. A transparent, floating rectangle might suddenly sprout a pointed roof and arched doorway, instantly producing a doghouse. These seminal influences are best seen in *The Magic Fluke* (1949) and *Robin Hoodlum* (1949), two interpretations of the same Grimm fable "The Fox and the Crow."

Searching for the antithesis of cute animal characters, Hubley introduced a befuddled and bullheaded character half inspired by an eccentric uncle and half based on the persona of vaudevillian screen star W. C. Fields. Mr. Magoo first stumbled onto the screen in *Ragtime Bear*; he proved so popular that he would be resurrected in *Spellbound Hound* (1950) and *Fuddy Duddy Buddy* (1951).

By 1951, Hubley and UPA had turned the animation world on its ear. Because they were a fledgling group trying to compete with established studios, Hubley eliminated much of the work required in cel-based animation while retaining the style's look. They worked smarter, cutting costs significantly in their production by a process dubbed "limited animation." Rather than create twenty-four frames for every second of film, they used fifteen frames per second. Rich, lavish background paintings were reduced to shapes of color and repeated often. This studio model worked well within restrictive budgets, generating compelling, lively films for a fraction of the cost of rival shorts. When television forced theatrical film studios to cut costs, they quickly adopted limited animation techniques, and to do it convincingly, they borrowed heavily from Hubley's examples. Limited animation became the predominant production method in the industry and is used almost exclusively in animated television programming today.

Successful films like *Gerald McBoing Boing* (1951) and *Rooty Toot Toot* (1952) signaled that limited animation techniques did not shave time and money at the expense of entertainment. With *Rooty Toot Toot,* a highly stylized Frankie and Johnnie spoof set to jazz music, Hubley won an Academy Award and commanded the attention of his peers. Ironically, *Rooty Toot Toot* would be Hubley's last for UPA, but by then he had already created a worldwide shake-up.

His cartoon sequences for live-action films, including *The Four Poster* (1952), would inspire Saul Bass and other graphic designers to rethink title sequences. The Zagreb studios of Czechoslovakia revered him and imitated his stark, graphic look. Most important, his inventive processes were efficient.

Every major cartoon studio, including Disney, would go back to their story-boards and adopt the economical style to compete with television studios that were learning the time-saving tricks of UPA's limited animation. Even master character animator Chuck Jones's *The Dot and the Line* (1964) owed a debt to Hubley's work.

In 1955, Hubley left UPA under the dark cloud of McCarthyism and created his own studio. His wife Faith became a full-time collaborator and helped him start Storyboard, their own cartoon production company. Some of their most experimental and personal films were made independently. Oscar-winning shorts like *Moonbird* (1959), *The Hole* (1962), and *The Windy Day* (1967) further inspired a new breed of animators. These films cleverly used sound recordings of the Hubleys' children at play; animated sequences accompanied the touching, innocent words of the soundtrack, bringing their fanciful comments and colorful dreams to life. Shown on college campuses and at animation festivals, these celebrated works were accompanied by other showcase cartoons from around the world. By the 1970s, a grass-roots movement had secured a place for short films, and today's independent animators enjoy international fame and commercial success largely due to these early groundbreaking films.

John Hubley remains the most significant animator in the second half of the twentieth century. No other single person has done more to free the form of its early stylistic constraints, to bring creative individuals to the craft, and to make animated films a deeply personal art.

100

JOHN CASSAVETES

Born: December 9, 1929, New York, NY
Died: February 3, 1989, Los Angeles, CA

He was a maverick every time he stepped behind the camera.

—Michael Barson

John Cassavetes was a television writer whose raw style was in demand in the untamed environment of TV's golden age. His angry, emotional teleplays gave birth to the kind of live-wire performances that kept families glued to their couches and kept movie theater owners fretting over the powerful lure of home entertainment. Cassavetes was also a skilled actor and director who had worked on more than eighty film and television projects before a startling performance with Sidney Poitier in Martin Ritt's interracial tale *Edge of the City* (1957) threw him into the spotlight, where he would remain for thirty-five years. He was a double threat—an actor whose sheer intensity would foreshadow such seventies superstars as Al Pacino and Robert De Niro, and a fiercely original director who would become a hero of the burgeoning independent film industry in America.

Taking to the streets of New York with a 16mm black-and-white camera, Cassavetes began making features with *Shadows* (1960) and launched a different style of American film. Harkening to the cinema verité of the French New Wave, he brought the method actor's perspective to the director's chair. Despite working from a detailed script, Cassavetes relied heavily on improvisation, so that the story's strength emanated from an analysis of the characters. On his sets, crews were instructed to follow the whims of the actors, even if this meant traveling over electrical cords and around corners. This free-wheeling method often required the use of hand-held cameras, which gave many shots an erratic feel. *Shadows* was an instant classic even before it captured the Critics Award at the 1960 Venice Film Festival, and its realistic quality would influence many New York City "street" films of the following decade, most notably William Friedkin's *The French Connection* (1971) and Martin Scorsese's *Mean Streets* (1973).

After directing a pair of studio-financed flops, Cassavetes vowed to make movies on his own terms. Paying for his personal projects by taking acting assignments on commercial films, including *The Dirty Dozen* (1967) and *Rosemary's Baby* (1968), he returned to independent productions with *Faces* (1968), a film mostly seen in small venues. Slowly, Cassavetes was building a reputation as an uncompromising artist with a unique gift for storytelling. Actors, particularly those who practiced the Stanislavsky method, were eager to work with him—even without pay. Many actors even also pitched in with set, costumes, and promotional efforts.

Husbands (1970) gave him the chance to be on both sides of the camera, and his growing respect and popularity made acting in mainstream Hollywood movies unnecessary. His steady output of independent work began paying for itself, and John Cassavetes continued to add new dynamics to his films. *Minnie and Moskowitz* (1971) and *A Woman Under the Influence* (1974) both included Cassavetes's wife, Gena Rowlands, among a group of distinguished actors. The ensemble casting was powerfully effective, and Robert Altman and Woody Allen adopted it almost exclusively in their subsequent pictures.

Cassavetes's trademark style was cause for some confusion. He became so identified with the improvisational method that his roles in films like Elaine May's *Mikey and Nicky* (1976) and Paul Mazursky's *Tempest* (1982), which were made with the free-form approach, were often mistaken as Cassavetes's own directorial efforts.

Wider audiences enjoyed Cassavetes's *The Killing of a Chinese Bookie* (1976), a gritty film about a Los Angeles nightclub owner who has to kill a bookmaker to repay a mob loan. In art houses, he gained an underground following that blossomed into cult status, and the arrival of videocassette rentals helped get his work in front of film students and critics, who rediscovered his impressive career after his death in 1989. Following the family tradition, director Nick Cassavetes would later adapt one of his father's unfinished scripts into *She's So Lovely* (1997), starring Sean Penn, and remake a version of *The Killing of a Chinese Bookie* (1998).

Before his untimely death, Cassavetes's unique style was an institution. He was less interested in creating films with commercial appeal than in capturing something raw and immediate. He aspired to nothing more than putting

two characters in a close space and leaving them to sort through an emotional puzzle while a nearby camera watched patiently for something to
happen. By placing character exploration ahead of traditional storylines, his
focus on interaction and relationships enhanced the artistry of film. In word
and deed, he represented the spirit of the modern independent filmmaker,
embracing the notion that the process of making movies was an opportunity
for discovery. By avoiding the conventional, Cassavetes blazed a refreshingly
new path nearly a hundred years after the advent of moving images, and a
new wave of documentarists and feature film directors picked up their cameras and followed.

INDEX